D1383811

Facilitating Early Social Communication Skills:
From Theory to Practice

Pamela Rosenthal Rollins, MS, EdD, CCC-SLP

Instructional Units (Chapter 5) by
Michelle Neilon McFarlin, MS, CCC-SLP
Pamela Rosenthal Rollins, MS, EdD, CCC-SLP
Carol Hamer Trautman, MA, PhD
&
Emily Kerr, MS, CCC-SLP

WITHDRAWN
TOURO COLLEGE LIBRARY
Kings Hwy

AAPC
PUBLISHING

P.O. Box 23173
Shawnee Mission, Kansas 66283-0173
www.aapcpublishing.net

7305

KH

PUBLISHING

©2014 AAPC Publishing
P.O. Box 23173
Shawnee Mission, Kansas 66283-0173
www.aapcpublishing.net

All rights reserved. No part of the material protected by this copyright notice may be reproduced or used in any form or by any means, electronic or mechanical, including photocopying, recording, or by any information storage and retrieval system, without the prior written permission of the copyright owner.

Publisher's Cataloging-in-Publication

Facilitating early social communication skills : from theory to practice / Pamela Rosenthal Rollins ; instructional unit (chapter 5) by Michelle Neilon McFarlin, Pamela Rosenthal Rollins, Carol Hamer Trautman & Emily Kerr. -- Shawnee Mission, Kansas : AAPC Publishing, [2014]

pages ; cm.

ISBN: 978-1-937473-84-6
LCCN: 2014944693
Includes bibliographical references and index.
Summary: This text presents a developmental social-pragmatic approach to facilitating language and social communication. Consistent with the SCERTS model (Social Communication Emotional Regulation and Transactional Supports; Prizant et al.), it makes a major contribution to the training and support of young children on the autism spectrum, ages 3-5. While the focus is on the preschool environment, suggestions are provided for how to extend the approach to the home and other environments where the child spends time.--Publisher.

1. Autistic children--Education. 2. Autistic children--Language--Study and teaching. 3. Language disorders in children--Treatment--Study and teaching. 4. Autism spectrum disorders in children--Treatment--Study and teaching. 5. SCERTS model. 6. Verbal ability in children--Study and teaching. 7. Communicative competence in children--Study and teaching. 8. Interpersonal communication in children--Study and teaching. 9. Interpersonal communication in infants--Study and teaching. 10. Teachers of children with disabilities--Handbooks, manuals, etc. I. McFarlin, Michelle Neilon. II. Trautman, Carol Harmer. III. Kerr, Emily, 1986- IV. Title.

LC4717.8 .R651 2014   2014944693
371.94--dc23   1408

Art and Photographs: ©Thinkstock Photos; www.thinkstockphotos.com

Illustrations in visual supports: LessonPix; www.lessonpix.com

This book is designed in Myriad Pro.

Printed in the United States of America.

10|3|19

Table of Contents

Acknowledgments

I became interested in working with children with ASD in 1982 when I was a graduate student in communication disorders at the University of Wisconsin-Madison. I have now spent more than 30 years engaged in research, teaching, and clinical practice in service of young children with ASD and their families.

I would like to thank all of the children I have worked with; you have been my teachers and my guides. A special thank-you goes to Danny M, Michael Cohcrane, Michael B, Lane C, Eliot, Will, Shumli, and their families. I would also like to thank my graduate students, who believed in me and brought the Early CLASS environment with them as they set up their own classrooms and clinical practices; and the graduate students who worked in the lab while I was writing this book, Kimberly Fogle, Kayli Self, Steven Darroh, Cristina Rangel Uribe, Kate Merrifeld, Alafiya Nasrulla, Lauren Brockman, and Emily Kerr. I could not have done it without you. To Carol Trautman and Michelle McFarlin for partnering with me in the Early CLASS, you make me better at what I do. And finally, to my husband, Jon, and daughter, Michaela, for all the love and support, I thank them most of all.

Pamela Rollins

Introduction

The Early Communication, Language, and Social Skills (Early CLASS) program was developed at the University of Texas at Dallas (UTD)/Callier Center for Communication Disorders as a preschool-based intervention program for young children on the autism spectrum (ASD), ages 3-5. The Early CLASS is a developmental **social-pragmatic approach** to facilitating language and social communication, and is rooted in the SCERTS model (Prizant, Wetherby, Rubin, Laurent, & Rydell, 2006). In our preschool at UTD, Michelle Neilon McFarlin, a certified speech-language pathologist, and Carol Hamer Trautman, a special educator, worked with me to run the classroom and develop the curriculum. We were assisted by graduate students in speech-language pathology and early childhood education, who participated as part of their practicum rotation. I chose to deliver speech therapy services within the classroom environment because the classroom is a functional and naturalistic environment for preschool children. Therefore, in this book I do not distinguish between teacher and speech-language pathologist in the classroom, and use both *teacher* and *therapist* to refer to the adults working in the classroom. In our preschool at UTD, the involvement of graduate students made it possible to maintain a 1:1 student-teacher ratio. While I recognize that this ratio is difficult to maintain in many settings, it is nevertheless important to maintain a low student-teacher ratio so that young children with ASD just learning to communicate and share experiences with people around them can receive consistent responses to their communicative signals.

The purpose of this volume is to support teachers and speech-language pathologists in developing language and social communication-based preschool classrooms. That said, the approach and techniques described in this book may also be used with older children with ASD who are functioning at the early social communication levels described. In addition, speech-language pathologists working within a traditional (less functional) pull-out model can adapt the approach for use within individual or Small Group therapy sessions. Lastly, the Early CLASS approach can and should be extended to the home and other environments where children spend most of their time.

The book is divided into five chapters representing the theoretical and organizational framework of social pragmatic intervention as well as 12 instructional units each focused on a particular theme chosen to be developmentally appropriate and functional in the lives of the children (i.e., bed time, birthday party, restaurant, grocery store).

Chapter 1:
Dimensions of Treatment

Learner Objectives:

After reading this chapter, the learner should be able to:

- Define autism spectrum disorder.

- Describe the three types of evidence that comprise evidence-based practice (EBP).

- Define focused interventions and explain why they are important.

- Describe the continuum of comprehensive treatment strategies from discrete to naturalistic.

- Compare and contrast components of a naturalistic behavioral approach and a transactional approach.

- State the three core principles of a universally designed curriculum.

- Explain why the social-pragmatic approach best meets many of the criteria set by the Division for Early Childhood (DEC) and the National Association for the Education of Young Children (NAEYC) for high-quality inclusive early childhood programs.

Autism spectrum disorder (ASD) is a heterogeneous neurodevelopmental disorder that severely compromises the development of social relatedness, reciprocity, social communication, **joint attention**, and learning. The Centers for Disease Control and Prevention (CDC) estimates that 1 in 68 children are on the autism spectrum (CDC, 2014) and that ASD is almost five times more likely to occur in boys than in girls. While it is now possible to reliably diagnose ASD by 2 years of age, there continue to be barriers to early screening and diagnoses that delay access to quality treatments (Interagency Autism Coordinating Committee, 2012). As a result, the average age at diagnosis is reported to be between 3 and 6 years, and even later for children who are culturally or linguistically diverse or who have higher IQs (Mandell, Novak, & Zubritsky, 2005; Shattuck et al., 2009). While there is no cure for ASD, early identification and intervention makes a significant difference in improving a child's level of functioning, thereby ensuring better long-term outcomes (Dawson et al., 2010; Reichow, 2012; Wallace & Rogers, 2010; Warren et al., 2011).

Evidence-Based Practices

Identifying and implementing appropriate **evidence-based practices (EBP)** are important priorities. Historically, evidence-based practices originated in the medical community because of concerns about limited research into treatments that had positive outcomes (Dollaghan, 2007; Odom, Collet-Klingenberg, Rogers, & Hatton, 2010). These concerns led to the development of several organizations, whose mission was to summarize systematic reviews of medical and health care interventions (Odom et al., 2010). This focus on EBP has led many government and professional organizations to undertake major efforts to identify the best available external scientific research (Dollaghan, 2007).

Several systematic reviews of intervention practices for children with ASD are available. The most notable reviews on educational and behavioral practices for school-aged children include the National Standards Project (NSP) completed by the National Autism Center (NAC, 2009) and the National Professional Development Center on Autism Spectrum Disorders (NPDC, n.d.).

The NPDC was funded by the U.S. Department of Education, Office of Special Education Programs, with the twofold goal of conducting systematic reviews using rigorous criteria of focused practices (Odom et al., 2010) and translating practices with sufficient scientific evidence into usable resources for service providers (NPDC, n.d.). To date, the NPDC has identified 24 **focused interventions** as meeting the criteria for scientific evidence. *Focused interventions* are practices that are used to promote a specific skill (Odom et al., 2010). Not all focused practices have been found to be effective for all skills or all grade levels, however. Table 1.1 lists each of the 24 identified practices by outcome (i.e., Academics & Cognition, Behavior, Communication, etc.) and grade level (i.e., Early Childhood (EC), Elementary (EL) and Middle School [MH]).

Often these focused treatments are the building blocks for comprehensive treatment models. A **comprehensive treatment model** "… consists of a set of practices designed to achieve a broader learning or developmental impact on the core deficits of ASD" (Odom, Boyd, Hall, & Hume, 2009, p. 426). Comprehensive treatment models have been evaluated based on "quality of the procedures and implementation, the number of replications of the model, and the associated evidence generated by the efficacy of focused interventions that are components of the models" (Odom et al., 2009, p. 432). In addition, comprehensive treatments fall along a continuum from discrete to naturalistic (Yoder & McDuffie, 2006) (see Figure 1.1). Viewed through the lens of history, this continuum reflects theoretical changes in the field of psychology from the late 1950s to today.

Chapter 1. Dimensions of Treatment

Table 1.1
Evidence-Based Practice by Outcome and Grade Level

Evidence-Based Practices	Academics & Cognition			Behavior			Communication			Play			Social			Transition		
	EC	EL	MH	EC	EL	MH	EC	EL	MH	EC	EL	MH	EC	EL	MH	EC	EL	MH
1. Antecedent-Based Interventions	■	■		■	■	■	■											
2. Computer-Assisted Instruction	■	■	■				■											
3. Differential Reinforcement				■	■	■	■	■		■			■	■	■			
4. Discrete Trial Training	■	■		■	■		■	■		■	■		■	■				
5. Extinction				■	■	■	■	■										
6. Functional Behavioral Assessment				■	■	■	■											
7. Functional Communication Training				■	■		■	■										
8. Naturalistic Interventions							■	■		■	■		■	■				
9. Parent-Implemented Interventions							■	■		■			■	■				
10. Peer-Mediated Instruction/Intervention							■	■		■	■		■	■	■			
11. Picture Exchange Comm. System				■	■		■	■					■	■				
12. Pivotal Response Training	■	■		■	■		■	■		■	■		■	■				
13. Prompting	■	■	■	■	■	■	■	■		■	■		■	■				
14. Reinforcement	■	■	■	■	■	■	■	■		■	■		■	■				
15. Response Interruption & Redirection	■	■	■	■	■	■												
16. Self-Management	■	■		■	■	■	■						■	■		■	■	
17. Social Narratives	■	■		■	■	■	■						■	■				
18. Social Skills Groups							■	■					■	■				
19. Speech-Generating Devices (VOCA)							■	■										
20. Structured Work Systems	■	■		■	■											■	■	
21. Task Analysis	■	■		■	■								■	■				
22. Time Delay		■					■	■					■	■				
23. Video Modeling	■	■		■	■		■	■		■	■		■	■				
24. Visual Supports	■	■	■	■	■	■	■	■	■	■	■	■	■	■	■	■	■	■

Reproduced with permission from the National Professional Development Center on Autism Spectrum Disorders. (n.d.). *Evidence-based practice by outcome matrix*. Chapel Hill, NC: University of North Carolina at Chapel Hill, Frank Porter Graham Child Development Institute.

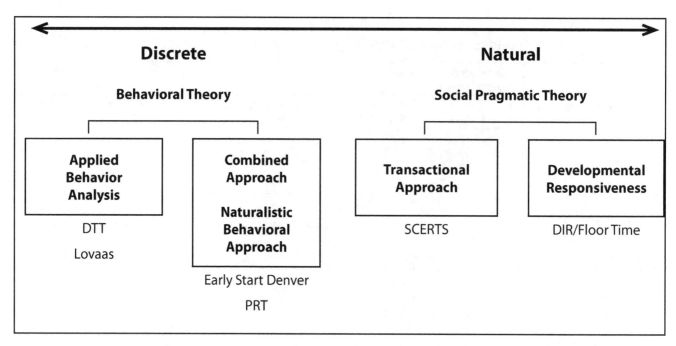

Figure 1.1. **Comprehensive treatment models: dimension of intrusiveness.**

At the far left of the continuum are the discrete trial applied behavioral analysis (ABA) programs. These programs use a method of teaching based on the theoretical work of B. F. Skinner. Discrete Trial Training (DTT; Smith, 2001) and Lovaas program (Lovaas, 1987) are both examples. DTT simplifies skills into discrete and structured steps. The program is considered **adult-directed** because the interventionist identifies the skill to be taught and the targeted correct response from the child. Correct responses are followed by something that is motivating to the child to reinforce the behavior. This may be an external reinforcer such as food/candy or an internal reinforcer such as social praise (e.g., "good talking"). These more traditional behavioral programs rely on one-to-one drills of preselected tasks outside of the child's natural environment (Prizant, Wetherby, & Rydell, 2000), and treat language and communication just like any other behavior that can be trained in discrete steps using Skinner's analysis of verbal behavior (Skinner, 1957). However, while Skinner's description of language was revolutionary for its time, it has been rejected by more contemporary psycholinguists (Tomasello, 2003) in favor of theories based on research conducted in the last 30 years.

Many of the comprehensive treatment programs on the right of the continuum (see Figure 1.1) view language and communication through the lens of contemporary research, which emphasizes developmental readiness, social interaction, and the language learning environment as the primary sources of language acquisition (Tomasello, 2003). As illustrated, **naturalistic programs** such as The Developmental, Individual Difference, Relationship-Based (DIR®) Model (DIR/Floortime) (Greenspan & Wieder, 1997) are at the far right of the continuum. These types of programs are based on developmental and **social-pragmatic theory**, which focuses on social/emotional and communication development within the context of the child's everyday interactions (Prizant et al., 2000).

Social-pragmatic theories of language describe language and communication as a usage-based system (Bruner, 1983; Tomasello, 2003). Therefore, rather than focusing on isolated skills and behaviors chosen by the adult, these programs focus on the child interacting with a communicative partner within the context of her surroundings. A core tenet of the social-pragmatic approach is that all children, including children with ASD, develop skills in a similar sequence (Rollins, 1994a). Where children with ASD differ from typical children is in the rate of development – both within and across domains (e.g., language vs. motor development). Stated differently, while individual skills may be slow at developing, the rate of development may differ from one skill to the next (Rollins, 1994a, 1994b), and it is for this reason that naturalistic approaches use the developmental sequence of a particular skill as the road map for intervention (Prizant et al., 2000). The social-pragmatic approach views communication within affectively based reciprocal social interactions and uses teaching strategies that facilitate language and communication development in typically developing children (Prizant et al., 2000). Specific strategies include use of routines, following the child's attentional focus regarding interests and activities, contingent responses, modeling, and wait time (also see Chapter 3).

The two approaches in the center of the continuum share many components (Ingersoll, Meyer, Bonter, & Jelineka, 2010; Yoder & McDuffie, 2006). **Naturalistic behavioral approaches** are rooted in the theory of ABA but are influenced by the social-pragmatic theories of language and communication development. Pivotal Response Treatment (PRT; Koegel & Koegel, 2006) and the Early Start Denver Model (Rogers & Dawson, 2010) are both excellent examples. **Transactional approaches**, in turn, are rooted in social-pragmatic theory but use some teaching strategies based on the principles of behavioral theory. The Social Communication, Emotional Regulation and Transactional Supports (SCERTS) model (Prizant et al., 2006) exemplifies the transactional approach.

In practice, both naturalistic behavioral approaches and transactional approaches (a) target social communication within more naturalistic and ongoing activities; (b) set up the environment to maximize teaching/facilitative techniques; (c) follow the child's focus of attention in choosing materials/activities; and (d) use natural reinforcers (Ingersoll et al., 2010; Prizant et al., 2000; Rogers, 2006). Despite similarities, however, there are important theoretical differences between two approaches with regard to what motivates and facilitates communication and language development (Ingersoll et al., 2010). For example, naturalistic behavioral approaches target isolated measurable skills, and only the targeted skill is reinforced (Ingersoll et al., 2010). In contrast, transactional approaches view skills as developing through motivating interactions with a responsive adult and don't consider an overt behavioral response as necessary for learning (Ingersoll et al., 2010). Further, transactional approaches focus on intentional communication and respond to all communicative attempts, including unconventional forms (Prizant et al., 2000).

With so many focused practices and comprehensive models to choose from, how does a parent, teacher, or therapist decide on which approach is best for the children in his or her care? True EBP requires that scientific evidence be viewed through the lens of professional expertise/experience and child/caregiver characteristics (Dollaghan, 2007; Odom et al., 2010). Dollaghan (2007) stressed the importance of integrating all three components of EBP – scientific evidence, professional expertise, and child/caregiver characteristics – by using the abbreviation E[3]BP. E[3]BP cannot be successful if support for the intervention is not available within the school and community (Odom, 2009). School support is an especially important consideration when children with ASD are integrated into the general education classrooms.

Access to High-Quality Inclusive Programs

An expansion of the mandates of the Individuals with Disabilities Educational Improvement Act (IDEA) of 2004 relates to serving young children with disabilities in natural environments with access to the general education curriculum (Division for Early Childhood [DEC], 2007). Accordingly, many young children with ASD are being integrated into typical daycare/preschool environments that, therefore, must meet the educational needs of children with ASD (DEC, 2007).

To this end, the **National Association for the Education of Young Children (NAEYC)** worked with the **Division for Early Childhood (DEC)** of the Council for Exceptional Children (CEC) to produce guidelines for high-quality inclusive services for early childhood programs (DEC, 2007; DEC/NAEYC, 2009). High-quality inclusion requires providing accommodations and supports to allow the child to participate in classroom activities. Specifically, DEC (2007) recommended adopting a curriculum with a universal design. The term *universal design* originates from the architecture literature on designing physical spaces but is now also applied to curriculum. In universally designed early childhood classrooms, the curriculum is developed with thoughtful modifications in place from the outset in order to meet the needs of all children (DEC, 2007). This is in contrast to adapting an existing curriculum to meet the needs of an individual child with disabilities, which is often more costly and difficult for the teacher to manage.

DEC (2007) outlined three core principles of a universally designed curriculum: (a) multiple means of representation, (b) multiple means of engagement, and (c) multiple means of expression. These principles, along with NAEYC's philosophy of developmentally appropriate practices, make the developmental social-pragmatic approach (see Figure 1.1) for working with children with ASD a good model for successful inclusion.

The Early CLASS Program

The Early CLASS program (described in Chapters 4 and 5) uses a developmental social-pragmatic approach to facilitating language and social communication and is rooted in the SCERTS model (Prizant et al., 2006). Consistent with the SCERTS model, the program uses a team approach, whereby teachers, speech-language pathologists, and other therapists work collaboratively in the classroom and with parents (Prizant et al., 2006). This collaborative model helps to maintain a low student-teacher ratio, which is important to ensure that children with ASD receive consistent responses to their social communication signals.

These qualities are also consistent with NAEYC standards and DEC recommendations for promoting positive outcomes. Table 1.2 illustrates how the early CLASS learning environment and teaching strategies meet many of NAEYC's standards. Consequently, many of the techniques described in Chapters 3, 4, and 5 are useful when setting up a universal design for learning. The developmental social-pragmatic approach provides an E^{3}BP framework for children with ASD that meets many of the criteria set by DEC and NAEYC for a high-quality inclusive early childhood programs.

Table 1.2
National Association for the Education of Young Children (NAEYC) Standards and Ways
Early CLASS Meets the Criteria

Standards	Description	Early CLASS Learning Environment and Teaching Strategies
1. Relationships	Building positive relationships among teachers and families	Teachers work in partnership with families to establish goals; regular two-way communication facilitated by My Day at School forms, weekly newsletter, Talk About Bags (see Chapters 4 and 5)
	Building positive relationships between teachers and children	Teacher individualizes each activity to meet the developmental level of the child through the key program components (see Chapter 3)
	Helping children make friends	Joint action routines during gym, Snack Time, and Center Time; Small Group activities (see Chapters 4 and 5)
	Creating a predictable, consistent, and harmonious classroom	Use of visual schedules; clearly defined spaces for each activity; activity-based intervention; joint action routines; core vocabulary; visually marking core vocabulary (see Chapters 3, 4, and 5)
	Addressing challenging behaviors	Break area; replace unconventional communication with conventional symbols (see Chapter 3)
	Promoting self-regulation	Get Ready Time (see Chapter 4); clearly defined spaces for each activity; core vocabulary; embedding core vocabulary into routines; predictable sequence of events; use of visual schedules; language addressed to child appropriate to comprehension level; use of naturalistic prompt hierarchy (see Chapter 3)
2. Curriculum	Essential characteristics	Written program philosophy (see Chapters 2 and 3) with clearly stated curriculum framework (see Chapters 4 and 5)
	Areas of development: Social-emotional development	Emotional words as part of core vocabulary; Small Group activities (see Chapter 4 and 5)
	Areas of development: Language development	All key program components and the instructional units (see Chapters 3, 4, and 5)
	Early literacy	Decreasing context embeddedness (see Chapter 3), Book of the Week, Book Time, Small Group activities (see Chapters 4 and 5)
	Creative expression and appreciation for the arts	Art & Music Center, Small Group activities; Music Time (see Chapters 4 and 5)
3. Teaching	Designing enriched learning environments	Theme and core vocabulary reinforced throughout the day during Large Group, Small Group, and Special Activities; classroom infused with other theme-related materials available during individual time; materials may include additional theme-related books in the book area, manipulative in the play dough area or block center, and theme-related songs (see Chapters 4 and 5)
	Supervising children	Classroom has a low teacher-student ratio (see Introduction)
	Using time, grouping, and routines to achieve learning goals	Teachers engage in all activities with children, including snack and playground; classroom infused with theme-related materials the child can select from (see Chapters 4 and 5)
	Responding to children's interests and needs	Joint activity routines and predictable schedule (see Chapters 3, 4, and 5)
	Making learning meaningful for all children	Parents and teachers work together on child's goals; child-centered goals around child's developmental level, core vocabulary (see Chapter 3)
	Using instruction to deepen children's understanding and build their skills and knowledge	Core vocabulary; embedding core vocabulary into routines; predictable sequence of events; use of joint activity routines; use of visual schedules; language addressed to child appropriate to comprehension level (see Chapters 3 and 4)
4. Assessment of Child Progress	Creating an assessment plan	First step of writing individual communication, language, and social skills goals is to perform in-depth functional communication assessment to understand and document child's developmental levels across various domains of social communication and language (see Chapter 3)
	Using appropriate assessment methods	SCERTS assessment process or functional communication assessment (see Chapter 3 and Appendix A)
5. Families	Sharing information between staff and families	Newsletter, My Day at School form (see Chapters 4 and 5)

Before explicating social-pragmatic interventions for children with ASD, in Chapter 2 we will review the development of social communication in young infants and toddlers and the consequences that protracted development has on children with ASD.

Chapter Highlights

- Autism spectrum disorder (ASD) is a heterogeneous neurodevelopmental disorder that severely compromises the development of social relatedness, reciprocity, social communication, joint attention, and learning.

- It is now possible for ASD to be reliably diagnosed by 2 years of age; however, there continues to be barriers to early screening and diagnosis that delay access to quality treatments.

- While there is no cure for ASD, early identification and intervention make a significant difference in improving a child's level of functioning, thereby ensuring better long-term outcomes.

- Identifying and implementing the appropriate evidence-based treatment strategies (EBP) are important priorities.

- Several systematic reviews have been conducted of intervention practices for children with ASD. The most notable reviews on educational and behavioral practices for school-aged children are the National Standards Project (NSP) completed by the National Autism Center (NAC, 2009) and the National Professional Development Center on Autism Spectrum Disorders (NPDC, n.d.).

- Focused interventions are practices that are used to promote a specific outcome. Not all focused practices have been found to be effective for all skills or all grade levels.

- The National Professional Development Center on Autism Spectrum Disorders (NPDC) has identified 24 focused interventions as meeting the criteria for scientific evidence.

- Often focused treatments are the building blocks for comprehensive treatment models. A comprehensive treatment model is designed to achieve a broader learning or developmental impact on the core deficits of ASD.

- Comprehensive treatments fall along a continuum from discrete to naturalistic. Viewed through the lens of history, this continuum reflects theoretical changes in the field of psychology from the late 1950s to the current day.

- To the far left of the continuum are discrete trial applied behavioral analyses (ABA) programs. These programs are based on the work of B. F. Skinner and rely on one-to-one drills of adult-selected tasks outside of the child's natural environment. Language and communication is treated like any other behavior that can be trained in discrete steps using Skinner's analysis of verbal behavior.

- While Skinner's description of language was revolutionary for its time, it has been rejected by more contemporary psycholinguists.

- To the far right of the continuum are naturalistic programs based on developmental social-pragmatic theory, which focuses on social/emotional and communication development within the context of the child's everyday interactions.

- A tenet of the developmental social-pragmatic approach is that all children, including children with ASD, develop social communication and language skills in a similar sequence. Consequently, it uses the developmental sequence of a particular skill as the road map for intervention.

- Children with ASD differ from typical children in rate of development, both within and across domains (e.g., language vs. motor development).

- Teaching strategies that facilitate language and communication development in typically developing children are used with students with ASD. Strategies include use of routines, following the child's attentional focus regarding interests and activities, contingent responses, modeling, and wait time.

- Naturalistic behavioral approaches and transactional approaches share many of the same components. The former are rooted in the theory of ABA but are influenced by the developmental social-pragmatic theory. In contrast, transactional approaches are rooted in social-pragmatic theory but are influenced by behavioral theory in some of their teaching strategies.

- True EBP requires that scientific evidence be viewed through the lens of professional expertise/experience and child/caregiver characteristics. This is referred to as E^3BP.

- Many young children with ASD are being integrated into typical daycare/preschool environments, and the quality of these settings must meet the educational needs of children with ASD.

- High-quality inclusive programs use a universally designed curriculum with thoughtful modifications in place from the beginning in order to meet the needs of all children.

- The Division for Early Childhood of the Council for Exceptional Children (DEC, 2007) outlined three core principles of a universally designed curriculum: (a) multiple means of representation, (b) multiple means of engagement, and (c) multiple means of expression.

- The developmental social-pragmatic approach provides an E^3BP framework for children with ASD that meets many of the criteria set by DEC and the National Association for the Education of Young Children (NAEYC) for high-quality inclusive early childhood programs.

Chapter Review Questions

1. What are the three types of evidence that comprise evidence-based practice (E³BP)?

2. What is a focused intervention?

3. State three principles of discrete trial programs.

4. What are the three main principles of the developmental social-pragmatic approach?

5. Compare and contrast the components of a naturalistic behavioral approach and a transactional approach.

6. What are the three core principles of a universally designed curriculum?

7. Why does the developmental social-pragmatic approach best meet many of the criteria set by DEC and NAEYC for a high-quality inclusive early childhood program?

Chapter 2:
Early Social Communication Development

Learner Objectives:

After reading this chapter, the learner should be able to:

- Describe the three major periods of social-cognitive development during the first two years of life.

- State the developmental progression of pragmatic skills during the first two and a half years of life.

- Describe three levels of development based on the interrelationship among social-cognitive development, social pragmatic development, and changes in word learning strategies.

- Explain the difference between labeling and commenting.

- Describe how children's sensitivity to word learning cues changes during the first two years of life.

- State which communicative intentions facilitate isolated words/phrases but not true language.

- List which communicative intentions facilitate true language.

- State the four components necessary for a joint cooperative activity.

A core tenet of the developmental social pragmatic approach is that all children, including children with ASD, develop social communication and language skills in a similar sequence. Because social communication is a core deficit area for children with ASD, it is important for teachers and therapists who work with children on the spectrum to be familiar with the developmental course of three interrelated components of social communication: **social cognition**, communicative intentions, and the process of word learning. When considered together, these three components give rise to three distinct levels of early social communication development (see Figure 2.1).

	Level 1: 2-6 months	Level 2: 6-10 months	Level 3: 10-24 months
Social-Cognitive Capability	Sharing Emotion	Sharing Perception & Pursuing Goals	Sharing Attention & Intention
Communicative Intention	NONE	Behavior Regulation (Request, Protest) Labeling	Direct Attention (Point & Show) Share Attention (Comment)
Process of Word Learning	Perceptual Salience Temporal Pairing	Perceptual Salience Temporal Pairing	Eye Gaze Social Context
Expressive Language	NONE	Isolated Words/ Phrases	True Language

Figure 2.1. **Levels of early social communication.**

The remainder of this chapter outlines the developmental course of as well as the interrelationships among social cognition, communicative intention, and the process of word learning during the first year of life, as laid out in Figure 2.1. This is followed by a description of how these three levels provide a framework for understanding social communication and language skills in children with ASD.

Many children with ASD have extraordinary difficulties moving from Level 2 to Level 3. It is not until the child reaches Level 3 that we observe true social communication. True social communication occurs when the child is capable of meaningfully sharing and **commenting** on objects, events, or information with another person.

Early Social Cognition and the Development of Communicative Intention

Over the first year of life, typical infants undergo several qualitative changes in how they monitor, control, and predict the behavior of others, culminating in the ability to engage in mutual or **shared understanding** and cooperation with people around them. These gradual qualitative changes have been quantified as movement from "sharing emotions" to "sharing perceptions and pursuing goals" to "sharing attention" and "sharing intention" (Tomasello, Carpenter, Call, Behne, & Moll, 2005).

Sharing Emotions

Around 2 months of age, infants across cultures become increasingly alert and begin to smile in response to social stimuli (Spitz, 1965; Wolff, 1987). The onset of social smiling, coupled with an increase in gazing at the partner's face, is highly significant to Western caregivers, launching **dyads** into a new quality of shared experiences (Rochat & Striano, 1999; Stern, 1977, 1985). These dyadic, face-to-face interactions reflect well-balanced, reciprocal, and rhythmic exchanges of affect and emotions (Brazelton, Koslowski, & Main, 1974; Stern, 1985; Trevarthen, 1977, 1979). The sensitive caregiver responds to the infant as a communicative partner, and these interactions take on a conversational quality (Snow, 1977), so much so that they have been referred to as **"proto-conversations"** (Bateson, 1975; Trevarthen, 1979). Protoconversations, thought to be a universal feature of caregiver-infant interaction (Keller, Schölmerich, & Eibl-Eibesfeldt, 1988; Tomasello et al., 2005; Trevarthen, 1993), involve a range of affect, emotions, social expectations, and rounds of vocal turn-taking (Murray & Trevarthen, 1985; Trevarthen, 1980).

The infant's initial pattern of social responsiveness propels the caregiver and child into a **"complex joint anticipatory system"** (Bruner, 1983). The young infant responds differentially to familiar and unfamiliar persons (Dunn, 1982), and by 4 months becomes more sensitive to the timing and organization of the protoconversational envelope (Rochat, Querido, & Striano, 1999). Caregivers learn to adjust to the child's fledgling responsiveness, and over the next few months, protoconversations become livelier, with predictable routines such as peek-a-boo or patty-cake, providing opportunities for the partners to exchange roles (Bruner, 1978, 1983). It is within the protoconversational envelope that the young infant learns to initiate and terminate protoconversational exchanges and learns the rules for conversational turn-taking (Bateson, 1975).

Sharing Perceptions and Pursuing Goals

Intuitively, some caregivers begin to include objects in their play (Adamson & Russell, 1999) and exploit the infant's fascination with the appearance and disappearance of interesting toys (Bruner, 1983). By 6 months of age, infants have mastered complex upper-body motor skills and are able to focus on distal objects within the immediate environment. A broad array of attentional options are now available, and infants spend increasing amounts of time focused on objects with no indication that they want to share them with the caregiver. Nonetheless, the infant-caregiver collaboration can continue, expanding toward the end of the first year to include **triadic interactions** that incorporate the object (Trevarthen & Hubley, 1978).

Bakeman and Adamson (1984) described these early triadic interactions (child, caregiver, object) as **"passive joint engagement."** Infants are thought to be passive because they do not explicitly acknowledge their caregiver's contribution to the interaction by looking back at the caregiver and smiling. Stated differently, what makes these interactions appear to be shared is the caregiver's active following of the child's focus of attention. That is, the sensitive caregiver actively supports the infant's perceptions by expanding the child's solitary focus to include caregiver verbal and nonverbal information about the attentional target. Thus, from 6 to 10 months, triadic interaction involves the infant and caregiver jointly perceiving an object or an event toward which they both direct their actions, and in so doing share a goal (Tomasello et al., 2005).

Young children begin to understand that their caregivers engage in *intentional actions*. As a result, they can now monitor their caregiver's actions and make predictions about what is coming next in the interaction exchange, as illustrated in the following example.

The caregiver and infant are both looking at a block. The caregiver starts to build a block tower. The 6- to 10-month-old infant begins to understand that the caregiver has a goal in mind of building a tower and can now share in that goal by monitoring the caregiver's behavior and join in an alternating sequence of placing blocks on the tower. After the caregiver places a block on the tower, the child predicts it is her turn and does the same. However, while they are both perceiving the blocks and experiencing the same activity of building the tower, the child does not yet look back at the caregiver and coordinate her attention between the object and adult. The child does not yet have the understanding that they are sharing their attention and intention to build the tower, the awareness to understand that it is a shared and cooperative experience.

Bruner (1978, 1983) described these early triadic interaction exchanges as evolving in concert with the child's changing interests and abilities. Responsive caregivers tailor their behavior to mesh with the social and cognitive advancement of the child (Bruner, 1978, 1983). For example, variations of peek-a-boo games exploit the child's growing awareness of the permanence of unseen objects and people (Bruner, 1983). As predictable sequences occur, routines are established, and each participant anticipates the actions of the other (Bruner, 1983). Within learned routines, roles are exchanged, and the infant learns to initiate and regulate social conventions that will later serve as the platform for conventional language (Bruner, 1978, 1983). See Figure 2.2.

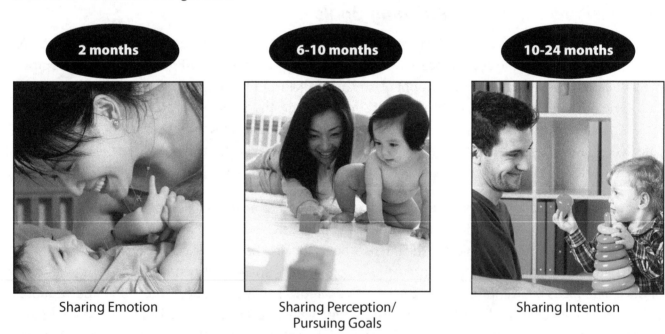

2 months	6-10 months	10-24 months
Sharing Emotion	Sharing Perception/ Pursuing Goals	Sharing Intention

***Figure 2.2.* Levels of early social cognition.**

Somewhere around 9 months of age, the infant's gestures and vocalizations to initiate and respond in these interactions become intentional (Bates, Camaioni, & Volterra, 1975; Bates, Benigni, Bretherton, Camaioni, & Volterra, 1979). Elizabeth Bates' seminal work on the early pragmatic development (Bates, 1976; Bates et al., 1975) suggested that the earliest **preverbal** intentions served both **proto-imperative** and

proto-declarative functions. There is now ample evidence to suggest that proto-imperatives (i.e., nonverbal forms of requesting and protesting) appear earlier in development than proto-declaratives; this phenomenon is related to the infant's nascent social-cognitive abilities (Camaioni, 1993; Rollins & Snow, 1998).

Nine-month-old infants who have the social-cognitive ability to share perceptions and pursue goals can regulate or influence the behavior of others (i.e., **request** and protest) but cannot yet influence their mental states (Camaioni, 1993). Influencing another's behavior requires little more than the attribution of agency to the social partner and the ability to share perceptions of an intended goal (Camaioni, 1993; Tomasello et al., 2005). When children are capable of sharing perceptions and pursuing goals, they have the will to affect the caregiver by some purposeful behavior (Ninio & Snow, 1996). From a communication standpoint, these children are capable of requesting (actions, objects or assistance) and protesting.

Sharing Attention and Intention

As the infant transitions to sharing attention and intentions, around 10 months, he is not only capable of monitoring the caregiver's behavior but is also able to actively monitor the caregiver's attentional focus (Bakeman & Adamson, 1984; Carpenter, Nagel, & Tomasello, 1998; Hubley & Trevarthen, 1979; Tomasello, 1995). This milestone, sometimes referred to as **"responding to joint attention" (RJA)** (Mundy & Thorp, 2008), marks the child's recognition that the caregiver's attention is different from his own (Tomasello, 1995; Trevarthen & Hubley, 1978).

Soon (10-12 months), the infant becomes socially motivated and checks for the caregiver's focus of attention by actively looking back and forth between the caregiver and the object of attention (Bakeman & Adamson, 1984; Carpenter et al., 1998). During these episodes, known as **"coordinated joint engagement"** (Bakeman & Adamson, 1984), the infant coordinates his attention between the caregiver and an object of mutual interest. This newly acquired social competency is a form of **cooperative intersubjectivity**, as it includes the active sharing of thoughts and emotions about an outside entity (Trevarthen & Aitken, 2001). Tomasello et al. (2005) referred to this development as "shared intention," reflecting an understanding that other persons have unique attentions, intentions, and goals.

This new level of social-cognitive skill, which emerges around the child's first birthday, is a monumental achievement not observed in nonhuman primates (Gomez, 1990; Tomasello et al., 2005; Tomasello & Call, 1997) and found to be extraordinarily difficult for children with ASD to acquire (Camaioni, 1993; Rollins & Snow, 1998; Rollins, Wambacq, Dowell, Mathews, & Reese, 1998; Tomasello et al., 2005). Many young children with ASD develop the communication skills needed for instrumental purposes, but their development of joint intention and shared cooperative activities is deficient and severely protracted (Mundy, Sigman, & Kasari, 1992; Rollins, 1994a, 1999; Rollins & Snow, 1998; Rollins et al., 1998; Wetherby, 1986; Wetherby, Yonclas, & Bryan, 1989). The development of joint intention requires that both the adult and the child know that they are doing something together in relationship, marking the emergence of a mutual cooperation (Tomasello et al., 2005).

When the preverbal child is capable of understanding that others have attentions and intentions different from his own, true intentionality in communication emerges (Camaioni, 1993). That is, children who are capable of shared intention are able to direct the caregiver's attention with gestures by showing an object or pointing to an object for the purpose of sharing interest (Bates et al., 1975; Ninio & Snow, 1996; Tomasello, Carpenter, & Liszkowski, 2007; Wetherby et al., 1988). As the young child learns words, her early communicative repertoire continues to reflect the unfolding of **shared intentionality** and the mutual understanding that she is communicating with somebody else. Directing the other's attention (also referred to as "initiating joint attention," see Mundy & Thorp, 2008) and a new skill of **discussing a joint focus of attention** continue into the second year of life.

These early discussions of the here-and-now often take the form of commenting on objects or events in the immediate environment while interacting around toys or looking at picture books together. As children's early vocabularies grow and they become able to use more words to convey intentions, the sophistication of these discussions increases. Soon, naming games take on a different quality as caregivers begin to question the child about her knowledge about events, objects, and pictures with which the dyad is engaged. For example, caregivers may request information about animal sounds or some shared past event. With adult assistance, the child is now engaging in communicative intentions that are less embedded in context (Ninio & Snow, 1996). Thus, at 20 months of age, most children "discuss" objects and events that are not in the environment but are somehow related to objects, events, and pictures that are present (Snow, Pan, Imbens-Bailey, & Herman, 1996).

The trend of incorporating discussions that are less embedded in the immediate context continues to 32 months of age, when children begin to discuss objects and events that have no perceivable reference in the environment (i.e., discuss something nonpresent), as well as talk about thoughts and feelings (Snow et al., 1996). The developing child's pragmatic understanding is now reflective of underlying motivations for cooperation and shared intentionality (Ninio & Snow, 1996; Snow, 1999; Tomasello, Carpenter, & Liszkowski, 2007). As children begin to understand others' mental states, they can take others' perspectives and understand what knowledge is shared and with whom (Baron-Cohen 1989; Ninio & Snow, 1996). In short, they move from joint perceptual focus to more **decontextualized** communicative intentions.

Communicative Intention and Its Relationship to Language

In the previous section we discussed the relationship between shifts in social cognition and the development of communicative intention. We found that the developmental progression of communicative intention emerges in an orderly fashion (see Figure 2.3) and is dependent on the child's underlying social-cognitive skills.

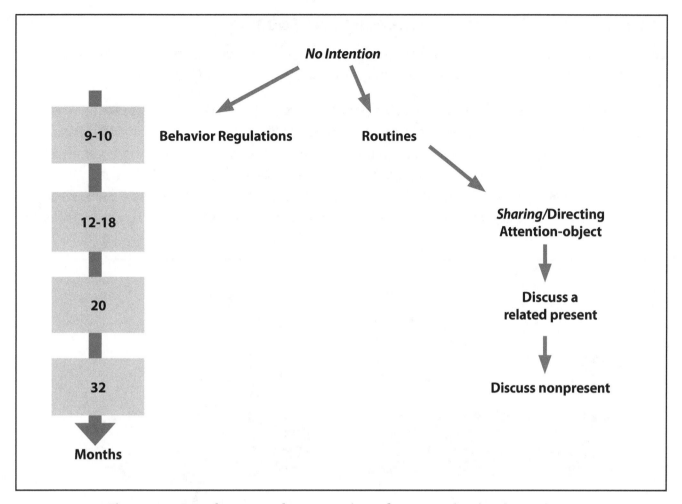

Figure 2.3. Developmental progression of communication intentions.

Adapted from Ninio & Snow; 1996, Rollins, 2009, 2014; Rollins & Snow, 1998.

We turn now to examining the relationship between early social communication and language development. We will learn that words are not enough for the development of true social language.

The earliest communicative intentions to emerge are **"behavioral regulations"** (communicative acts that are intended to regulate or control the behavior of another person) and only require the early developing social-cognitive skill of pursuing goals. Examples of behavioral regulations include requests (to get someone to give you an object or engage in an activity) and **protests** (to get someone to stop an activity).

Around the same time, children begin engaging in ritualized or routine exchanges. Many children on the autism spectrum seem to get stuck in the phase of sharing perceptions and pursuing goals. That is, they are able to use words to request and protest and learn to label objects/events in their environment.

The Distinction Between Commenting and Labeling

Commenting denotes that the child is sharing information with another person, whereas *labeling* does not. **Labeling** appears not to be for the benefit of anyone besides the child herself.

When a child with ASD is labeling, she is not using words with the intent to communicate with another person; there is no communicative intention behind her words. While many children with ASD use words or word combinations to regulate another's behavior and to label, they often do not go on to communicate verbally or nonverbally for the purpose of sharing information (Rollins & Snow, 1998; Rollins et al., 1998; Tomasello, 2003). That is, many children with ASD develop extensive use of words to regulate another's behavior and to label but fail to develop true language and to share information (see Figure 2.4). How can this be?

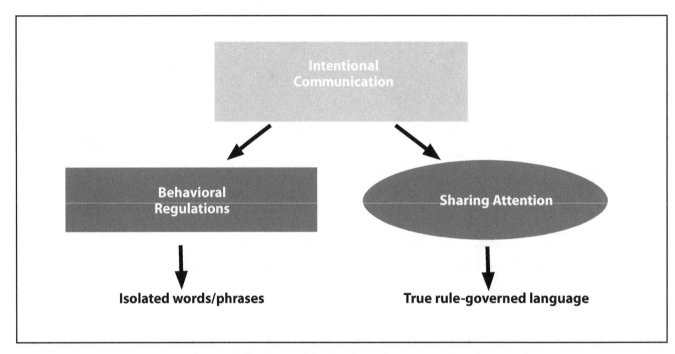

Figure 2.4. **Differential affect of intentional communication on language.**

Recent advances in our understanding of word learning make clear the apparent dissociation of words used for requesting/labeling from words used for true social language observed in children with ASD. We now recognize that children use a combination of perceptual, cognitive, social, and linguistic inputs or cues for word learning and that their sensitivity to these cues changes in the process of development (Hirsh-Pasek, Golinkoff, & Hollich, 2000; Hollich et al., 2000).

Across the early word learning period (under 2 years), children use both perceptual and **social cues** to identify word and meaning relations (see Figure 2.1). Perceptual cues (i.e., temporal pairing of what we hear with what we see) appear to dominate early in development before 10 months of age with a progressive shift toward reliance on social factors around 12 months (Hirsh-Pasek et al., 2000; Hollich et al., 2000; Rollins, 2003). This means that young infants and children with ASD who have acquired the skill of sharing perceptions and pursuing goals learn words by temporal pairing of hearing the word while looking at perceptually salient objects and events (Hirsh-Pasek et al.,2000; Rollins, 2003; Rollins & Trautman, 2011).

Children with ASD who are at Level 2 (see Figure 2.1) are able to acquire many words through this early perceptual word-learning process. Caregivers, teachers, and therapists may support the child's perceptions of objects and events while naming the object or event. This, in turn, facilitates the acquisition of many words and isolated phrases but does not lead to rule-governed language (Tomasello, 2000). True integration of vocabulary with grammar does not happen until a child is able to share attention and intention (Bates & Goodman, 1997, 1999; Rollins, 1999, 2003; Tomasello, 2000). In fact, many correlational studies have found a relationship between joint attention and later language (Carpenter et al., 1998; McArthur & Adamson, 1996; Mundy et al., 1990, Rollins, 2003; Rollins & Snow, 1998). That is, children who are able to share attention and intention (Level 3) begin to rely more heavily on social cues. For example, they learn new words in situations where the adult looks at and labels an object that the child is not looking at. Here, the child must look up and determine the adult's focus of attention for word learning to take place (Baldwin, 1993). Level 3 children who share attention and intention (see Figure 2.1) can also learn the names of objects that the adult *intends* to find. For example, children can learn new words in situations where the adult announces that he is going to find a novel object and searches for the object in several places before finding it (Tomasello & Barton, 1994).

Development of Social Communication and Language in Children With ASD

Our understanding of how social cognition, communicative intentions, and the process of word learning change over time in typically developing children provides a framework for understanding social communication in children with ASD. That is, just as with typically developing children, the early social communicative capabilities of children with ASD fall along a continuum that can be divided into three levels, each corresponding to the child's underlying social-cognitive skill (see Figure 2.5).

	Level 1:	Level 2:	Level 3:
Social-Cognitive Capability	Sharing Emotion	**Sharing Perception & Pursuing Goals**	**Sharing Attention & Intention**
Communicative Intention	NONE	**Behavior Regulation (Request, Protest)** **Labeling**	**Direct Attention (Point & Show)** **Share Attention (Comment)**
Process of Word Learning	**Perceptual Salience Temporal Pairing**	**Perceptual Salience Temporal Pairing**	**Eye Gaze Social Context**
Expressive Language	NONE	**Isolated Words/ Phrases**	**True Language**

Figure 2.5. Social communication levels in children with ASD.

Figure 2.5 is the same as Figure 2.1 with two exceptions. First, the ages have been taken off in Figure 2.5 because children with ASD typically move through these levels at varying ages. Second, the social-cognitive capability of sharing emotions is in white type to signify that Level 1 children with ASD do not have the **social reciprocity** seen in typically developing Level 1 children.

Level 1 Children

The Hanen program (*More Than Words;* Sussman, 1999) calls Level 1 the "Own Agenda" stage. This is a perfect description of the Level 1 child. The Level 1 child does not communicate directly with others because he does not have communicative intention. He has not learned that communicative signals can be used to pursue goals so that he can get what he wants. While he may interact with a partner for a brief moment, he does not yet demonstrate the social emotional reciprocity that we see in typical children who are sharing emotion.

Intervention for the Level 1 child is not the focus of this book and is not discussed in later chapters. Briefly, however, goals for the Level 1 child should stress social-emotional reciprocity and requests. To facilitate social-emotional reciprocity, the teacher, parent, or therapist can set up activities requiring mutual responsiveness with the child. To accomplish this, the adult should position herself in face-to-face interactions with the child and engage in **social sensory routines** to facilitate reciprocal interactions with shared affect (Rollins, 2013). Social sensory routines are routines that are created from sensory activities like tickle games, swinging, or bouncing on a large ball. They may also include finger plays like "patty-cake," "open, shut them," and "I'm going to get you."

In addition, several key ingredients discussed in Chapter 3 may be used when implementing social sensory routines, such as (a) using a core vocabulary, (b) embedding the core vocabulary within social sensory routines, and (c) being mindful of keeping the child emotionally regulated while participating in the routines.

Several programs are available for the Level 1 child. For example, *Picture Exchange System* (Bondy & Frost, 1996) is a helpful program for facilitating requests. In addition, *More Than Words* (Sussman, 1999) and *An Early Start for Your Child With Autism* (Rogers, Dawson, & Vismara, 2012) both include strategies to facilitate requests and social sensory games.

Level 2 Children

Level 2 children are not yet social. They are able to pursue their goals using conventional or unconventional signals. They understand others' intentions regarding actions on objects in the environment (Aldridge, Stone, Sweeney, & Bower, 2000), can monitor their caregiver's actions, and can make predictions about what is coming next in the interaction. For example, if an adult puts a block on top of another block, the child understands the person's actions of stacking blocks and may be motivated to put a block on the tower, too. However, Level 2 children cannot yet "coordinate their attention among self, partner, and task (joint attention abilities) and formulate shared goals and intention with the partner" (Liebal, Colombi, Rogers, Warneken, & Tomasello, 2008, p. 226).

Children developing typically and children with language impairments who do not have social deficits transition in and out of Level 2 when they are between 6 and 12 months old. Most typical children are not yet using words at this age but do request and protest using gestures and other nonverbal means.

Many children with ASD never move beyond Level 2. Others remain in Level 2 well into preschool or elementary school. Because children with ASD remain in Level 2 for a protracted period of time, they are able to learn and produce words through the early word learning mechanism of perceptual salience and temporal pairing. Therefore, unlike children without social deficits, Level 2 children with ASD use words to label objects, request, and protest.

Level 3 Children

Level 3 children are truly social. They have a mutual understanding with their communicative partner. They understand that they have shared goals and can interact together in a relationship. Level 3 children can direct others' attention to pictures, objects, and events for the purpose of sharing interests, as if to say, "Wow, do you see what I see?" They can also comment on pictures, objects, and events that are present and in their view. Level 3 children continue to struggle with incorporating their language into discussions about past or future events where there is no discernible **referent** in the environment and maintaining topics of conversation.

Facilitating the Transition From Level 2 to Level 3

By the time children without social deficits enter preschool, they are functioning at Level 3 (or higher) and are very capable of using language to share attention, thoughts, and feelings with others. Many teachers, therapists, and parents do not understand the nuanced differences between verbal Level 2 children with ASD and Level 3 children. As a result, they may implement Level 3 intervention strategies with Level 2 children. Unfortunately, this results in the child being asked to communicate outside of her developmental capabilities.

Some intervention philosophies stay within the developmental capabilities of Level 2 children with ASD but require them to label pictures and objects or ask them to request using progressively longer utterances. The former facilitates vocabulary development using the word-learning processes available to a child at Level 2. As such, this approach enables the child with ASD to build a large vocabulary but without movement to true language. The latter strategy facilitates multiword requests but often fails to increase the repertoire of communicative intentions. That is, the child may request using three words but fails to show (verbally or nonverbally) her communicative partner what interests her or to share her interests. Both of these intervention strategies fall short of creating a developmentally appropriate environment that will support movement to true social communication.

Chapters 3 and 4 focus on **social-pragmatic** intervention strategies designed to facilitate development of true social communication for children who are functioning at Levels 2 and 3. The goal of intervention changes from getting something done (i.e., label or request) to *sharing* together in relationship with others. This requires structuring the environment to facilitate engagement in a joint cooperative activity. According to Tomasello and colleagues, engaging in joint cooperative activities with shared goals and shared intentions is the driving force of true human communication (Moll & Tomasello, 2007; Tomasello et al., 2005). Based on the work of Bratman (1992), Tomasello and colleagues (2005, p. 680) outline the components necessary for a joint cooperative activity as follows:

1. The interactants are mutually responsive to one another.

2. There is a shared goal (mutual knowledge) that they are jointly committed to doing together.

3. Both participants understand both roles of the interaction (role reversal) and can take reciprocal and complementary roles in order to achieve the joint goal.

4. Participants are motivated and willing to help one another accomplish their roles (mutual support).

Joint cooperative activities provide a framework for setting up the environment when doing social-pragmatic intervention. Thus, all activities are filtered through this lens of a joint cooperative activity. For Level 2 children, this typically means arranging the environment and using strategies to facilitate mutual responsiveness and understanding. This requires creating an environment that is as comprehensible as possible so that the child can understand the expectations and opportunities around him.

Several key components, or treatment strategies, described in Chapter 3 may be used to structure the environment to facilitate joint cooperative activities. For example, developmentally appropriate interactions that (a) use a core vocabulary, (b) embed the core vocabulary in functional routines, (c) follow a predictable sequence of events, (d) use visual supports, and (e) keep the child emotionally regulated help create an environment that helps the Level 2 child to be mutually responsive and have mutual understanding and to participate in a shared goal.

Functional routine exchanges are characterized as being mutually supportive, whereby both partners are committed to the joint activity (Steps 1 and 2 of a joint cooperative activity; i.e., facilitating that the communicative partners are mutually responsive to one another and providing a shared goal or mutual knowledge to which both partners are committed to doing together). Often children do not understand both roles of the interaction and cannot assume reciprocal and complementary roles until late in Level 2 and into Level 3 (Step 3 of a joint cooperative activity; i.e., understanding and participating in both roles of the interaction). As children begin to participate in functional and motivating routines, the expectation of reciprocity emerges. That is, they begin to take their turn in the interaction by responding to the adult or initiating the interaction itself. They begin to learn complementary roles and become motivated to support the other in reaching a shared goal.

Chapter Highlights

- Over the first year of life, typical infants undergo several qualitative changes in how they monitor, control, and predict the behavior of others, culminating in the ability to engage in mutual or shared understanding and cooperation with people around them.

- The development of social cognition, communicative intentions, and the process of word learning are three strands of development that, when combined, give rise to three distinct levels of early social communication development.

- Sharing Emotions develops around 2 months of age. Infants and caregivers begin to engage in face-to-face interactions reflecting well-balanced, reciprocal, and rhythmic exchanges of affect and emotion.

- Sharing Perceptions and Pursuing Goals develops around 6 months of age. Within these triadic interactions, the infant and caregiver jointly perceive an object or an event, but the infant does not yet explicitly acknowledge the caregiver's contribution to the interaction by looking back at the caregiver and smiling.

- Children who have the cognitive capability of Sharing Perceptions and Pursing Goals are goal-directed and will persist until their goal is met. They understand others have goals and can predict what comes next. These infants can regulate or influence the behavior of others (i.e., request and protest) but cannot yet influence their mental states by pointing or showing.

- The earliest communicative intentions to emerge are "behavioral regulations." They only require the early developing social-cognitive skill of Sharing Perceptions and Pursuing Goals.

- There is now ample evidence to suggest that nonverbal forms of requesting and protesting appear earlier in development than showing or pointing.

- Sharing Attention and Intention emerges around 10 months of age.

- The development of joint intention requires that both the adult and the child know that they are doing something together in relationship, marking the emergence of a mutual cooperation.

- Sharing Attention and Intention is the underlying social-cognitive skill needed for true rule-governed language.

- Many children with ASD get stuck in the phase of Sharing Perceptions and Pursuing Goals. They are able to use words to request and protest and learn to label objects/events in their environment but fail to develop true language and to share information.

- *Commenting* denotes that the child is sharing information with another person, whereas *labeling* does not. Labeling appears not to be for the benefit of anyone besides the child herself.

- Children use a combination of perceptual, cognitive, social, and linguistic inputs or cues for word learning, and the child's sensitivity to these cues changes in the course of development.

- Young infants and children with ASD who have acquired the skill of Sharing Perceptions and Pursuing Goals learn words by the temporal pairing of hearing the word while looking at perceptual salient objects and events.

- True integration of vocabulary with grammar does not happen until a child is able to share attention and intention.

- The Level 1 child does not communicate directly with others because he does not yet have communicative intention.

- Intervention for a Level 2 child should structure the environment to facilitate engagement in a joint cooperative activity.

- To facilitate social-emotional reciprocity for a Level 1 child, the teacher, parent, or therapist can set up activities requiring mutual responsiveness with the child. To accomplish this, the adult should position herself in face-to-face interactions with the child and engage in social-sensory routines to facilitate reciprocal interactions with shared affect.

- Level 2 children are able to pursue goals with conventional or unconventional signals. They can monitor their caregiver's actions and can make predictions about what is coming next in the interaction. But they cannot yet engage in joint attention.

- Level 3 children have a mutual understanding with their communicative partner. They understand that they have shared goals and can interact together in a relationship.

- Joint cooperative activities provide the framework for setting up an effective classroom environment for Level 2 children.

Chapter Review Questions

1. What are the three stages of early social cognition during the first two years of life?

2. Compare and contrast Sharing Perceptions and Pursuing Goals with Sharing Attention and Intention.

3. What word learning strategy do children use when they have the cognitive skills of Sharing Perceptions and Pursuing Goals?

4. What communicative intentions do children use when they have the cognitive skills of Sharing Perceptions and Pursuing Goals? What communicative intentions are missing for true communication to emerge?

5. What communicative intentions are associated with Sharing Attention and Intention?

6. What is the difference between labeling and commenting?

7. How does the goal of intervention change from Level 1 to Level 2?

Chapter 3:
Key Program Components

Learner Objectives:

After reading this chapter, the learner should be able to:

- State eight key components of classroom-based developmental social-pragmatic intervention for Level 2 children.

- Describe why a functional communication assessment is a necessary first step to intervention.

- List and describe the four components of a goal.

- Explain the different ways to measure a goal and their advantages and disadvantages.

- Explain why using a core functional vocabulary is beneficial for children with ASD.

- Explain how to develop a core functional vocabulary for a child with ASD.

- Explain why use of visual graphic symbols is beneficial for children with ASD.

- List two rules governing how to choose picture symbols.

- Describe why pairing spoken language with pointing to picture symbols is recommended for children with ASD.

- Explain why having a predictable sequence of events is beneficial for children with ASD.

- Describe and give examples of nonlinguistic comprehension strategies.

- Explain how routines support comprehension and social communication for children with ASD.

- Define *decontextualization*.

- Explain why Discuss a Related Present is an extremely important communicative intention.

- Define a pseudo-conversation and describe techniques to help the child maintain a topic of conversation.

- Explain how the naturalistic prompt hierarchy is used in spontaneous interactions.

- List and describe at least three language stimulation/modeling techniques.

- Define *emotional regulation* and explain how it affects children with ASD.

- List two classroom strategies to support emotional regulation.

This chapter focuses on several key components used to facilitate social communication through the lenses of joint cooperative activities. Key components are implementation strategies, that when used together, form the backbone of a developmental social pragmatic classroom for Level 2 and Level 3 children (see Figure 3.1).

1. Individualized goals with a developmental approach to goal hierarchy
2. Activity-based intervention: embedding goals in meaningful routines and activities
3. Core functional vocabulary
   a. Use of visual-graphic symbols
4. Functional joint action and joint attention routines
5. Discussing a Related Present: Decrease in context embeddedness
6. Natural prompt hierarchy and language modeling
7. Emotional regulation

Figure 3.1. Key components.

Individualized Goals With a Developmental Approach to Goal Hierarchy

The purpose of this textbook is to support teachers and/or therapists in developing a language and communication-based preschool classroom for the Level 2 and 3 children. As such, much of the book is concerned with setting up the classroom and specific classroom activities. Volume 1 of the SCERTS manual (Prizant et al., 2006) is an excellent resource for social communication goals that are consistent with the classroom activities for Level 2 and 3 children. Because each child's individual goals are embedded into classroom activities, a few points about writing goals are addressed here.

1. Assess Functional Communication

The first step of writing individual communication, language, and social skills goals is to perform an in-depth functional communication assessment to understand and document the child's developmental levels across the various domains of social communication and language.

An early communication, language, and social skills functional communication checklist is provided in Appendix A. This checklist assists in assessing speech, language, and social communication in young children. Pulling from a variety of sources, it assesses the child along a developmental continuum so that a teacher or therapist can plan activities that are fine-tuned to the child's developmental level within and across the various component parts of social communication and language. The functional communication checklist delineates each component of social communication (e.g., articulation/phonology, language comprehension, **nonlinguistic comprehension strategies**, means for relating to objects, **symbolic play**, communicative means and intentions, reciprocity, **repair strategies**, **social affective signaling**, and emotional regulation). This type of in-depth information may also be obtained using the SCERTS Assessment Process observational scale (Prizant et al., 2006).

A functional assessment shapes goals that focus on the child's level of development within and across domains. The classroom is then structured so that each child's goals can be embedded within the context of the ongoing routines and activities.

2. Ensure Goals Are Functional and Achievable

Short-term goals are written in small increments to ensure the child will be successful and show progress. This means two things: First, it is important to break down the long-term goal into small incremental parts along the developmental continuum. If the child is not making progress, it is often because the teacher or therapist has set the goal too high. Second, it is important to remember that language and communicative functioning in children with ASD varies systematically, depending on the social (i.e., familiar vs. unfamiliar communication partner, interaction with another person 1:1 vs. interaction in a group) and communicative (i.e., regulating behavior, routine, joint attention) context (see Figure 3.2).

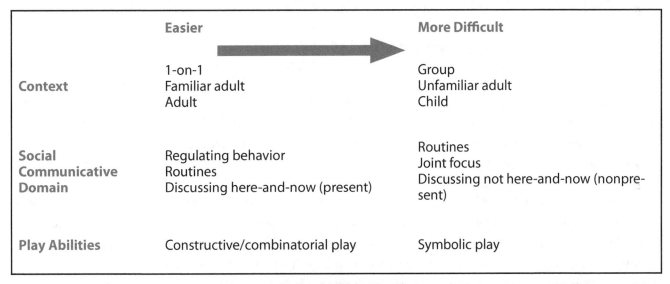

Figure 3.2. Social communication varies systematically by social demand.

Sam was a 4-year-old boy with ASD. He could initiate requests using four words (i.e., "I want cookie, please") but could only respond to a bid for joint attention by pointing to a picture. A student teacher was new to the classroom and did not know that a child's language ability can vary depending on the communicative context. During Snack Time, the student teacher observed Sam's language as he requested cookies and punch using three- and four-word phrases (e.g., "I want cookies please").

Based on this observation, at Book Time, she prompted Sam to use multiword utterances (e.g., "a red hat") when talking about pictures in a book. Sam became highly agitated and echoic because the language expectation was too high for the joint attention context. The classroom teacher facilitated a different interaction by prompting Sam to point to pictures she named in a "where is _____" routine. Sam calmed, and they engaged in a reciprocal inter- action around the pictures.

The take-home message here is that children are variable in their communicative competency with changes in social and communicative contexts. Therefore, goals must reflect this by targeting the communicative context at the level of intention, conversation, and communicative means as well as the social context. Goals should state:

- The *communicative intention* (routine, joint attention, etc.)

- The *conversational level* (response, initiation, continuation)

- The *communicative means* the child will use if it is an expressive goal (conventional gesture, pic- ture symbol, vocal syllabic formation, word, utterance length)

- The *specific social condition* (1:1/group, adult/child, familiar/unfamiliar person)

3. *Ensure Goals Are Observable and Measurable*

To ensure that goals are observable, you must state the antecedent needed to observe the behavior (e.g., in the presence of a picture, when asked a question, when shown a picture and the word is mod- eled, or spontaneously) and the nonsocial conditions (or context) in which you expect the behavior to occur. The nonsocial condition may include materials (e.g., table toys, blocks) or specific activities (e.g., Snack, Hello Circle, symbolic play activity).

To ensure that goals are measurable, you need to specify how often you want to see the behavior. There are different ways to measure a goal. A common way is to specify frequency (e.g., 8/10 times or 80%). However, it is difficult to measure exact percentages in naturalistic environments such as a classroom setting (see Rogers & Dawson, 2010, for a similar discussion). Another way to take data is by using a time sampling method whereby you specify how often a behavior occurs during a specific time interval and for how many days you might expect to see that behavior.

For example:

<Child's name> will respond to turn-taking routines for 3 turns with a familiar child when playing with table toys by saying "my turn," when provided with a picture symbol of "turn," 2 times/days for 2 weeks.

The above goal sets the communicative intention (i.e., routine), the conversational level (i.e., respond), the communicative means (i.e., verbal "my turn"), and the social context (i.e., familiar child). The anteced- ent for the behavior to occur is also stated (i.e., when provided with a picture symbol of the word "turn") along with how the goal will be measured (i.e., 2 times/day for 2 weeks). Further, the goal is written so that it can be worked on during meaningful activities, which is the topic of the next section.

Data on treatment goals are collected often, and goals are evaluated for mastery criteria. Once a goal is mastered, a new goal is written according to the developmental trajectory for the particular skill.

Activity-Based Intervention: Embedding Goals in Meaningful Routines and Activities

Once goals are established, each child's individual goals are embedded into meaningful activities within the broader classroom environment. This is a basic tenet of activity-based intervention (ABI; Bricker & Cripe, 1992). ABI is defined as a "child-directed, transactional approach that embeds intervention on children's individual goals and objectives in routine, planned, or child-initiated activities, and uses logically occurring antecedents and consequences to develop functional and generative skills" (Bricker, Pretti-Frontczak, & McComas, 1998, p. 11).

A preschool environment based on ABI offers many planned activities throughout the day; for example, Hello Circle, Remember Time, Small Group, Snack, and Music Time, to name a few. Other activities are more child-initiated such as Center Time and Gym. All activities incorporate functional vocabulary (later referred to as the "core functional vocabulary") and routines that can be scheduled to occur every day and be replicated at home or in other settings. For example, each of the planned activities may include routines for "check your schedule," "sit down," "waiting," and "look."

Routines can be simple songs that correspond to specific action words. As a child learns several short routines, two or more can be chained together. For example, transition between activities can chain three routines in a predictable way: "clean up," "check schedule," and "sit down" (see the section on transitions in Chapter 4 for more details).

In addition, all planned activities such as Hello Circle and Small Group have a meta-structure, which provides a predictable sequence of events with a clear beginning and end. The content of these activities changes from day to day, which allows for planned varied repetition (see Chapter 4 for more specific information on implementation).

Core Functional Vocabulary

Caregivers simplify their language when they talk to young typically developing children (Nelson, 1974). That is, they use more restricted vocabulary, use shorter, less complex utterances, make more references to the here-and-now, and speak in a high-pitched, sing-song voice (see Pine, 1994, for a review). Similarly, a core functional vocabulary simplifies the language used to address Level 2 and 3 children on the spectrum. The simplification ensures that the child receives multiple exposures (i.e., repetition) to each word in multiple contexts. Stated differently, the core functional vocabulary (Rollins et al., 1998) consists of a relatively small number of words that are embedded into meaningful/functional classroom routines and activities that require active learning and shared engagement. It constitutes the majority of the content words the child and communicative partners use while communicating (see Figure 3.3).

Example of "Choice"

Choice board at Center Time   **A choice at Music**

Figure 3.3. **Core functional vocabulary across the curriculum.**

A core functional vocabulary should be developed with each child's caregivers and, if possible, other professionals involved with the child. For children in Levels 1, 2, and 3, three principles based on language development in typically developing infants and toddlers guide the selection of core vocabulary words.

First, the core functional vocabulary is based on objects and actions relevant to the child's daily routines, as well as relational words consistent with the semantic relations observed in the early vocabularies of typically developing children (Owens, 2008; Paul, 2001; Prizant et al., 2006). **Early semantic relations** include words that denote existence (e.g., *look*), recurrence (e.g., *more*), cessation (i.e., *finish*), and general-purpose words (e.g., *choice* and *different*).

Using a vocabulary based on early semantic relations provides the child opportunities not only to talk about objects and actions but also to talk about the relationships among objects (Lahey & Bloom, 1977). A deviation from typical development is that while the categories of words reflect the early semantic relationships, the word choice is functional for the child and appropriate for her chronological age (see Table 3.1).

The second principle for developing a core vocabulary is choosing only one word for each communicative function (Ninio & Snow, 1996). For example, both *all done* and *finished* can be used to signify the termination of an activity; however, only one of these words (e.g., *finished*) might be chosen as part of the core vocabulary.

The third principle is that every attempt should be made to focus on words that can be replicated across the various activities in which the child engages (within school) and environments (school, home, place of worship), and by different communication partners (teacher, therapists, and parent). For example, the core vocabulary word *choice* is introduced at Choice Time (refer to Chapter 4), which is a time when children make a choice about what center(s) they will go to during Center Time. The core word *choice* is then used every time the child has to choose among two or more items. Children are asked to make a choice at Music regarding what song they want to sing and to make a choice at Snack Time regarding what food they want to eat. Once they comprehend the core word *choice*, they can learn that some things are "not a choice." The core vocabulary word *choice* is easily integrated into the home or other environments.

Table 3.1 lists other core functional vocabulary words that might be used within a preschool environment. Further, Table 5.1 in Chapter 5 provides an example of how the core vocabulary is expanded over time as children's comprehension of previously learned words and experiences increases.

Table 3.1
Early Semantic Relationships: Example of Core Classroom Words (Early Level 2)

Type		Words
Name for a Thing/Person		
Object		schedule, calendar, tv
Places/Activities		Small Group; Hello Circle, Early CLASS, home, gym, playground, snack, cleanup
Body Part **Agent (person/animal)**		mom, teacher, friend
Existence		look
Nonexistence/Disappearance		no, finished
Recurrence		more
Rejection/Refusal		no, stop
Social Interaction		hi, bye-bye, please, thank you
Action		want, give, help, wait, listen, watch, share, play, look, open, eat, drink, jump, wash, sit, choice, call, move, break (as in take a), sing
Modifier	Attribute Possession Location Denial Emotion words	different mine (turn) in, out not happy, mad, okay
Wh-word	Asks questions	where

Adapted from Lahey & Bloom (1977), Owens (2008), and Prizant et al. (2006).

Use of Visual Graphic Symbols

Visual graphic symbols are an effective learning tool for preschool children with ASD (Hume, 2008). Intervention for Level 2 and 3 children pairs spoken core vocabulary with visual graphic symbols during engaging and motivating classroom activities. This approach capitalizes on the word learning strategy available to Level 2 children – the pairing of the spoken words with interesting and motivating visual stimuli (refer to Chapter 1). Stated differently, spoken language is paired with pointing to the visual graphic symbol of core vocabulary during natural interactions to visually mark core vocabulary words. The adult language model consists of synchronized spoken and visual input for core vocabulary words. This is similar to natural aided language modeling described in the augmentative communication literature (Cafiero, 1998; Drager et al., 2006).

It is helpful for each child to have an individualized language board (see Figure 3.4) with visual graphic symbols available at all times; activity-specific boards are also available (i.e., book boards for reading books, placemats for snack, game boards for board games, etc.). Other visual supports in a classroom include schedules, turn identifiers, and supports to encourage and maintain play interactions (see Figure 3.4).

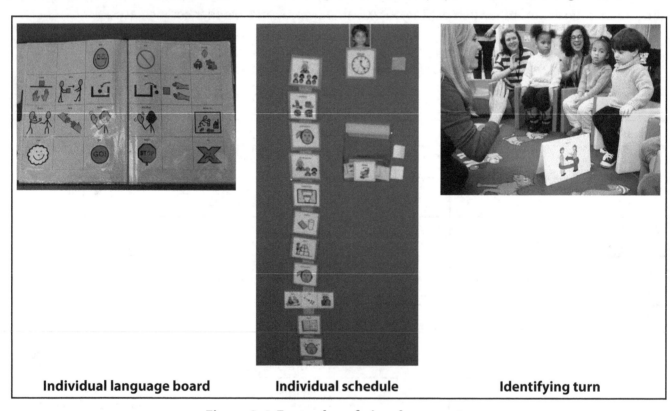

Individual language board **Individual schedule** **Identifying turn**

Figure 3.4. **Examples of visual supports.**

A child may use any form of language and communication in interactions. Specifically, he may touch the word(s) on a language board, say the word(s), use a word approximation, and gesture or combine any of these elements. It is important not to require children to use the visual language system if they desire to communicate in a more natural way because the goal is to develop language and communication, not to use a language board.

Further, control of the visual language boards is shared between the child and the adult during interactions. This is very important because language is bidirectional. Very often teachers and therapists take full control of the visual communication system. Some teachers carry the pictures around with them, forgetting to put the board out for the child to use. Other teachers and therapists hang picture cards from their belt to use when the child is not behaving. These situations do not foster communication because they do not allow the Level 2 child with ASD to use the visual system when he is ready and willing to communicate. It also can send the message to the child that language flows in only one direction – toward the child for controlling her behavior.

Choice of Visual Graphic Symbol

While there are many choices with regard to visual graphic symbol systems, the Mayer-Johnson Picture Communication Symbols (Mayer-Johnson, 2000) or LesssonPix (n.d.) are good choices. These symbols are generic visual representations and not representations of any real objects/actions in the environment. In addition, many of the symbols are iconic and have been found to be more easily understood than other visual graphic symbol systems by nonverbal children with ASD (Mirenda & Locke, 1989) and young, typically developing children (Mizuko, 1987). They also depict a variety of parts of speech, including nouns, adjectives, verbs, and prepositions, and they are easily available and easily reproducible, allowing consistency of the symbol across environments.

We have two rules about how to choose symbols for specific words when the goal is to facilitate language. First, the picture symbol used to represent an individual word must always be the same. For example, Boardmaker® (Mayer-Johnson, 2000) and LessonPix (n.d.) offer several different symbol options to represent the word *no,* but only one of these options is used with the children. Just as the spoken word for *no* is the same each time it is said, the symbol for the word *no* should not vary. Second, there is only *one word per picture symbol* (see Figure 3.5). For example, we use the symbols for *water* and *table* when the children are playing at the water table rather than combining the two symbols into one pictorial representation. Similarly, we use the symbols for *sand* and *table* when the children are playing at the *sand table*. In this way, we are focusing on the individual word mappings, visually highlighting that there are different types of tables in the real world, and on the *concept* of modifer+noun. Both of these rules are important because we are trying to facilitate generative language across people, locations, and environments.

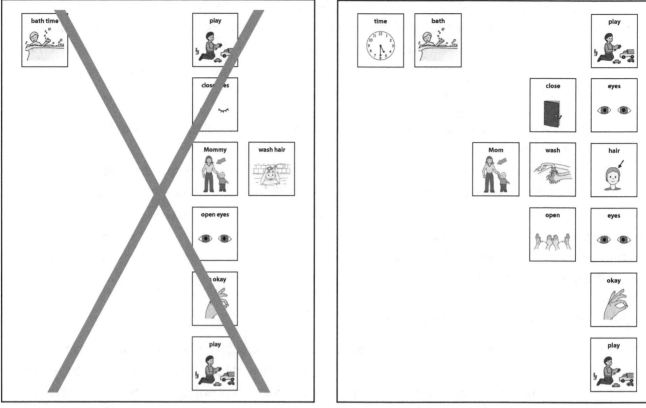

Figure 3.5. Example of incorrect and correct use of the one word per symbol rule.

Implementing Functional Joint Action/Activity Routines

Core functional vocabulary may be placed in linguistically meaningful and *functional* routines for the Level 2 child to scaffold more sophisticated social communication. Using joint action/activity routines has been advocated by many intervention programs for children on the autism spectrum (Prizant et al., 2006; Rogers & Dawson, 2010; Rollins et al., 1998; Snyder-McLean, Solomonson, McLean, & Sack, 1984). From a developmental social-pragmatic perspective, routines facilitate language comprehension and constitute an early emerging communicative intention (refer to Figure 2.2). Consequently, routines create a context for shared mutual knowledge.

The language comprehension abilities of typical children functioning at Levels 2 and 3 are often limited to understanding a few words within routines or embedded in a specific context (Chapman, 1978). For example, a child may appear to understand the word *smell* when holding a flower, the word *throw* when holding a ball, and the word *kiss* when receiving an embrace, but fail to understand these words out of these very specific contexts.

Often children rely on **nonlinguistic comprehension strategies** to understand the language around them (Chapman, 1978; Miller & Paul, 1995). For example, young children may look at the object the adult is holding or do what is typically done with the object in a given situation (i.e., child smells a flower when handed a flower or brushes teeth when given a toothbrush). Using functional core vocabulary within routines facilitates comprehension of classroom activities such as "clean up," "check your schedule," "sit," "wait," "look," "hello," "turn," and "finish," and can be used functionally in other environments (e.g., home) as well.

Because core vocabulary routines present a lower level of demand than the spoken word, they can be used as a scaffold to understanding language (see naturalistic prompt hierarchy). Stated differently, core vocabulary routines are often made up of simple songs that are used consistently and correspond to a specific action, such as the clean-up song used in many preschools. This facilitates the use of routines as a strategy when a child does not comprehend the word without context.

> *Andrew entered the classroom. His teacher greeted him, "Hi, Andrew," and waited for Andrew to respond with an appropriate greeting. When Andrew began to walk away, his teacher sang "♪ ♫ ♫ Hello Andrew, Hello Andrew ♪ ♫ ♫." Andrew turned to the teacher and supplied the appropriate response to the routine by saying, "Hello, Miss Sally." Andrew was successful at saying "hello" within the appropriate social context because his response, "Hello, Miss Sally," was embedded within the routine/song, a skill that is developmentally less sophisticated but socially appropriate for the context.*

From a language-use standpoint, routines are an early emerging communicative intention. Young typically developing children engage in many social routines such as "peek-a-boo" and reading books. Social routines alert the child to information he should attend to and define what he can presuppose (Bruner, 1995). That is, when children participate in social routines, they know what to expect and can predict what comes next. Therefore, routines provide the contexts for a shared goal (mutual knowledge), which both partners are jointly committed to doing together – the second requirement of *a joint cooperative activity* (see Chapter 2). In addition, as routines are learned, caregivers allow the child to take over more control of the interaction. This helps the child to understand that there are two roles in the interaction and that each participant can take either role (role reversal) – the third requirement of *a joint cooperative activity.*

As with the example of the "hello" routine above, routines have specific speech uses, and children recognize these as belonging to the routine. The sensitive caregiver provides opportunities for the child to contribute a turn within routine activities (Ninio & Bruner, 1978; Ninio & Snow, 1996; Snow, Perlman, & Nathan, 1987). The predictable patterns of these socially constructed routines make it possible for young children to participate in conversational turn-taking exchanges well before they can add new information to the interaction (Ninio & Snow, 1996).

Similarly, routines support comprehension and social communication for children with ASD functioning at Level 2 and early Level 3. Routines facilitate context-embedded, shared meaning that may scaffold joint cooperative activities. While the early routines used with typically developing children are often meaningless (e.g., peek-a-boo), routines developed for children with ASD are functional and based on the child's core functional vocabulary. The core vocabulary decreases the linguistic load and the routine decreases the cognitive load (Rollins et al., 1998). Functional routines are embedded into meaningful activities that can occur across the child's various activities and environments (e.g., home, school, playground) and across persons (parent, babysitters and teachers). This facilitates comprehension and mutual knowledge, and helps the child to predict what is coming next.

Within a preschool environment, the first routines developed are often those that help a child understand classroom and behavioral expectations (e.g., clean up, check schedule, sit down, look); social routines (e.g., hello/goodbye, anticipating actions, my turn), as well as joint activity routines (e.g., birthday party, restaurant, store). Later developing joint focus routines, such as book reading routines (Ninio & Bruner, 1978; Snow et al., 1987), can be adapted using the core functional vocabulary to simplify the linguistic content of books for meaningful joint attention routines (see Book of the Week section in Chapter 4).

Implementing Activity Routines

Engaging in an activity one time does not make it a routine, and just because the teacher or therapist knows an activity is a routine does not mean that the child understands it is a routine. While this sounds obvious, teachers and therapists often give up because a child does not participate in the "routine" when first introduced. Initially, the child may need to watch others participating in the routine. Video modeling (D'Ateno, Mangiapanello, & Taylor, 2003) also works well for this. For example, make a video of core functional routines used in the preschool for children to watch prior to entering the program. Joint activity routines (e.g., birthday party routines or going to the grocery store routines) also lend themselves well to video modeling.

To establish a routine, children need modeling and prompting. Once the child is able to participate in the routine, it should be varied to promote new learning (Prizant et al., 2006; Snyder-McLean et al., 1984). For example, you can add varied repetition by doing the same routine with different materials or in different contexts. In addition, once an activity routine is mastered, it is expanded, but the meaning or purpose remains consistent. Expanding a routine can be accomplished by interrupting or violating it, omitting necessary materials, initiating the routine and "playing dumb" (Prizant et al., 2006; Snyder-McLean et al., 1984), or by adding new and more mature constituent parts.

Michael was a Level 2 child who was very motivated by music. He always chose to listen to music and sing songs for his first Center Time activity. This became an established routine for Michael.

One day his speech therapist violated the routine by not having a CD in the player. That meant Michael had to "look" for a CD. First, the therapist arranged it so that Michael found a CD in the first place they looked. Later, Michael had to search in two or three locations. Once the routine of looking for the CD was established, the routine of "look" was expanded on.

Now Michael had to knock on the office door and "wait" for someone to answer and bring him the CD. When this routine was established, the therapist expanded the routine again by requiring Michael to say "hello" to the person answering the door and request a CD. Michael's routine of listening to music was expanded over several iterations. With the addition of each new component of the routine, he needed initial modeling and prompting. While the routine varied over time, the meaning and purpose of the routine remained the constant.

Discussing a Related Present: Decreasing Context Embeddedness

As we have discussed, linguistically meaningful and functional routines for the Level 2 child facilitate comprehension and shared engagement, both of which are necessary for joint attention. As Level 2 children begin to elaborate and expand on their routines, they may transition to Level 3. The Level 3 child begins to share attention and interest with teachers, therapists, and parents by pointing, showing, or commenting on something in the immediate environment. These early object-mediated displays of sharing interest do not require the child to maintain the conversation. Many early conversations of typical children and their caregivers require minimal response on the part of the child, who may simply provide a point, shrug yes/no, or give a one-word answer to an adult question (Eisenberg, 1981; Uccelli, Hemphill, Pan, & Snow, 2005) (see Figure 3.6).

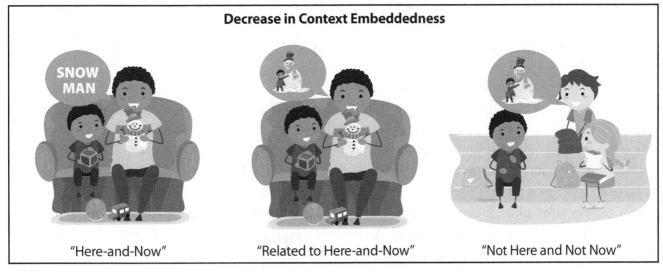

Figure 3.6. Decrease in context embeddedness.

Typical children do not maintain the topic of conversation by adding new information until they are 20 to 32 months old, when their language becomes increasingly more proficient (Bloom, Rocissano, & Hood, 1976). From 20 to 32 months of age, typical children engage in social communication that represents a decrease in context embeddedness. That is, children and their caregivers begin to incorporate discussions about objects and events that, while not currently present in the child's environment, are somehow related to it (e.g., Discuss a Related Present in Figure 2.3). Next they engage in discussions about objects and events, that have no perceivable reference in the environment (e.g., Discuss Nonpresent in Figure 2.3) as well as talk about nonobservable thoughts and feelings.

In many older pragmatic coding schemes, Discuss a Related Present and Discuss Nonpresent are collapsed and not seen as separate developmental steps (Ninio & Snow, 1996; Ninio, Snow, Pan, & Rollins, 1994). However, recent literature on the development of social-pragmatic skills in typically developing children emphasizes that Discuss a Related Present is important for promoting shared knowledge necessary for learning how to maintain a topic of conversation (Ninio & Snow, 1996; Rollins, 2014; Uccelli et al., 2005).

Young children's fledgling conversational skills are enhanced by a responsive and cooperative adult partner. For example, a caregiver may point to a picture of a lion in a book and say, "A lion, did we see a lion?" The child nods, and the caregiver continues, "That's right, at the zoo." The child repeats "zoo," and the caregiver asks, "What did the lion say? Did he say roar?" Uccelli et al. (2005) suggested that the shift in conversations from Discussing a Joint Focus to Discussing Related Present provides the child with a rudimentary opportunity to remember past events and bring them into the present, which is the beginning of narrative development.

Children on the autism spectrum have extraordinary difficulties maintaining a topic of conversation and often engage in **pseudo-conversations**. In a pseudo-conversation the child initiates a topic and the adult responds. Rather than moving the conversation on, the child brings up a new topic, and the adult responds again. This sequence of the child bringing up new topics of conversation followed by an adult response is often repeated several times. The adult is so happy that the child is conversing that he continues to respond, often not realizing a true conversation is not taking place.

To help address pseudo-conversations, intervention can maximize the social interchange of Discussing a Related Present for Level 3 children. Discussing a Related Present promotes mutual knowledge and helps with topic maintenance when talking about future and past events. Discussing a Related Present also promotes complex language forms (past and future tense, temporal vocabulary) and literacy development (Snow, Burns, & Griffin, 1998). Opportunities for children to Discuss a Related Present can be scheduled to occur several times during the day. Specific Discuss a Related Present routines may include Remember Time, Calendar Time, Choice Time, and filling out My Day at School forms. Talk About Bags and Picture Diaries can also be developed to structure cross-context communication between the home and school environments. All of these activities are discussed fully in the Daily Schedule section in Chapter 4.

Naturalistic Prompt Hierarchy and Language Modeling

One goal of meaningful social communication is to keep the conversation moving forward (Ninio & Snow, 1996). Using the naturalistic prompt hierarchy (see Figure 3.7), the teacher provides the child with spontaneous communication opportunities within the context of an ongoing activity. If the child does not respond or offers a response that is inappropriate for the situation, the teacher can scaffold the child's response to facilitate successful communication by reducing the level of linguistic demand. The left side of Figure 3.7 describes what happens when the child does not respond or offers an inappropriate response – the clinician drops down to an antecedent that has a lower level of demand.

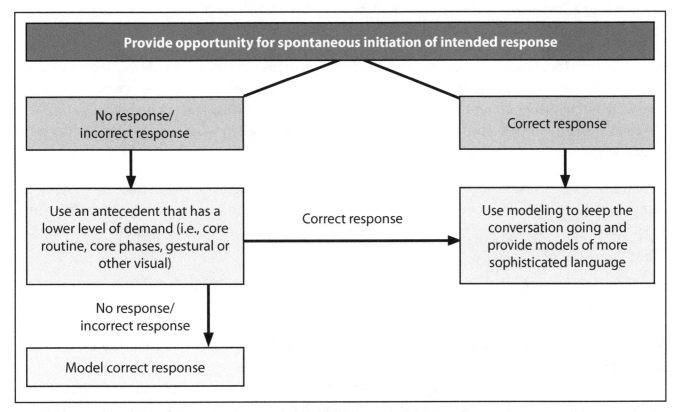

***Figure 3.7.* Naturalistic prompt hierarchy.**

Andrew was asked to look for his folder. When he did not respond, his teacher sang the "Look" song (to the tune of the first line of "Skip to My Lou"), "♪ ♫ ♫ Look, look, look for your folder, look, look, look for your folder ♪ ♫ ♫," one time. The antecedent of the "Look" routine, with its lower level of demand, resulted in Andrew comprehending the request and looking for his folder. The teacher continued singing until the folder was located (see Chapter 4 to learn how the "Look" routine is established during Hello Circle). If Andrew did not respond to the "Look" song, the teacher would have gently guided him to the folder to keep the interaction moving forward.

The right-hand side of the response hierarchy is used when the child produces/approximates an appropriate response or spontaneously communicates. It is important to note that in a developmental social-pragmatic program, all communicative attempts are responded to (not just specific therapy targets), and language modeling techniques are used within the socially motivating interactive context.

Language modeling consists of synchronized verbal and visual input similar to natural aided language modeling (Cafiero, 1998; Drager et al., 2006). Specifically, core vocabulary is visually and verbally marked. Visually marking vocabulary allows the child to see the words creating perceptual salience, whereas verbally marking vocabulary allows the child to pair what she sees with what she hears (refer to the section on Word Learning in Chapter 2). While only the core vocabulary is visually marked, language models continue to be grammatically correct to avoid **telegraphic speech**. Other strategies include talking about what the child is looking at, slowing down your rate of speech, and leaving pauses for the child to add new information.

Remember the focus here is on Level 2 and 3 children. Therefore, all language modeling occurs in interactions where you are facilitating mutual responsiveness. This suggests that you are interacting face-to-face with the child, supporting his attention to objects and events in his view. Sitting behind or next to the child and narrating what he is doing may be facilitative for children who have well-established joint attention, but not for children in Level 2.

Finally, we recommend limiting the use of wh-questions as the first level demand on the prompt hierarchy (see Figure 3.7). Asking questions only requires a child to respond without leaving space for him to initiate conversation. Children with ASD have difficulties initiating, so it is important to give them opportunities to do so.

Several modeling strategies are discussed in the literature. The strategies we have found successful are as follows.

Replacing unconventional communication with conventional symbols: The clinician interprets the child's behavior as meaningful and intentional and models the correct conventional symbol. For example, the child reaches for the play dough, and the teacher or therapist responds by showing the child the picture for play dough and saying, "Play dough, want the play dough." Or the child falls down on the floor to protest, and the teacher or therapist responds by showing the child the picture for "mad" and saying "mad."

It is important to be responsive to all of the child's communicative attempts, not just the conventional ones. This is one way the child learns the value, function, and meaning of his communicative expressions – verbal or nonverbal. Being responsive to the child's communication does not mean, however, that the child always gets what he wants or talks about only what he is interested in.

> *Sam was a Level 2 child who used many nonconventional signals. One day, when the teacher was reading the Book of the Week during Hello Circle Time, Sam was making big X's with his finger in the air. A speech therapist working with the children in the classroom noticed that Sam was looking toward the calendar that had X's crossing off each day that had gone by. The speech therapist acknowledged Sam's behavior by saying "you see X's, X's are on the calendar," and redirected him to the book reading activity.*

Expansion: The teacher or therapist repeats the child's communicative attempt/utterance back to her with the correct grammatical markers and semantic details that would make it an acceptable adult utterance.

Extension: The teacher or therapist comments on the child's utterance while adding semantic information.

Buildups: The teacher or therapist gradually expands the child's sentence to its full grammatical form. This technique allows the clinician to gradually increase the complexity of her utterance to include additional information while also providing a lot of repetition within the action or activity (e.g., "Coat. Coat on. Put your coat on. We need to put your coat on."). Use of buildups helps the child to identify key words within your longer utterances.

Breakdowns: The teacher or therapist gradually *decreases* the complexity of her utterance into several phrase-sized pieces (e.g., "We need to put your coat on. Put your coat on. Coat on."). Breakdowns are also helpful to many children when learning to segment longer utterances while providing a great deal of repetition of target vocabulary.

Recasting: Similar to expansions, the teacher or therapist reformulates the child's utterance so that it is grammatically correct.

Actively Supporting the Child

Several language stimulation techniques are not mentioned here, such as **self-talk** and **parallel talk**. These techniques are often used in interactions where the teacher or therapist is sitting slightly behind the child or next to the child, not face-to-face with the child. As mentioned, such interactions are productive for children who have well-established joint attention (late Level 3 and beyond) and can readily share objects and events with others in their environment. For children who are not yet initiating and maintaining joint attention with a communicative partner (Levels 1, 2, and early 3), however, it is important that the adult actively supports the child's attention by creating an interaction that helps the child understand that she is doing something in relationship with another person (see Figure 3.8).

Figure 3.8. Adult actively supporting the child's attention by creating an interaction that helps the child understand he is doing something together in relationship with another person.

Emotional Regulation

Many developmental social-pragmatic interventions highlight the importance of supporting a child's emotional regulation because regulation is essential for optimal attention and social and communication development (Prizant et al., 2006). When a person is well regulated, his emotional arousal (positive or negative) is "redirected, controlled, modulated and modified to enable the person to function adaptively" (Cicchetti, Ganiban, & Barnett, 1991, p. 15).

As depicted in Figure 3.9, there is an optimal degree of arousal where children learn best. Thus, children who are under- or over-aroused are less available for learning (DeGangi, 2000; Prizant et al., 2006). Emotional regulation skills fluctuate in everyone; just think about how difficult it is to pay attention and learn during a long lecture when you are tired, or to listen and remember what is being said when you walk into a crowded, unfamiliar place, and you are hungry!

Children with ASD have substantial difficulties with self- and emotional regulation. Transitions from high to low arousal (or vice versa) may be very quick or very slow. In addition, it may be difficult for them to recover from dysregulation (see Prizant et al., 2006, for a complete discussion).

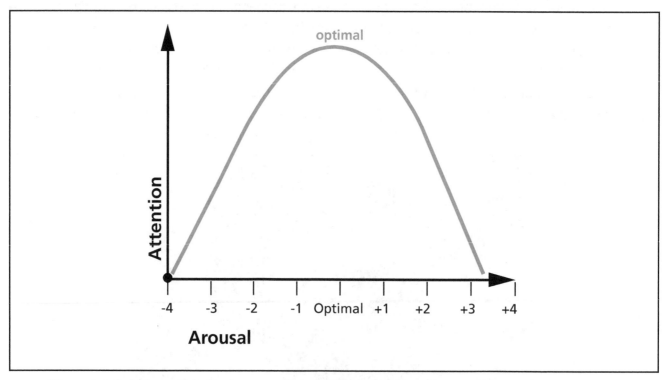

Figure 3.9. Relationship between arousal and attention region of optimal attention for learning. (Prizant et al., 2006; Rollins & Greenwald, 2013).

There are many things that caregivers, teachers, and therapists can do to support emotional regulation. Recently, Rollins and Greenwald (2013) found that some caregivers of typical infants functioning at Level 2 were more skilled at supporting their infant's attention by using calm interactions without over-arousing them. Further, they found that well-attuned, low-intensity interactions promoted under-standing of joint attention, whereas moderate-intensity interactions not only deregulated the children but also had a strong negative relationship with joint attention. These findings point out that there is an optimal level of arousal that facilitates understanding of the attention and learning, and that the level of arousal may be influenced by the pattern of interaction between the child and his environment.

The SCERTS model suggests several qualities of the language and physical environment to support emotional regulation. For example, Prizant et al. (2006) recommended preorganizing the child by pro-viding a predictable structured routine and visual supports. They also suggested simplifying the lan-guage addressed to the child and making sure that it is appropriate to her comprehension skills.

All of the key components described in this chapter attend to these emotional regulation suggestions. That is, core functional vocabulary, embedding core vocabulary into functional joint action/activity routines, the use of visual graphic symbols, the naturalistic prompt hierarchy, and language modeling techniques all support the child's emotional regulation.

The physical space is also important. The classroom is organized to answer the question: "Where should I be?" (Mesibov & Shea, 2014). To accomplish that, each area should have clear boundaries; areas should be clearly labeled and physically delineated with carpets or barriers so there is no question where in the room an activity is taking place (see Figure 3.10). This means the classroom is well organized around specific kinds of materials and/or types of play, such as a table-toys area (for puzzles, pegboards, and board games); a book area; a blocks area; a movement area (for trampolines, rocking boards, scooter boards); a music area; an art area; a play dough area; and a pretend area (for dramatic play materials).

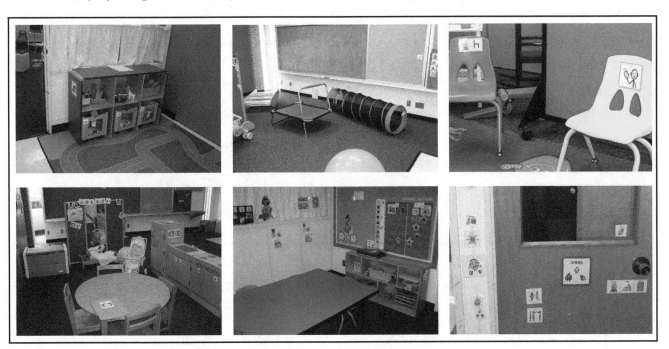

Figure 3.10. Examples of clearly defined space.

The classroom should have a quiet, relaxing area to be used when the child is feeling dysregulated and needs a break. A book area or a tent may be sufficient. If space permits, there may be a "break room" with a ball tent, weighted blanket, and bean bag chairs to help the children regulate.

Finally, children with ASD also need to know where to put their bodies within the space at all times. That means there should be a designated spot for the child to sit or stand (chair, carpet square, etc.). For example, the children's picture can be laminated onto their chair, and there may be a "watching chair" for the child who is getting deregulated and needs to move away from the group and a "hello chair" to sit in when singing hello.

Chapter Highlights

- Eight key components of classroom-based developmental social-pragmatic interventions for Level 2 children are (a) individualized goals with a developmental approach to goal hierarchy, (b) activity-based intervention, (c) a core functional vocabulary, (d) visual graphic symbols, (e) joint activity routines, (f) discussion about object or events not in the immediate environment but somehow related to it, (g) a naturalistic prompt hierarchy, and (h) strategies to keep the child regulated.

- The first step of writing individual communication, language, and social skills goals is to perform an in-depth functional communication assessment.

- Social communication goals must be functional and achievable as well as observable and measurable.

- Goals state the *communicative means, communicative intention, conversational level,* and the *specific social condition.*

- Child goals should be embedded into meaningful activities within the broader classroom environment using logically occurring antecedents and consequences.

- A core functional vocabulary simplifies the language addressed to young children and ensures that they receive multiple exposures (i.e., repetition) to each word in a variety of naturalistic contexts.

- Core vocabulary is visually and verbally marked. Visually marking vocabulary allows the child to see the words, thereby creating perceptual saliency. Verbally marking vocabulary allows the child to pair what she sees with what she hears.

- Embedding core functional vocabulary into routines helps increase the child's comprehension and overall social-emotional reciprocity.

- Routines facilitate context-embedded, shared meaning that may scaffold joint cooperative activities.

- To establish a routine, children need modeling and prompting. Once the child is able to participate in the routine, it is varied to promote new learning.

- When using picture symbols to facilitate language, it is important to use only one word per picture symbol and ensure that the picture symbol used to represent an individual word is always the same across various contexts.

- Pairing spoken language with picture symbols during natural interactions capitalizes on the word learning strategy available to Level 2 children.

- Discussing a Related Present promotes mutual knowledge and helps with topic maintenance when talking about future and past events.

- Discussing a Related Present promotes complex language forms (e.g., past and future tense, temporal vocabulary) and literacy development.

- A naturalistic prompt hierarchy first provides opportunity for spontaneous initiation of a target response, followed by use of prompts with lower levels of linguistic demand.

- Children with ASD have substantial difficulties with self- and emotional regulation. Children who are under- or over-aroused are less available for learning.

Chapter Review Questions

1. Name two key components of classroom-based developmental social-pragmatic intervention and explain why they are important for Level 2 children.

2. What are the four criteria for writing a goal? Give an example goal.

3. How would you choose the words to include in a child's core functional vocabulary?

4. How do routines support comprehension and social communication for children with ASD?

5. What are nonlinguistic comprehension strategies?

6. What are the two rules governing how to choose picture symbols for Level 2 children?

7. How would you use the naturalistic prompt hierarchy?

8. Why is Discussing a Related Present an important communicative intention?

9. What is emotional regulation, and why is it important to be aware of this when working with children with ASD?

10. List two classroom strategies to support emotional regulation.

Chapter 4:
The Early CLASS Daily Schedule

Learner Objectives:

After reading this chapter, the learner should be able to:

- Explain why it is beneficial to alternate between activities that require the child with ASD to sit and attend and activities that require the child to move.

- Explain why it is important to structure transitions from one activity to the next.

- Describe a functional activity that can be used to facilitate joint attention.

- Explain why having a mixture of 1:1 with adult, small- and large-group activities is beneficial for a child with ASD.

- Describe a functional teaching/therapy activity that can be used to facilitate an understanding of reciprocal roles and role reversibility.

- Explain how to rewrite children's books to facilitate a child's comprehension and joint attention.

- Describe a functional therapy activity that facilitates negotiating mutual attention.

- Describe at least two functional activities that increase children's use of Discussing a Related Present to structure cross-context communication between home and school environments.

- Describe ways to modulate children's arousal levels through activity planning.

The Early CLASS program was developed as a preschool-based intervention program for young children on the autism spectrum, ages 3-5. Specifically, the Early CLASS activities were designed for young children whose social communication functions were at Levels 2 and 3. Most children entered the program capable of using consistent means (i.e., words, pictures, conventional/nonconventional gestures) to request. Some used words to label objects and events without regard for their communicative partner.

As a developmental social-pragmatic preschool, the program was designed to facilitate reciprocal interaction, joint attention, and shared understanding using the key components described in Chapter 3. In this chapter, we use the Early CLASS to demonstrate how these components can be integrated within a preschool class.

The Daily Schedule

- Get Ready
- Hello Circle
- Choice Time
- Center Time
- Remember Time
- Small Group Time
- Bathroom Time
- Snack Time
- Gym Time
- Book Time
- Music Time

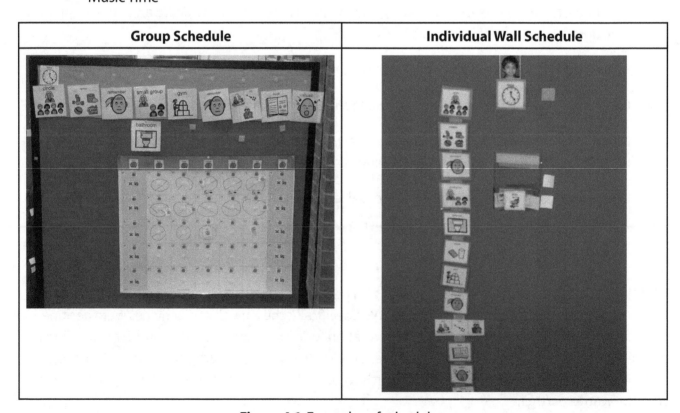

Group Schedule	Individual Wall Schedule

Figure 4.1. Examples of schedules.

Children with ASD are often more emotionally regulated and available (attentive) for learning when they know what to expect. In the Early CLASS, therefore, there is a predictable sequence of events across the entire day (i.e., the daily schedule) and activity schedules are followed within specific activities. Transitions between activities are clearly marked through core vocabulary, or by pairing spoken language with picture symbols. Finally, the core vocabulary and routines are used to mark initiation of activities, steps within activities, completion of activities and transitions.

Rationale for the Sequence of Activities

The daily schedule consists of a mixture of small- and large-group activities. In addition, there are several opportunities in the schedule for children to participate in activities with a single teacher (e.g., Center Time). The latter facilitates individualized instruction with the teacher or a therapy session (e.g., occupational or speech) within the context of the classroom. Varying the group size allows children to use their nascent communication, language, and social skills within a variety of social contexts.

Also, the Early CLASS alternates between group activities that require children to sit, pay attention, and interact and activities that allow the children to move around the room. Such alternating of activities is important to prevent children from having to sit and attend for long periods of time without a break. Further, the planned times to move around give children the opportunity to engage in specific activities (i.e., jumping on a trampoline, pushing a weighted chair, crawling with a scooter board) that will help keep them regulated and attentive during the next activity. Finally, wherever possible, less challenging and preferred activities are alternated with more challenging, less preferred activities.

Get Ready Time

The purpose of Get Ready Time is to help the children regulate when they first come to the classroom. Children often get to school dysregulated because of the rushed morning routine from home to school, having to leave a favorite toy at home, transitioning away from parents, and a myriad other reasons. The first 7 minutes of the school day are relaxed in order to help children negotiate these transitions. Thus, the children are able to go (or be led) to the type of activity that helps them best regulate. Some children need to jump on a trampoline while others need to sit quietly with a book or a table toy. This is not a time for active teaching/therapy; it is a time for transition and regulation.

Figure 4.2. Helper of the day schedule and check-in board.

At some point during Get Ready Time (usually toward the beginning), when the child is comfortable, he moves his picture on the check-in board from the home location to the school location and looks for his folder. The teacher or therapist says, "Time to move your picture" and "Look for your folder."

Children in the classroom who are functioning at Level 3 have the opportunity to be "helpers." As such, they check the helper-of-the-day schedule (in far left of Figure 4.2). The helper-of-the-day schedule features pictures of each of the Level 3 children in the room to the left and the helper jobs to the right.

The picture above depicts five helper jobs for a given day – calendar, line leader, snack, TV, and light helper. If the child is a helper that day, she takes the picture of the helper job and places it in her folder to help her remember. If the child is not a helper, the teacher/therapist says, "You're *not* a helper," pointing to "not" and "helper" in the child's folder.

Transitions

Transitions refer to the times between activities. Transitions are not inconsequential and should be structured so that the children understand the organization of the transition (moving from one space to another) and know what is coming next (by checking their schedule). For example, the transition between Get Ready Time and Hello Circle is a four-part functional routine, as follows:

Two minutes/clean up/check schedule/sit down

1. Teacher/therapist gives 2-minute warning and flashes lights saying, "Two minutes, two minutes 'til clean-up."

2. After 2 minutes, the teacher/therapist flashes lights and says, "Time to clean up!" Everyone sings "Barney: Clean-Up Song"(Barney & Friends, n.d.) "♪♫♫ *Clean up, Clean up, Everybody, Everywhere, Clean up, Clean up, Everybody Do Your Share*♪♫♫ ."The song is repeated until everyone has finished cleaning up. Everything in the classroom has a logical place in small bins on shelves or in cubbies. During the song, the teacher encourages children to clean up their activity. Early in the year, when the clean-up activity routine is new, it may involve the teacher actively modeling or prompting the child. With time, the clean-up activity routine may include having children who finish cleaning up their area early help other children clean their areas.

3. When the room is cleaned up, the teacher says: "Clean-up is finished; time to check your schedule." Everyone sings the "Check Your Schedule" song to the tune of "Frère Jacques.""♪♫♫ Check your schedule, check your schedule./Check it now, check it now./ Time to check your schedule, time to check your schedule./Check it now, check it now.♪♫♫ " As children check their individual schedules, a teacher, therapist, or aide in the classroom assists as needed. The song is repeated until the majority of the children have checked their schedule (if a child requires more time, an assistant may continue singing to the child while the rest of the class moves on to the next activity).

4. When children have checked their schedule, the teacher sings: "♪♫♫ Everybody sit down, sit down, sit down/Everybody sit down/Find your chair. ♪♫♫" to the tune of "London Bridge Is Falling Down."The song is repeated until the majority of the children sit down (if a child requires more time, an assistant may continue singing to the child until he sits down).

Hello Circle

We start Hello Circle with music meant to attract and engage the children as they arrive to Hello Circle. We use "Greg and Steve's Good Morning" song (YouTube, dagr8vixster, 2012) for this purpose. The teacher initiates an imitation activity, "Stretch up, wiggle fingers, touch the floor, wave." The music and imitation activity let the children arrive at their own pace, while keeping early comers engaged. Each child's picture is on his chair to provide the children the opportunity to "look" for their chair. In addition, the pictures ensure that children sit in a predetermined location without disrupting the flow of the activity. This is especially important when you want a child to sit in a specific seat. For example, you may want a highly distractible child to sit directly in front of the teacher or to make sure that specific children do not sit next to each other.

Hello Circle has a meta-structure to keep a predictable sequence of events, while allowing for varied repetition. It may include "Hello" song, "Days of the Week" song, Calendar Time, Look, Book Time, and the introduction of Special Activity.

Figure 4.3 shows an example of the Hello Circle meta-schedule on a pocket chart next to the chair where the teacher sits facing the children. The specific elements of Hello Circle may change depending on the level of the children and their ability to attend. As the children are able to attend for longer periods of time, elements are added. For example, at the beginning of the year, Hello Circle may consist of the Hello song and the book; weeks later, the "Days of the Week" song may be introduced followed by Calendar Time and Look. Having the meta-schedule displayed next to the teacher (see Figure 4.4) allows the teacher to mark the initiation and completion of each element of the Hello Circle with core vocabulary and visual means (i.e., "It's *time* to sing hello," pointing to the hello picture; "'Hello Song' is *finished*," turning the Hello picture over; "now it's *time* to sing days of the week," pointing to the days of the week picture). A sample script for Hello Circle may be found in Appendix B.

Figure 4.3. Example of Hello Circle meta-structure.

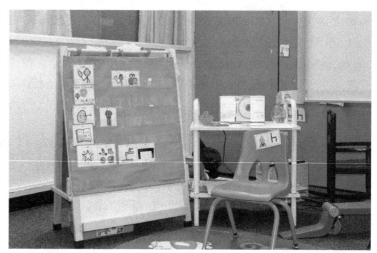

Figure 4.4. Meta-schedule next to teacher.

Rationales for Each Component in Hello Circle

"Hello" Song: The "Hello" song teaches the children a routine song, which can be used as a prompt when a child does not spontaneously say "hello" in response to an adult's greeting when entering the classroom or greeting a person for the first time (see the naturalistic prompt hierarchy, Figure 3.7). During Hello Circle, each child takes his turn sitting in the "hello chair" while the other children sing the "Hello" song (refer to song glossary for words and music). The "hello chair" is located next to the teacher's chair and faces the group. It is labeled with the "Hello" picture symbol to help the children know where to sit when it is their turn. The "hello chair" provides the children with a visual cue that there is a sender of the hello message and a receiver of the hello message. Use of the "hello chair" facilitates an understanding that there are reciprocal roles in the interaction and that these roles can be reversed. Role reversibility is a component of a joint cooperative activity discussed in Chapter 2.

Taking Turns: *Turn* (as in "my turn") is a core vocabulary word. At Hello Circle as well as other times during the day, turns are visually marked with a "turn" symbol to let the children visually see who has the floor and how turns move from one person to the next. For example, in large-group activities, a large picture symbol for "turn" is placed on both sides of a manila folder. The folder is then propped open like a tent and placed in front of the child who is taking a turn (see Figure 4.5). Alternatively, a folded index card with two small picture symbols for "turn" works well for table top activities.

Visually marking a child's turn facilitates an understanding of more than one role in an interaction as well as role reversibility (both are components of a joint cooperative activity discussed in Chapter 2). We use predictable routine language for turn-taking, marking the beginning and ending of a child's turn (i.e., "Whose turn?" "It's _____ turn." "_____'s turn is finished.").

Figure 4.5. Turn-taking.

"Days of the Week" Song and Calendar Time: Singing the "Days of the Week" song (KidsTV123, 2009) or Greg & Steve's Days of the Week (Troy DaBoss, 2011) one time provides a routine song for learning the days of the week. This is important for future activities the child will be asked to participate in (e.g., see the What's Our Work Today section later in this chapter). Calendar Time serves several purposes. It helps the children learn a routine activity that they will engage in for many years in school. For Level 3 children, Calendar Time is also a time to talk about special events,

such as field trips, birthdays, special activities, or news such as "Josh has new shoes." Special events are drawn on the calendar. This gives the teacher the opportunity to talk about past and future events with a visual reference. The teacher can visually mark temporal vocabulary such as *today, tomorrow, next week, last week, begin, end, before,* and *next.* These vocabulary words are easier for the children to understand when the teacher is able to point to the appropriate place on the calendar.

Look: Before the children come to school, the teacher tapes a picture of an object to the wall in a location the children can easily see during Hello Circle. When it is time for the Look routine, the teacher tells the children it is "time to look for _____," naming the object in the picture. The teacher shows the children a picture that is identical to the one that is taped on the wall. The class sings to the tune of the first line of "Skip to My Lou," "♪♫♫ Look, look, look for the _____, look, look, look for the _____ ♪♫♫" until the teacher locates the target picture on the wall. Everyone is encouraged to point to the picture and say "there it is." The Look routine encourages children to respond and initiate joint attention.

Book of the Week: Books provide a shared attention routine with opportunities for varied repetition throughout the week. (Appendix C includes suggestions for how to vary the reading of the book to facilitate discussions around a joint focus of attention.) Each week, we read a different book that corresponds to the theme of the week. We use commercially available books but rewrite them, simplifying the language using core vocabulary with known routines and repetitive phrases.

Each instructional unit in Chapter 5 begins with a suggested book title and recommendations for how to simplify the book using specific core vocabulary, routines, and repetitive phrases. We have found that the simplified vocabulary and known routines increase the children's ability to attend to the book and prevent them from getting overloaded and tuning out when new vocabulary and concepts are introduced. It also facilitates comprehension and shared mutual knowledge of core concepts. The use of repetitive phrases catches the child's attention and helps with comprehension. Once a child gets used to a repeated phrase, the repeated phrase signals a new vocabulary word. New language forms/target words are embedded within repeated phrases to increase comprehension and attention.

Because we rely on core vocabulary and core routines, the books we use early in the semester consist of fewer words than those used later in the semester. Successive books build on earlier concepts and, therefore, contain more vocabulary, concepts, and syntax (see pages 80-81 for a list of core vocabulary words used with each book). At times, we use the books to help teach specific routines that are performed in the classroom or that the parents want the children to learn to use at home (e.g., going to a restaurant or grocery store). In these instances, the goal is to acquaint the children with a routine so that they are familiar with it when they hear it in the classroom or some other environment. For example, during the first week of class, the theme is "school." Classroom routines and songs are taught because the children do not yet know the classroom routines. The "school" book incorporates the "Hello," "Check Schedule" and "Goodbye" songs (refer to the song glossary in Appendix E for a complete list of Early CLASS songs), which are not yet well established for the children. These new routines are further supported within Small Groups and activities that are individualized for each child.

To ensure that each adult reading a book is familiar with the core vocabulary, routines, and repetitive phrases chosen for a given book, we add picture symbols as guides. In addition, each child receives a book board so that he can simultaneously hear and see the words. The latter facilitates comprehension for words, capitalizing on the word learning strategy used by Level 2 children. As mentioned in Chapter 2, the pairing of hearing with seeing an object or picture is one of the underlying word-learning strategies used by Level 2 children. Finally, we send the book board home so that caregivers can read the books to their children.

Transition to Choice Time

After the book is finished, the children are dismissed from Hello Circle and told to check their schedule: "Hello Circle is finished; it's time to check your schedule, ♪ ♪ ♪Check your schedule, check your schedule. Check it now, check it now. Time to check your schedule, time to check your schedule. Check it now, check it now♪ ♪ ♪" (sung to the tune of "Frère Jacques"). The song is repeated until the majority of the children have checked their schedule. Each child's individual schedule is vertically aligned on the wall in a designated location (see Figure 4.1). The schedule includes an activity card for each component of the daily schedule. Each activity card can be moved next to the "time for" symbol or the "finished" symbol. A portable copy of the daily schedule in children's individual folders facilitates the use of a visual support to talk about the schedule at any time and/or during any activity throughout the day. For some children, the portable schedule provides a bridge from a wall schedule to a notebook schedule.

Choice Time, Center Time, Remember Time

Choice Time and Remember Time bracket Center Time. Choice Time allows practicing communicating about future experiences, whereas Remember Time allows communicating about past experiences. That is, Choice and Remember Times allow opportunities for decontextualized language by communicating about objects and events that are not in the immediate environment. Using pictures, visual graphic symbols, or objects (see Figure 4.6) creates a bridge so that the child can communicate about past and future events with a referent present (i.e., Discussing a Related Present) and helps to scaffold language with decreased context embeddedness (see page 41).

Figure 4.6. Choice Time visual support.

Choice Time: Choice Time precedes Center Time. The goal of Choice Time is to help the child talk about future events as well as to aid her in making a plan and carrying it out. We do not expect all children to be able to make a plan; children may be at different levels in the planning process. Facilitating the process of planning during Choice Time is an example of a joint activity routine (discussed in Chapter 3) that can be systematically varied and expanded while keeping the purpose of the activity consistent over time.

Page 1 and 2 of an individual schedule for a child's folder.

time 	early CLASS 		schedule 	small group 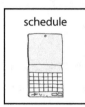

circle

bathroom

choice

snack

| center  | music  | blocks | playground | |

| | dress-up  | art | remember  | |

| | cars and trucks  | table toys  | book 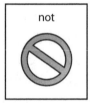 | not  |

| | movement  | house | music  | no  |

remember

finish

What follows is an example of how the Choice Time functional activity routine may be varied. Once the child can participate successfully in a given phase of the routine, that phase is expanded, but the intent of the routine remains the same. In all phases of this activity routine, the teacher/therapist makes sure the child *looks* at the choice board before she speaks.

Phase 1: No planning

o   Child goes to center of his choice; the teacher puts the visual symbol of the choice on the choice board and models for the child by pairing verbal and visual symbols (e.g., "NAME's choice is blocks" or "It's *time* for blocks.").

o   Child leaves the first center and goes to second center; the teacher pairs verbal and visual symbols to say the previous center is finished, puts the visual symbol of the second choice on the choice board, and models for the child by pairing verbal and visual symbols ("Blocks is *finished*; now it's *time* for music.").

o   Repeat as child moves to subsequent centers.

Phase 2: Forced-choice planning in one center

o   Teacher pairs verbal and visual symbols and asks the child to make a choice between two centers ("Make a choice – blocks or music?").

o   Teacher and child walk to the chosen area.

o   Child either indicates he is finished playing at the center using the word, visual symbol, or both ("finished"), or the activity is completed as in Phase 1 above.

o   Repeat as child moves to subsequent centers.

Phase 3: Child plans one center, choosing from an array

o   Teacher shows child several visual symbols of center activities and asks the child to make a choice ("make a choice").

o   Child indicates his choice verbally or using the visual symbol. Child and/or adult put(s) the child's choice on choice board. Teacher uses appropriate language models.

o   Child either indicates he is finished playing at the center using the word, visual symbol, or both ("finished"), or the activity is completed as in Phase 1 above.

o   Repeat as child moves to subsequent centers.

Phase 4: Child plans two or more centers, choosing from an array

o   Same as Phase 3, but now the child plans two or more centers on his choice board and is expected to follow through with the plan.

o   When child is finished with each center, the teacher prompts him to look at his choice board for the next activities.

Center Time: Centers are organized around specific kinds of materials and/or types of play, such as a table-toys area (for puzzles, pegboards, and board games); a book area; a movement area (for trampolines, rocking boat, scooter boards); a music area; an art area; a play dough area; a block area; and a pretend area (for dramatic play materials).

As described in the Emotional Regulation section in Chapter 3, the room is organized so that each area or center has clear boundaries. Areas are labeled and marked so the child knows where to go, and everything within the center has a place in bins, cubbies, or on a shelf. The latter helps to reduce clutter and facilitate clean-up when an activity is finished. During Center Time, the child is free to choose which activities to engage in. Nonetheless, the teacher and therapists should identify specific activity routines to engage in within each of the centers.

Remember Time: As described above, Remember Time is a time for the children to talk about past events with a referent in the immediate environment. There are many ways to do this. In our program at UT-Dallas, one of the teachers videotapes each of the children during Center Time, and the video is played back to the children on a monitor during Remember Time. This activity bridges discussing a joint focus of attention to less context-embedded discussions about a related present. Remember Time is also scheduled into other activities such as Small Group. During Small Group Remember Time, we ask the children to talk about the activity they just participated in using the Small Group visual supports. These visual supports provide the referent about the past event needed to create the space for mutual knowledge while scaffolding talk about the past.

Small Group

Small Group is an opportunity to reinforce vocabulary and concepts from the book of the week. Each instructional unit in Chapter 5 includes a sample Small Group lesson that reinforces vocabulary and concepts introduced in the book of the week. Small Groups typically have either a boardgame format or a pretend play format. Both formats emphasize new theme vocabulary and core vocabulary, and provide opportunities to practice taking turns, waiting, and attending to others. As an example, during the restaurant Small Group, core vocabulary words are combined to facilitate comprehension of the functional activity of going to a restaurant. The restaurant Small Group may go as follows (core functional vocabulary words are italicized while theme words are underlined):

> The children will *walk* into the pretend <u>restaurant</u> and *wait* to be told to *sit* at a *table*. They will *look* at a <u>menu</u> and make a *choice* about what they *want to eat*. They will *wait* for the <u>waiter</u> (another child or a teacher). When the <u>waiter</u> arrives, they say *hello* and take turns *tell*ing the <u>waiter</u> their *choice* of *food* to *eat*. After all of the children *tell* the <u>waiter</u> their choice of food, they *wait* for the *food*; when the food arrives, the children pretend to *eat*.

This activity allows the children to practice the appropriate behaviors and the language needed at a restaurant while requiring them to comprehend three new words (*restaurant, menu, waiter*). Reducing the linguistic requirements scaffolds a joint cooperative activity (see page 26 for a definition of a joint cooperative activity). That is, when the children comprehend the core vocabulary words (or core routines associated with each word), they are more likely to be mutually responsive to one another and have shared knowledge about the activities taking place. In addition, if the children have reached Level 3, they may be capable of being the waiter, which allows them to practice taking on reciprocal and complementary roles (i.e., role reversibility) in the interaction in order to achieve a joint goal. Parents are encouraged to use this simple restaurant activity routine when going out to a restaurant, and are given suggestions on how they may expand the routine over time.

As with Hello Circle, Small Group has a meta-structure to keep a predictable sequence of events, while allowing for varied repetition. The meta-structure (see Figure 4.7) includes "who's here, what's our work today, time to do our work, time to remember, and clean up." The rationale for the latter three components of Small Group have already been discussed. Therefore, we only elaborate on "who's here" and "what's our work today?" The specific elements of Small Groups are adjusted to the developmental/attentional level of the children in the group.

Figure 4.7. Small Group meta-structure support.

"Who's here" is a functional joint activity routine that requires the children to respond verbally to their names when called, be aware of and attend to other children in the environment, and practice the concept "not" (e.g., Jonnie is *not* here today). When children are in early Level 2, this functional joint activity routine may be embedded in a song such as "Where Is Thumbkin," substituting the child's name and having the child respond with "here I am." For example, the teacher may say, "Where is Jonnie" and then begin to sing ♪♫♫"Where is Jonnie, where is Jonnie,"♪♫♫ pausing after two repetitions and leaving space for Jon to say, "Here I am."

As with all other functional joint activity routines, as the child becomes able to participate in the routine, it is varied to promote new learning and to increase the sophistication of the activity while the meaning and purpose of the activity remain constant. That is, once the child can participate successfully in a given phase of the routine, that phase is expanded, but the intent of the routine remains the same.

"What's our work today?" provides opportunity for children to talk about future activities. When children are functioning in early Level 2, "what's our work today" may be omitted or be very simple: "Today we will play pretend restaurant." As the children develop Level 3 skills, the "what's our work today?" component of Small Group can generate a decontextualized discussion around a related present. Recall from Figure 2.3 that Discuss a Related Present emerges before Discuss Nonpresent and is important for promoting a shared knowledge necessary for learning how to maintain a topic of conversation. Consequently, "what's our work today?" is built around a carefully constructed visual support.

Figure 4.8 illustrates an example of a "what's our work today?" visual support for a full week of Small Group activities. By pointing to the relevant picture, mutual knowledge is facilitated, and group members can talk about what they will do on a given day (i.e., today). Further, they can talk about what they will do tomorrow or what they did yesterday. For example, the teacher using the support in Figure 4.8 can point to Tuesday and say, "Look, *today* is _____, Tuesday (as a repetition or model), what will we do today?" After talking about painting the grass and animals, the teacher can move her finger to Monday and continue with, "Look, *yesterday* was____, Monday (as a repetition or model), remember, what we did *yesterday*?"

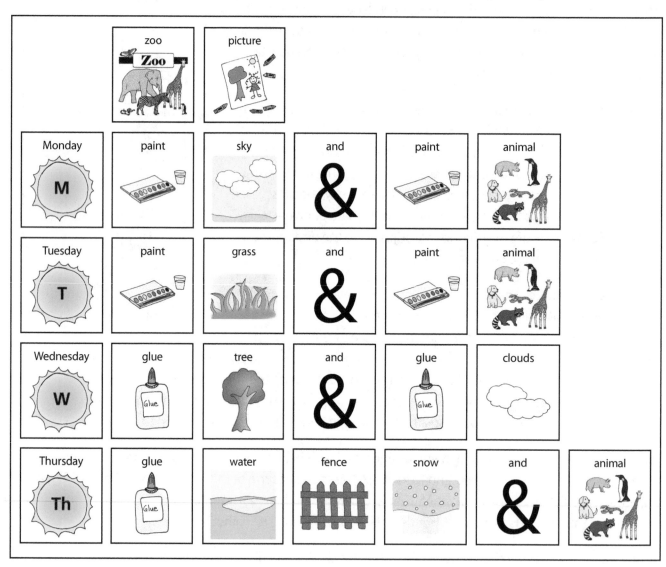

Figure 4.8. Example of Small Group weekly schedule.

This allows the teacher/therapist to co-construct a discussion about what they did the day before. The visual support allows the teacher/therapist and children to co-construct a discussion about future and past events with a referent in the environment. Similarly to Calendar Time, the visual pointing helps to create perceptual saliency to difficult temporal vocabulary such as *today, tomorrow, begin, end, before,* and *next*.

Snack

Snack is a great time for children to request what they want to eat, especially when several options are available (animal crackers, pretzels, Goldfish®). Children can increase their utterance length by specifying how many (i.e., "I want 2 pretzels") or if they want a lot or a little. However, Level 2 children already know how to request, so it is important to be creative about facilitating other types of communicative intentions.

Because snack is often very motivating to children, it is a good time to facilitate **"negotiating mutual attention"** (i.e., getting another person to look at you before you speak to them) by calling the Snack leader's name. This can be accomplished through a functional joint activity routine. The adult leading Snack turns her back on the target child so that calling her name to gain her attention is functional for the child. When the child calls the correct name, the adult attends to the target child and asks what he wants for snack. As with all joint action routine, this is varied over time and brought into different environments until the child is able to negotiate mutual attention spontaneously.

Once snacks have been passed out, the children with ASD eat, and there is very little communication going on. Conversely, typical children often talk about past experiences, upcoming events, or favorite TV shows while they are having snack. This suggests that Snack may be a good time to engage in decontextualized talk about past or future experience with a referent present (i.e., see Chapter 3, Discussing a Related Present). In addition, children are often seated and focused while they are eating, which gives them the set to attend. In the Early CLASS, activities used to increase the number of different communicative acts targeted during snack include My Day at School forms, Talk About Bags, and Picture Diaries.

My Day at School

The My Day at School form was designed to encourage the children to discuss past events while they have a referent in the immediate environment. The form provides the focus for an activity where the child reviews the day with her teacher as well as a vehicle for the child to answer the question, "what did you do in school today?" with parents and other caregivers. The My Day at School form is paired with a situational support containing words the child may need to communicate about her day (see Figure 4.9; Appendix D).

The communicative acts focused on during this activity change with the developmental level of the child. For example, the focus for Level 1 children is on creating a routine activity where they can anticipate what comes next and begin to fill in words. The focus for Level 2 children continues to be on the routines, but these children begin to use the activity to comment, first as responders and then as initiators. Finally, Level 3 children continue commenting on what they did, but they can now understand that they are talking about past events. The My Day at School form provides the visual referent needed to create space for mutual knowledge while scaffolding conversation about the past.

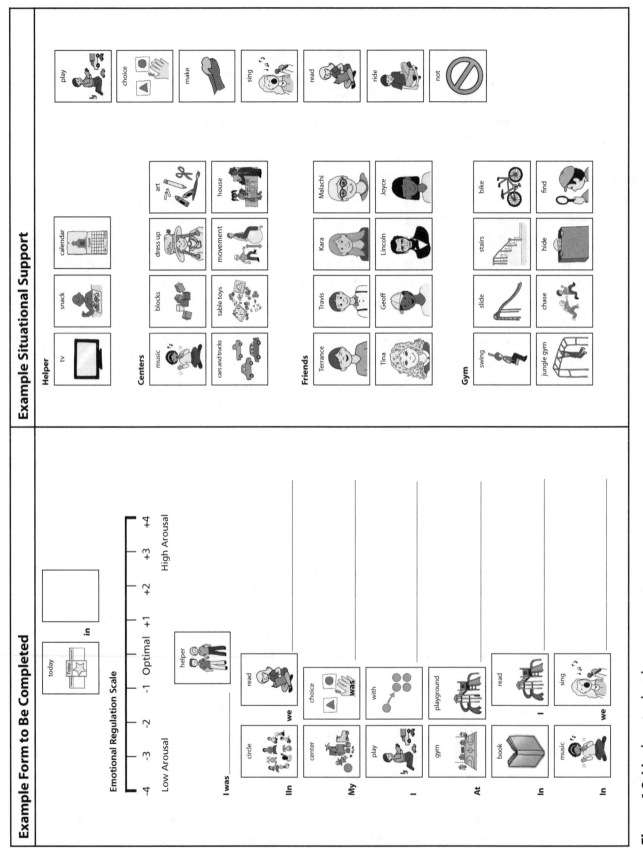

Figure 4.9. My day at school.

When it is time to go home, the teacher can help the child talk about her day with her caregiver, and the caregiver can take the form home and discuss with the child what happened in school. This facilitates conversation between caregivers and children.

Talk About Bags and Picture Diaries

The Talk About Bags activity is based on Gray (2004). It was designed to encourage discussions about past events that happened at home or in some other environment. We ask parents to create Talk About Bags for their child to bring to school. The caregiver places an item in a bag that will remind the child of what he did the day/night before and write details about the experience on the bag. This allows the child to engage in decontextualized talk about past events with a referent present when he is at school.

> *Michael's mother put the wrapper from a hamburger in a bag after they went to McDonald's. She wrote on the bag, "Michael went to McDonald's last night with family. We bumped into Jonny from the Early CLASS. They played together in the ball pit."*

Notice that Michael's mother gave enough details about the event to allow an adult who was not present to co-construct a past-event narrative with Michael. The next day in Early CLASS, the teacher took the wrapper out to "talk about" dinner at McDonald's with Michael.

Picture Diaries are similar, but now the parent puts pictures from the weekend, vacation, or other special family activities in the bag. Again, it is important that the parents give enough detail so that the clinician can co-construct an accurate story with the child.

Gym or Playground

Playground is a time to facilitate joint activity routines centered around social games among peers. A few games that our children enjoy include chase, hide-and-seek, and rolling a ball back and forth with another child. Playground joint activity routines are taught using core vocabulary and visual supports. For example, we use a version of the game "red rover," calling it "friend, friend run to me." As with the original game, it is played between two lines of children standing several feet apart. A strip of masking tape placed on the ground helps the children know where to stand. Teams alternate turns calling friends to run over and join their side. Every child on each team has a turn to make a choice about what friend she wants to call. The activity routine learned during Snack for "negotiating mutual attention" (i.e., getting another person to look at you before you speak to them) is used to call a friend. When the friend on the other team is ready (often with the help of an adult), everyone chants "friend, friend run to me," while the friend runs to join the other team.

Cautionary Note

Be careful not to over-arouse the children during Playground. In our experience, many children get very excited playing chase games; therefore, it is necessary to identify ways to help modulate the children's arousal levels. As a result, this version of the game does not involve physical contact among the players.

Book Time

Book Time is an opportunity to facilitate joint attention, discuss a Related Present, and reinforce various concepts. Books may include photo diaries, social narratives, and books about the theme of the week. Children can "make a choice" and choose a book to read with a therapist or teacher. It is good to have additional books on hand to be able to quickly shift the child's attention to a new book when the first is finished. During Book Time, be sure not to ask the child too many questions or have the child label rather than comment about the pictures (see page 22 for the distinction between labeling and commenting).

Music Time

Music Time is the last activity of the day. It is placed after Book Time because reading with another person is often a difficult activity for Level 2 and 3 children, whereas listening to music and singing songs is often very enjoyable for them. Music Time provides the children additional practice in taking turns and making choices. Some of the songs assist with functional vocabulary ("Brush Your Teeth" and "Goodbye"); others provide an opportunity to imitate the leader. The "Goodbye" song is similar to the "Hello" song. Each child has a turn to be sung to. When it is a child's turn, the child sits in the "goodbye chair." The "goodbye chair" is labeled as such, and faces the rest of the group (refer to the song glossary in Appendix E for words and music) . This gives the children a visual cue to indicate that there is a sender and a receiver of the goodbye message to help facilitate understanding that there are two roles in the interaction and that the roles can be reversed. (Role reversibility is a component of a joint cooperative activity discussed in Chapter 2.)

Once everyone has sung "Goodbye," the children are dismissed. At our preschool at UT Dallas, the children are released to their parents. This gives us the opportunity to review the My Day at Early CLASS form with the parents and to briefly discuss any other issues the parents may have to talk about.

Chapter Highlights

- The Early CLASS preschool was designed to facilitate reciprocal interaction, joint attention, and shared understanding using a functional curriculum rooted in the key components described in Chapter 3.

- The daily schedule and activity schedule provide a predictable sequence of events and, consequently, facilitate emotional regulation because the child knows what to expect.

- The daily schedule consists of a mixture of small- and large-group activities as well as 1:1 activities to allow children to use their nascent communication, language, and social skills within a variety of social contexts.

- Alternating between activities that require focused attention and activities that allow the children to move around the room helps them be available for learning and gives them the opportunity to engage in activities that help with emotional regulation without having to leave the group.

- Effective transitions are structured so that the children understand the organization of the transition and know what is coming next.

- Having children sit in a "hello chair" that faces the rest of the group is a way of arranging the environment to facilitate the understanding that there are reciprocal roles in the interaction and that these roles can be reversed. It also provides the children with a visual cue that there is both a sender and a receiver of the "hello" message.

- Books provide a shared attention routine with opportunities for varied repetition throughout the week. The use of repetitive phrases, core vocabulary, and core vocabulary routines increases the children's comprehension of functional activities and concepts represented in the book

- Choice Time and Remember Time provide opportunities for using decontextualized language. Using pictures, visual symbols, or objects allows for communicating about past and future events with a referent present (i.e., discuss a Related Present) and helps to scaffold conversations about nonpresent objects and events.

- Small Group is an opportunity to reinforce vocabulary and concepts from the Book of the Week. The format emphasizes new theme vocabulary and core vocabulary and provides opportunities to practice taking turns, waiting, and attending to others.

- The My Day at School form encourages the children to discuss past events while they have a referent present (i.e., discuss a Related Present) with caregivers when answering the question, "what did you do in school today?"

- The Talk About Bags activity encourages cross-context communication between home and school environments. It allows the child to engage in decontextualized talk about past events with a referent present (i.e., discuss a Related Present) when he is at school.

- Playground is a time to facilitate joint activity routines centered on social games among peers.

- Book Time is an opportunity to facilitate joint attention, discuss a Related Present, and reinforce various concepts.

- Music Time provides the children additional practice in taking turns and making choices.

Chapter Review Questions

1. What factors should be kept in mind when designing a schedule of activities?

2. Why is having a mixture of 1:1 with an adult, Small Group, and Large Group activities beneficial for a child with ASD?

3. What goals can be targeted during the "Hello" song?

4. How would you rewrite a children's book to facilitate a child's comprehension and joint attention?

5. Why are transitions important?

6. List two functional activities that can increase children's use of cross-context communication between the home and school environments.

Chapter 5:
Instructional Units

Learner Objectives:

After reading this chapter, the learner should be able to:

• Describe why and how themes were selected.

• Describe how the physical classroom is altered to reflect the unit/weekly theme.

• State which "times" of the classroom day are altered to reflect the theme.

• Describe the preparation for each weekly theme, both in classroom alteration and creation of new visual supports.

• List which visual supports should be added to the child's individual folder to support the weekly theme.

• Describe a "special activity" appropriate to a given weekly theme.

• State the core rationale utilized in rewriting books for each Early CLASS theme.

• Design a unit:

   ▪ select a picture book to rewrite

   ▪ describe a Small Group activity

   ▪ describe a special activity

   ▪ list materials to add to the classroom environment

   ▪ list theme-appropriate snack choices

   ▪ list theme-appropriate songs for Music Time

The Early CLASS curriculum may be divided into instructional units, each intended to take place for 1 week (5 sessions). Each unit is a theme, which – with input from the parents – is selected to be developmentally appropriate, functional, and motivating for the children. Each unit centers around a picture book that introduces a theme and new vocabulary. The theme and vocabulary are reinforced throughout the day during Hello Circle, Music, Small Group, and special activities. Further, we infuse the classroom with other theme-related materials to be available during individual time; materials may include additional theme-related books in the book area, manipulatives in the play dough area or block center, and theme-related songs (all Early CLASS songs referred to in this book are in the song glossary, Appendix E). Each week, a newsletter (see samples in the instructional unit section) communicates essential information to the parents, highlighting key information for better carryover at home, including the vocabulary presented during the week.

Each weekly theme unit requires the creation and implementation of specific classroom materials and individual supports consistent with the theme. In planning for a new curriculum unit, teachers must:

- identify a picture book that accurately illustrates the target concept(s), social skills, and vocabulary to be used as the Book of the Week

- rewrite the picture book with language appropriate for the developmental level of the children in the classroom

- create a picture symbol visual support to be distributed to each child's individual folder and utilized during Hello Circle

- design a special activity supporting the concepts, skills, and vocabulary presented in the Book of the Week

- create visual supports to be used during special activities, including the "schedule" detailing expectations for participation in the activity, and any additional picture symbol supports required for the activity

- infuse the classroom with the weekly theme by "resetting" the classroom with activities and play materials to support additional practice and extension activities for the weekly theme, creating visual supports as necessary

- identify songs for Music Time and the music center supportive of the weekly theme

- create visual supports to facilitate comprehension of words in songs and participation in the group activity

- create a parent newsletter to communicate the weekly theme and activities to parents, with suggestions for carryover activities to be used at home

Notes on Early CLASS Books

The books and book boards (see Book of the Week in Chapter 4) for each example unit included in this text are examples of how commercially available picture books can be rewritten to meet the needs of the children in our classroom (Level 2 and Level 3 children). You as the educator may choose different books to better meet the needs of the individual children in your classroom. To help you, on the introductory page to each example unit, we list additional recommended theme-related books. In selecting picture books to rewrite, look for books with simple pictures without too many visual distractions from the target vocabulary or concept. Also, pay attention to the flow of the story to make sure it illustrates a skill or routine the way you want it to.

In rewriting books for each Early CLASS theme, the following core rationale was utilized:

- Use simple language targeting developmentally appropriate core vocabulary.

- Incorporate familiar routines to facilitate increased comprehension, recognition, generalization, and attention. Consider using the book as a vehicle for introducing new routines, which are then generalized to the classroom through supported group and individual activities.

- Use repetitive phrases to catch the children's attention. Repetition also facilitates comprehension. Once the child gets used to a repeated phrase, the repeated phrase becomes a carrier for a new vocabulary word, which is then emphasized and highlighted.

- Embed new language forms/target words within repeated phrases to promote increased comprehension and attention.

- Reinforce classroom routines and concepts.

A case study to follow illustrates how all the various pieces are combined.

Notes on Taking Turns

As mentioned in Chapter 4, *turn* (as in "my turn" or "your turn") is a core vocabulary word. At Hello Circle as well as other times during the day, turns are visually marked with a "turn" card to let the children visually see who has the floor and how turns move from one person to the next. For example, in Large Group activities, a large picture symbol for "turn" is placed on both sides of a manila folder. The folder is then propped open like a tent and placed in front of the child who is taking a turn. Alternatively, a folded index card with two small picture symbols for "turn" works well for table-top activities.

turn

Visually marking a child's turn facilitates an understanding of more than one role in an interaction as well as role reversibility (both are components of a joint cooperative activity, discussed in Chapter 2). We use predictable routine language for turn-taking (see Figure 4.5), marking the beginning and ending of a child's turn (i.e., "Whose turn?" "It's _____ turn." "_____'s turn is finished.").

Case Study for Instructional Units: Picnic Theme

Preparation

Preparation for an upcoming theme week is completed on the Friday before the theme begins on Monday.

1. Each Friday afternoon before a new unit on Monday, support staff finalize and print the parent newsletter to be distributed to parents on Monday morning. In our example, on the Monday of the picnic theme, we distributed the newsletter on page 149.

2. Each child's folder is updated with:

   - **The book board for the book of the week.** This picture symbol book board is used to facilitate attention and participation during the large group book sharing activity in Hello Circle, and referenced as appropriate throughout the classroom day. See page pages 144-145 for an example book board for the picnic theme.

   - An **additional vocabulary sheet** with theme-related vocabulary to be facilitated during individual and Small Group activities. For the picnic theme, example supplemental vocabulary might be a variety of food words. Food words targeted should represent foods that would be appropriate to pack on a picnic, with examples of these pretend foods located in centers throughout the classroom (kitchen center, molds in play dough center).

3. Teachers and support staff "reset" the room to be facilitative of the upcoming target theme. The book center is essentially cleared of the previous theme (leaving one or two books from the previous week to support carryover). In their place, staff place books consistent with the new theme. Example supplemental reading is listed as "Additional Related Books" on the overview page for each unit. During the picnic theme, the book center might contain the book of the week for the grocery store theme (previous week), in addition to picnic theme-related books such as *Packing for a Picnic* by Mary Lou Roberts, *We're Going on a Picnic!* by Pat Hutchins, and *Teddy Bears' Picnic* by Jimmy Kennedy.

4. Centers to be visited during Center Time are altered to provide opportunities for theme-vocabulary use. For example, during the picnic theme, staff place plates and play dough molds to create food shapes at the play dough center. Activity supports reinforcing food vocabulary and pretend picnic activities are created to support the creation of play dough food, putting on plates, pretending to eat, etc. In the kitchen center, staff place a picnic basket, picnic blanket, and an activity support leading the child through packing a picnic, spreading out the blanket, passing out plates, passing out food, and pretending to eat, as will be facilitated and reinforced during Small Group activities.

5. Within the classroom, a "special activity" center is created that facilitates theme vocabulary and concepts. This center, with accompanying visual supports, is ready when the first child enters the classroom on Monday morning for the picnic special activity.

- Picnic Basket: Provide crayons, glue, pictures of food, and paper cutouts of picnic baskets. Children choose pictures of food to take on a picnic, color them, and glue them in a basket to show friends.

- Pretend Food: Provide paper plates, construction paper, glue, crayons, and scissors so that the children can make their own pretend food. Children with fine-motor challenges or those who struggle with attention during such craft activities may require additional support from teachers. The number of steps in the activity should be determined by the developmental levels and fine-motor abilities of the children in the classroom. Construction paper foods may be prepared in advance by support staff and teachers to limit fine-motor demands for the child and shorten activity time.

6. Songs in the music center are replaced with songs related to the picnic theme. Support staff prepare the music center to allow access to "The Cookie Song" and "The Peanut Butter and Jelly Song," as well as their song boards.

Theme Through the Classroom Day

As discussed in Chapter 4, the classroom day is as follows:

The Daily Schedule

- Get Ready
- Hello Circle
- Choice Time
- Center Time
- Remember Time
- Small Group
- Bathroom Time
- Snack Time
- Gym Time
- Book Time
- Music Time

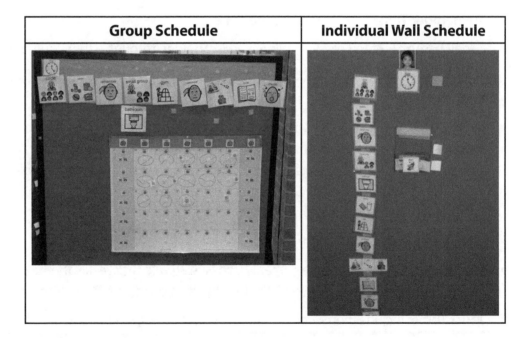

Group Schedule	Individual Wall Schedule

Theme vocabulary and concepts are infused into each step of the daily routine. The familiarity of the structure of the classroom day affords the child predictability and familiarity, better enabling students to focus on the *new, less-familiar* theme vocabulary and concepts.

For the picnic theme, routine parts of the daily schedule might be customized as follows:

The Daily Schedule (Picnic Theme)

- **Get Ready:** Child-centered routines stay the same, although child may go to centers that have been customized to support carryover of the weekly theme (picnic), including special activity.

- **Hello Circle**

  - Book of the Week: *Picnic* by Emily Arnold McCulley

- **Choice Time:** Routine remains the same

- **Center Time**

  - Special activity: Picnic basket – Provide crayons, glue, pictures of food, and paper cutouts of picnic baskets. Children choose pictures of food to take on a picnic, color them, and glue them in a basket to show friends.

  - Play dough center – Provide play dough molds for food, create activity support for making pretend play dough food.

  - Kitchen center– Provide picnic basket and picnic blanket. Provide activity support for packing a picnic basket, setting up for a picnic, and pretending to eat. Should be consistent with activities supported during Small Group.

- **Remember Time**: Routine remains the same.

- **Small Group:** Pretend picnic – children are scaffolded through a functional activity routine for going on a picnic (see page 146 for further explanation of this Small Group activity).

- **Bathroom Time:** Routine remains the same.

- **Snack Time:** Allow food options that would be appropriate for a picnic such as apples, grapes, small sandwiches. As much as possible, snack choices are consistent with choices of pretend food during Small Group. At midweek, teachers may begin setting up snack on a picnic blanket in the classroom. On Friday, if the students are ready, Snack will take place outdoors on a picnic blanket, with a routine consistent with that used in Small Group activities.

- **Gym Time:** Routine remains the same.

- **Book Time:** Limit access to be primarily books related to the weekly theme (*Packing for a Picnic* by Mary Lou Roberts, *We're Going on a Picnic!* by Pat Hutchins, and *Teddy Bears' Picnic* by Jimmy Kennedy).

- **Music Time:** Include theme-related choices such as the "Cookie" song and the "Peanut Butter and Jelly" song.

Instructional Units – Introduction

Twelve example instructional units are detailed on the pages to follow. For each example instructional unit, we provide:

- overview page outlining curriculum for the theme, including the book, Small Group, special activity, and suggested ideas for other items to be placed in the classroom. We have selected commercially available books and rewritten them to create joint attention routines for each theme. Therefore, we provide relevant information about the books that we have adapted on the theme overview page.

- book chart identifying symbols to be present on each page and adult spoken narrative (see Tables 5.1-5.12)

- "book board" to be included in the child's folder

- description of a Small Group activity that includes targets, visual supports, and a sample script. Note that Small Group activities for early Level 2 have fewer steps, whereas emerging Level 3 (Level 2-3) have more steps. We have provided a variety of examples. Please adapt the number of steps to the level of your children.

- Early CLASS Newsletter to send home to the parents on Friday of the previous week

---

Notes on Reading Book Charts (Tables 5.1-5.12)

For each book, we include a chart that details (a) words/symbols on each page, (b) what is to be spoken in the narrative, and (c) any notes about any routine songs to be included when reading.

Columns 2 and 4 list words/symbols to be present on each page. Each individual picture symbol is underlined. Please note that we use ONE symbol for each word, except in the case of phrases such as "clean up" and "thank you" that act as a single unit.

Columns 3 and 5 detail the narrative to be spoken.

Italicized words are optional and are often best added later in the week to expand on the book once the children understand and become familiar with the basic script.

Text that is preceded by an asterisk indicates a routine song to be sung as part of the narrative. Songs are used to help the children reestablish or maintain attention or as a support to comprehension.

In some books, we have not included a narrative for all of the pages. In such cases, the page numbers are indicated in Column 1, but the rest of the row is shaded to signal that we have skipped those pages and do not include them in the narrative.

Instructional Units Overview

Unit 1: School
   Book: I Love School
   Small Group Week 1: Early CLASS friends lotto game
   Small Group Week 2: Early CLASS centers lotto game

Unit 2: About Me
   Book: *Time to Wash* (adapted from *Bobby, Bobby What Did You Do?*)
   Small Group: Pretend bath

Unit 3: Bedtime
   Book: *Bedtime*
   Small Group: Pretend bedtime

Unit 4: Happy Birthday
   Book: *Happy Birthday, Jesse Bear*
   Small Group: Pretend birthday party

Unit 5: Restaurant
   Book: *Barney and Baby Bop Go to the Restaurant*
   Small Group: Pretend restaurant

Unit 6: Grocery Store
   Book: *At the Supermarket*
   Small Group: Pretend grocery store

Unit 7: Picnic
   Book: *Picnic*
   Small Group: Pretend picnic

Unit 8: Family
   Book: *I Can Do It, Too!*
   Small Group: Family lotto game

Unit 9: Airport
   Book: *Airport*
   Small Group: Pretend airplane

Unit 10: Feeling Mad/Calm-Down Time
   Book: *Calm Down Time*
   Small Group: Calm down game

Unit 11: Halloween
   Book: *Maisy's Trick-or-Treat*
   Small Group: Pretend trick-or-treating

Unit 12: Train
   Book: *Freight Train*
   Small Group: Sharing the train

Weekly Core Vocabulary

Type of Semantic Relationship	Week 1: School	Week 2: All About Me	Week 3: Bedtime	Week 4: Happy Birthday	Week 5: Restaurant
Names for Things/Persons					
Objects	schedule, blocks, book		toy, teeth, pajamas, blanket, pillow	present, cake	table, menu, food,
Places/Activities	Early CLASS, center, Music, art, playground, snack (time), Small Group, (make) choice, book (time), home	bath	bed, bathroom, bath	home, birthday, party	restaurant, home
Body Parts		arm, hand, stomach, leg, foot, face			
Agent	teacher, friends	Bobby, baby		friend	waiter
Relational Word					
Existence					
Non-Existence/Disappearance	finished	not, finished		finished	finished
Recurrence					
Rejection					
Social Interaction	good-bye, (my) turn		goodnight	hello, thank you, goodbye, happy birthday	thank you
Action	wait, sit, eat, drink, read	wash	brush, say, clean up	wait, eat, say, sing	wait, look, sit, make, eat, go, say, choice, tell
Modifier	time	time	time	time	time
Attribute		dirty, clean			
Possession					
Location			on		here
Denial					
Emotion				happy	
Wh-word					what

Week 6: Grocery Store	Week 7: Picnic	Week 8: Family	Week 9: Airport	Week 10: Feelings Mad/ Calm-Down Time	Week 11: Halloween	Week 12: Train
cart, list, chicken, grapes, milk, peanut butter, ice cream, food, bag	food, basket, blanket, grass, plates, cups	breakfast, cookie, book, song, bike	suitcase, airplane, seatbelt, sky		bag, treat, jack-o-lantern, costume, door	train
grocery store, home	picnic, outside	dress up	trip, airport, line	break	house, line, trick or treat, Halloween	tunnel, bridge
cashier		family, dad, sister, grandma, grandpa, uncle, mom, brother		boy, girl, friend	Maisy, cowboy, friend	
finish(ed)						
					thank you	share, goodbye
look, pay	wait, go, pass, eat	make, bake, read, sing, hug, ride	wait, go, stand, walk, sit, fly, hold	calm down, play, say, hug, count, breath	wait, dress up, paint, knock, say, stand, walk, choice	push
time			time	time		together
		same	fast			red, orange, yellow, green, blue, purple, black, fast, slow
		my				
there, in	in, on	on	on		in	through, on
				mad, happy, okay	what	

Table 5.0
Core Functional Vocabulary

Core Vocabulary	Early CLASS Songs (see glossary)	Notes
sit	Sit Down	
schedule	Check Your Schedule	
turn		
time		begins every activity with "Time for _____"
finish		end every activity with "_____ time is finished"
look	Look	
clean up	Clean Up	
stop, look and listen	Train	use phrase "stop, look and listen"
wait	Waiting	
give	Hat	use phrase from song "and give it to _____"
hello	Hello	
goodbye	Goodbye	
where	Where	attendance, when locating child
here I am	Where	
listen	Train	use phrase "stop, look and listen"
remember	Remember	
wash	Wash	
choice		
want		
no		
not		
different		
open		
yes		
more		
play		
emotion regulation		
calm down	Calm Down	used to help regulate new child
okay		
break		
mad		
happy		
developmentally later words		
in		
out		
share		
call		
same		
my		
Help		

Note: All words are visually supported.

Unit 1: School

Overview

Entering preschool is difficult for any young child, but it is particularly difficult for children with ASD. Every classroom is full of new people and has a unique vocabulary and routines that may be completely unfamiliar to the child. Unless properly supported, the child may become overwhelmed, resulting in dysregulation.

This unit is designed to introduce and reinforce classroom core vocabulary, routines, and activities, as well as to introduce Early CLASS classmates. Due to the high language load, in addition to the high emotional load of acclimating to a new environment, it is recommended that this unit be extended to take place over a two-week period. Based upon the developmental level and readiness of the students in your classroom, you may choose to do one book for two weeks or write another school-related book to be used in the second week of your unit. Recommended related books are below.

Book: *I Love School!* (adapted to follow the routine of the classroom)
Author: Philemon Sturges
ISBN#: 0-06-009286-6
Publisher: Harper Trophy

Table 5.1
Book Narrative Unit 1

Page Spread	Pictures Left	Narrative Left	Pictures Right	Narrative Right
Front Cover	TIME EARLY CLASS	I Love School		
p. 1/2				
p. 3/4				
p. 5/6				
p. 7/8				
p. 9/10	TIME EARLY CLASS	It's time for Early CLASS.	HELLO TEACHER HELLO FRIENDS	Hello Teacher. Hello Friends. *"Hello" song
p. 11/12	TIME CENTERS BLOCKS	Time for centers. Blocks. *"Build the tower up so high" song	CENTERS FINISH SCHEDULE	Centers are finished. Time to check your schedule. *"Schedule" song
p. 13/14	TIME ART	Time for Art.	ART FINISH TIME CLEAN UP SCHEDULE	Art is finished. Time to clean up. Time to check your schedule. *"Schedule" song
p. 15/16	TIME PLAYGROUND TURN WAIT	Time for Playground. "my turn" waiting for turn *"Waiting" song	PLAYGROUND FINISH SCHEDULE	Playground is finished. Time to check your schedule. *"Schedule" song
p. 17/18				

Page Spread	Pictures Left	Narrative Left	Pictures Right	Narrative Right
p. 19/20	TIME SMALL GROUP SIT FRIEND	Time for Small Group. Sit with friends. *"Everybody Come Sit Down" song	SMALL GROUP FINISH SCHEDULE	Small Group is finished. Time to check your schedule. *"Schedule song
p. 21/22				
p. 23/24	TIME SNACK EAT	Time for Snack. Eat.	DRINK SNACK FINISH SCHEDULE	Drink. Snack is finished. Time to check your schedule. *"Schedule" song
p. 25/26	TIME BOOK READ	Time for book. *"Everybody Come Sit Down" song Read. Teacher reads book.	BOOK FINISH SCHEDULE	Book is finished. Time to check your schedule. *"Schedule" song
p. 27/28	TIME MUSIC	Time for Music.	MAKE CHOICE MUSIC FINISHED SCHEDULE	Make a choice. Music is finished. Time to check your schedule. *"Schedule" song
p. 29/30	EARLY CLASS FINISHED TIME HOME	Early CLASS is finished. Time for home.	GOODBYE TEACHER GOODBYE FRIEND	Goodbye teacher. Goodbye friend. *"Goodbye" song
p. 31/32				
p. 33/34				
Back cover				

Book Targets:

1. To introduce Early CLASS daily routine and schedule

2. To introduce core vocabulary related to the classroom routine, schedule, and environment

3. To reinforce the classroom schedule and centers

4. To introduce social routines and songs that support transitions and comprehension

5. To introduce social routines within classroom activities (i.e., greetings, turn taking)

Early CLASS Songs (words and tunes may be found in the song glossary, Appendix E):

- "Hello" song
- "Check Your Schedule" song
- "Sit Down" song
- "Waiting" song
- "Build a Tower up so High" song
- "Goodbye" song

Small Group Week 1: Early CLASS Friends Lotto Game

The child matches a picture of an Early CLASS classmate to an identical picture on a lotto game board with a selection of classmate pictures. For increased difficulty, the game board can later be adapted using pictures of teachers.

Small Group Week 1 Targets:

1. To introduce/reinforce the names of classmates
2. To teach foundational skills of playing a lotto game (taking turns, waiting, watching friends, matching)

    Early CLASS Centers Lotto Game

    The child matches a picture of an Early CLASS center to an identical picture on a lotto game board with a selection of center picture symbols.

Small Group Week 2: Early CLASS Centers Lotto Game

The child matches a picture of an Early CLASS center to an identical picture on a lotto game board with a selection of center picture symbols.

Small Group Week 2 Targets:

1. To introduce/reinforce the names of Early CLASS centers
2. To teach foundational skills of playing a lotto game (taking turns, waiting, watching friends, matching)

Special Activity:

* Friend Book: The child makes a book using the pictures of peers in the classroom. The child glues pictures of peers and their names onto construction paper that has been folded into a book. The child then takes this book home and reads it with his parents to learn the names of the children in the class.

Related Songs: "Wheels on the Bus"

Additional Related Books:

* *Maisy Goes to School* by Lucy Cousins
* *My School* by Catherine Peters
* *Where Are Maisy's Friends?* by Lucy Cousins

Additions to Children's Folder:

* *I Love School* book supports
* School vocabulary supports

Unit 1: School
Child Book Board p. 1/3

time	Early CLASS

time	Early CLASS	hello	teacher	hello	friends

time	center	blocks
		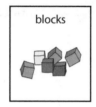

center	finished	schedule
		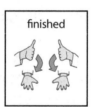

time	art	art	finished	schedule
	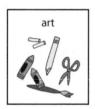			

time	playground	wait	turn
		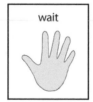	

playground	finished	schedule

Unit 1: School
Child Book Board p. 2/3

time	small group		sit	friend	

		small group	finished		schedule

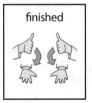  

time	snack		eat	drink	

		snack	finished		schedule

time	book		read		

		book	finished		schedule

Unit 1: School
Child Book Board p. 3/3

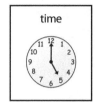
time

music

make

choice

schedule

music

finished

Early CLASS

finished

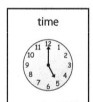
time

home

goodbye

teacher

goodbye

friend

Unit 1: School
Small Group Week 1: Early CLASS Friends Lotto Game

Targets:

1. To introduce/reinforce the names of classmates

2. To teach foundational skills of playing a lotto game (taking turns, waiting, watching friends, matching)

Explanation of the Activity:

The child matches a picture of an Early CLASS classmate to an identical picture on a lotto game board with a selection of classmate pictures. For increased difficulty, the game board can be adapted using pictures of teachers or centers in Early CLASS (instead of the students' photos).

Materials:

- Lotto board (see example on p. 91) with the digital photos of classmates surrounding the center "friend" picture/symbol

- Lotto cards with each child's picture on them (for "make a choice")

- Small Group activity schedules

- "Turn" support (see "Notes on Taking Turns," page 73)

How to Play:

On the first day of playing the game, the teachers model how to play.

- Teacher 1: "Time for work."

  - "Whose turn?" (talk only to the other teachers)

  - "It's <Teacher 2>'s turn." Place "turn" support in front of Teacher 2.

- Teacher 1: Holds the cards in front of Teacher 2 and says: "Make a choice."

- Teacher 2: Chooses a card.

- Teacher 1: "Look! What friend?"

  - Teacher 2: "It's <Name>."

  - Teacher 1: "Yes, your choice is <Name>."

- Teacher 1: "Look for <Name>." (Sing "Look" song.)

  - Teacher 2 matches the child's picture with the corresponding picture on the game board.

- Teacher 1: "<Name>'s turn is finished."

The cycle may repeat with each child taking a turn as on the second day (see below) or stop, depending on the children's attention.

On the second day of playing the game, the children play the game.

- Teacher 1: "Time for work."
    - "Whose turn?" (talking only to the children)
    - "It's <name>'s turn."
    - Place "turn" support in front of the child.
- Teacher 1: Holds the cards in front of the child and says: "Make a choice."
- Child: Chooses a card.
- Teacher 1: "Look! What friend?"
    - If the child does not respond: "It's <insert child's name>."
    - If the child responds: "Yes, it's <name>."
- Teacher 1: "Look for <name>." (Sing "look" song.)
    - If the child does not respond: Use the prompting hierarchy to cue the child to match the pictures.
    - If the child responds: "Look it's <name>!"
- Teacher 1: "<Name>'s turn is finished."

The cycle repeats until each child in the group gets a turn.

At the beginning of the week, the turns are short and heavily guided by the teacher. When the children have a longer attention span and have become familiar with and understand the game, the turns may become longer.

Unit 1: School
Week 1: Small Group Support – Lotto Game Board (Friend)

Place a photo of a child in each of the squares		
	friend	

Unit 1: School
Week 1: Small Group Activity Schedule – Early Level 2

friend	game

one	what	friend

two	look	friend
	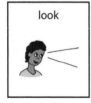	

three	finish

Unit 1: School
Week 1: Small Group Activity Schedule – Level 2

friend	game

one	who	turn

two	what	friend

three	look	friend

four	finish

Unit 1: School
Small Group Week 2: Early CLASS Centers Lotto Game

Targets:

1. To introduce/reinforce the names of Early CLASS centers

2. To teach foundational skills of playing a lotto game (taking turns, waiting, watching friends, matching)

Explanation of the Activity:

The child matches a picture of an Early CLASS center to an identical picture on a lotto game board with a selection of center picture symbols.

Materials:

- Lotto board (see example on page 94) with the centers' pictures surrounding the center support
- Lotto cards with each center picture (for "make a choice")
- "Turn" support (see "Notes on Taking Turns," page 73)

How to Play:

On the first day of playing the game, the teachers model how to play.

- Teacher 1: "Time for work."
  - "Whose turn?" (talk only to the other teachers)
  - "It's <Teacher 2>'s turn." Place "turn" support in front of Teacher 2.
- Teacher 1: Holds the cards in front of Teacher 2 and says: "Make a choice."
- Teacher 2: Chooses a card.
- Teacher 1: "Look! What center?"
  - Teacher 2: "It's <center>."
  - Teacher 1: "Yes, your choice is <center>."
- Teacher 1: "Look for <center>." (Sing "Look" song.)
  - Teacher 2 matches the center's picture with the corresponding picture on the game board.
- Teacher 1: "<Name>'s turn is finished."

The cycle may repeat with each child taking a turn as on the second day (see next page) or stop, depending on the children's ability to pay attention.

On the second day of playing the game, the children play the game.

- Teacher 1: "Time for work."
    - "Whose turn?" (talking only to the children)
    - "It's <name>'s turn."
    - Place "turn" support in front of the child.
- Teacher 1: Holds the cards in front of the child and says: "Make a choice."
- Child: Chooses a card.
- Teacher 1: "Look! What center?"
    - If the child does not respond: "It's <center>."
    - If the child responds: "Yes, it's <center>."

Teacher 1: "Look for <center>" (Sing "Look" song.)

- If the child does not respond: Use the prompting hierarchy to cue the child to match the pictures.
- If the child responds: "Look it's <center>!"

Teacher 1: "<Name>'s turn is finished."

The cycle repeats until each child in the group gets a turn.

At the beginning of the week, the turns are short and heavily guided by the teacher. When the children have greater understanding of the game and longer attention spans, the turns may become longer.

Unit 1: School Week 2
Small Group Support – Lotto Game Board (Centers)

Place a photo of one center in each of the squares		
	center 	

Unit 1: School Week 2
Small Group Activity Schedule – Early Level 2

center	game

one	what	center
1	**?**	
two	look	center
2		
three	finish	
3		

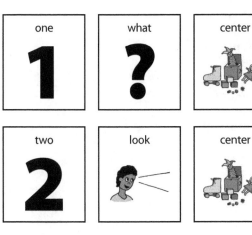

Unit 1: School Week 2
Small Group Activity Schedule Level – 2

center

game

one	who	turn

two	what	center

three	look	center

four	finish

Early CLASS News

Early CLASS Office Phone Number: < > **Date**

Welcome to the Early CLASS!

Important Dates
August 31-September 1: No Early CLASS
September 7: No Early CLASS

We are very excited to welcome you to the Early CLASS fall semester. We are very happy to have 3 new students and 4 returning students for this semester. We are also happy to have 10 fabulous new graduate student clinicians join our program. We hope you're as excited as we are about the fall <year> semester.

New Early CLASS Therapists!
Teacher 1	Teacher 6
Teacher 2	Teacher 7
Teacher 3	Teacher 8
Teacher 4	Teacher 9
Teacher 5	Teacher 10

Teaching Assistants:

Early CLASS Illness Policy
If you fear your child may be coming down with something, has a fever or virus, or has had a fever or virus within the past 24 hours, please keep him/her home. When the kids are not 100% well, they have difficulty learning and benefit less from being at school. Also, keeping them home helps prevent epidemics! If you know your child will be absent, please leave a message on the Early CLASS line. Thank you for your cooperation!!!

Theme: School

Book: *I Love School*
By: Philemon Sturges

Our book this week is about going to Early CLASS. If your child is new to Early CLASS, this book will help teach the routines and vocabulary we use in Early CLASS. If your child is returning, this book will help reacquaint him/her with the social routines and vocabulary of Early CLASS.

Vocabulary
Objects, places, activities: Early CLASS, circle, centers, playground, snack, small group, music, book, home, blocks, car, water, cookies, schedule,
Agents: Teacher, friends
Social: Hello
Actions: Say (hello), move (picture), ride, drink, eat, read
Modifiers: Time

Songs: "Wheels on the Bus," "Spider on the Floor," "Boogie Walk"

Lead: Teacher 1

Small Groups: In Small Group this week, we will use a lotto game format to learn the names of Early CLASS <friends/centers> and work on turn taking.

TOURO COLLEGE LIBRARY

Unit 2: About Me

Overview

This week, we facilitate learning the names of body parts within the familiar, naturalistic, and functional routine of Bath Time. The book allows the teacher to introduce a bath routine with repeated phrases and core vocabulary, which will then be reinforced during individual and Small Group activities. Knowledge of this familiar routine is used to facilitate development of a symbolic play routine and semantic relations at the level of (agent) + (action) (such as "baby" + "wash").

Book: *Time to Wash* [rewritten from *"Bobby, Bobby, What Did You Do?"* In *Storytime: Stories, Symbols, and Emergent Literacy Activities for Young Children With Disabilities* (Revised Edition)]
Author: Pati King-DeBaun
ISBN#: 0-9628290-2-1
Publisher: Creative Communicating

Table 5.2
Book Narrative Unit 2

Page Spread	Pictures Left	Narrative Left	Pictures Right	Narrative Right
Cover		Time to wash.		
p. 1/2	BOBBY DIRTY	Bobby is dirty.	TIME BATH	Time for a bath.
p. 3/4	DIRTY ARM	Dirty arms.	TIME WASH	Time to wash. *"Wash" song.
p. 5/6	DIRTY STOMACH	Dirty hands.	TIME WASH	Time to wash. *"Wash" song.
p. 7/8	DIRTY LEGS	Dirty tummy.	TIME WASH	Time to wash. *"Wash" song.
p. 9/10	DIRTY FEET	Dirty legs.	TIME WASH	Time to wash. *"Wash" song.
p. 11/12	DIRTY FACE	Dirty feet.	TIME WASH	Time to wash. *"Wash" song.
p. 13/14	DIRTY <?>	Dirty face.	TIME WASH	Time to wash. *"Wash" song.
p. 15/16		Dirty <body part>.	TIME WASH	Time to wash. *"Wash" song.
p. 17/18			BATH FINISHED BOBBY NOT DIRTY BOBBY CLEAN	Bath is finished. Bobby is not dirty. Bobby is clean.

Book Targets:

1. To introduce/reinforce body part vocabulary within the functional context of bathing

2. To introduce a routine for Bath Time that will support a scaffolded symbolic play routine during Small Group activities

3. To introduce routine songs for bathing

TOURO COLLEGE LIBRARY

Early CLASS Songs:

- "Wash" song

Small Group: Pretend bath

Supported by the teachers, routine songs, and visual supports, the children participate in a symbolic play routine for bathing a baby doll in a basin. The symbolic play routine follows the routine set out in the Book of the Week. The children are seated in a circle around the basin. When one child is finished washing one body part on the doll, it is the next child's turn to "wash the baby."

Small Group Targets:

1. To introduce/reinforce vocabulary for body parts within a naturalistic routine for bath time
2. To participate in a structured symbolic play routine
3. To practice game-playing skills (taking turns, waiting, watching a friend, etc.)

Special Activity:

- Water Table: A tub with water is placed in the special activity area. The children are provided with dolls, soap, and towels. The children can engage in symbolic play that imitates the Small Group activity. They can also expand on this activity by washing body parts that are not introduced in the book (hair, fingers, toes) and dressing the dolls. While labeling body parts on the dolls, they can identify their own body parts and their clinician's body parts to promote generalization of the skill.

- Body Part Book: The children color and glue body parts onto a coloring page. They can sing "Mat Man" while talking about the body parts ("Mat Man has one nose, one nose, one nose. Mat Man has one nose, so he can smell.")

Related Songs: "Wash" song, "Head, Shoulders, Knees, and Toes"

Additional Related Books:

- *From Head to Toe* by Eric Carle
- *Here Are My Hands* by Bill Martin Jr. and John Archambault
- *I Can* by Catherine Peters
- *Sometimes I Like to Curl up in a Ball* by Vicky Churchill
- *We've All Got Belly Buttons* by David Martin
- *Where Does Maisy Live?* by Lucy Cousins

Additions to Children's Folder:

- *Time to Wash* book supports
- About Me vocabulary supports

Unit 2: About Me
Child's Book Board

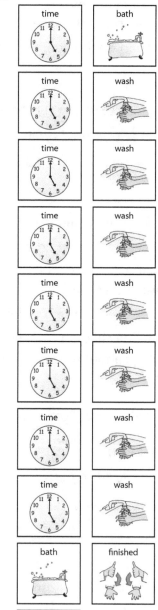

Unit 2: About Me
Small Group: Pretend Bath

Targets:

1. To introduce/reinforce vocabulary for body parts within a naturalistic routine for Bath Time
2. To participate in a structured symbolic play routine
3. To practice game-playing skills (taking turns, waiting, watching a friend, etc.)

Explanation of the Activity:

Supported by the teachers, routine songs, and visual supports, the children participate in a symbolic play routine for bathing a baby doll in a basin. The symbolic play routine follows the routine set out in the Book of the Week. The children are seated in a circle around the basin. When one child is finished washing one body part, it is the next child's turn to wash the baby.

Materials:

- Basin (bath tub), doll, towel, visual supports with each target body part on them
- Small Group activity schedules
- "Turn" support (see "Notes on Taking Turns," page 73)

How to Play:

At the beginning of the week, the turns are short and heavily guided by the teacher. When the children have demonstrated comprehension of the activity and have longer attention spans the turns may become longer.

On the first day of playing the game, the teachers model how to play.

- Teacher 1: "Time for work."
  - "Whose turn?" (talk only to the other teachers)
  - "It's <Teacher 2>'s turn." Place "turn" support in front of Teacher 2.
- Teacher 1: "Put in baby in bath."
- Teacher 2: Puts the baby in the basin.
- Teacher 1: "Wash <body part>." Chooses one body part for the teacher to wash, preferably one that was used in the *Time to Wash* book: arms, hands, stomach, legs, feet, face.
- Teacher 1: While Teacher 2 is washing the baby, sing the "Wash" song.
- Teacher 2: Pretends to wash the baby's body part by rubbing it with a towel.
- Teacher 1: "Bath is finished. Give baby to teacher."
- Teacher 2: Takes the baby out of the bath and gives it to Teacher 1.
- Teacher 1: "<Name>'s turn is finished."

The cycle repeats at least one more time with a child playing the game (instructions below), and stops when the children begin to lose focus.

On the second day of playing the game, the children play the game.

- Teacher 1: "Time for work."
    - "Whose turn?" (talks only to the children)
    - "It's <name>'s turn."
    - Place "turn" support in front of the child.
- Teacher 1: "Put baby in bath."
    - If the child does not respond: Use the prompting hierarchy to cue the child to put the baby in the basin
    - If the child responds: Move on to the next step
- Teacher 1: "Wash <body part>." Choose one body part for the child to wash, preferably one that was used in the "Time to Wash" book: arms, hands, stomach, legs, feet, face.
    - If the child does not respond: Use the prompting hierarchy to cue the child to wash the body part.
    - If the child responds: Sing the "Wash" song, while the child is washing the baby.
- Teacher 1: "Bath is finished. Give baby to teacher."
    - If the child does not respond: Use the prompting hierarchy to cue the child to give the baby to the teacher. (Sing "Give it to _____" from the "Hat" song. [See song glossary, Appendix E.])
    - If the child responds: Move on to next step.
- Teacher 1: "<Name>'s turn is finished."

The cycle repeats until each child in the group gets a turn.

Unit 2: About Me
Small Group Activity Schedule

pretend	bath

one	baby	in	bath
	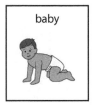		

two	wash	baby		arm	hand
	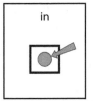	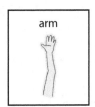		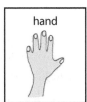	

three	bath	finished		stomach	leg
				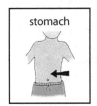	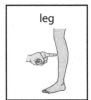

				foot	face
				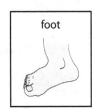	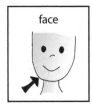

Early CLASS News

Welcome to the Early CLASS!

Important Dates
Dates when will not have therapy or dates when certain clinicians will not be in Early CLASS.

Taking Early CLASS Home

This week our theme is about washing body parts. At home, you might want to sing the "Wash" song as you wash your child's hands or give your child a bath. The song goes like this: "Dirty <body part> gonna wash, wash, wash" (repeat). Please also enjoy pretending to give a baby doll a bath, as we do in our Small Group activity this week.

The Early CLASS Lending Library!

This semester, we will be starting a lending library that will allow you access to recent research articles or other materials we think might be helpful to you. Please take a peek and see if you might be interested! We will place the lending library materials on top of our Early CLASS cubbies.

Early CLASS Illness Policy

If you fear your child may be coming down with something, has a fever or virus, or has had a fever or virus within the past 24 hours, please keep him/her home. When the kids are not 100% well, they have difficulty learning and benefit less from being at school. Also, keeping them home helps prevent epidemics! If you know your child will be absent, please leave a message on the Early CLASS line. Thank you for your cooperation!!!

Theme: About Me

Book: *Time to Wash*

By: Pati King-DeBaun

Our book this week is about a boy named Bobby who is dirty and takes a bath. He needs to wash his arm, hand, tummy, legs, feet, and face. We introduce the "Wash" song, which can be used at home when your child is washing his/her hands or taking a bath.

Vocabulary
Objects, places, activities: Bobby, bath, arm, hand, tummy, legs, feet, face
Actions: Wash
Modifiers: Time, dirty

Songs: "Wash" song; "Head, Shoulders, Knees, and Toes"

Lead: Teacher 1

Small Groups: In Small Group this week, we will act out the bath time routine from the Bobby book. The children will participate in a symbolic play routine to give a baby doll a bath. We wash all the body parts introduced in the book.

Unit 3: Bedtime

Overview

The theme of "Bedtime" was selected as a means to discuss and practice the bedtime routine. The bedtime routine reviewed in the book of the week sets up a framework for a symbolic play routine that will be practiced in Small Group and special activity. Symbolic play, particularly with "self" as actor, is a deficit area for most children with ASD. The symbolic play routines promote symbolic play with the object as the agent to the action and also the child as the agent. Practice with a symbolic play routine in individual and Small Group settings helps children learn to generalize this routine to their home, in addition to facilitating symbolic play skill development.

Book: *Bedtime*
Author: Elsa Warnick
ISBN-10 #: 152014713
Publisher: Browndeer Press

Table 5.3
Book Narrative Unit 3

Page Spread	Pictures Left	Narrative Left	Pictures Right	Narrative Right	Notes
Cover		Bedtime.			
p. 1/2					
p. 3/4	TIME BED	Time for bed.	CLEAN UP TOYS	Clean up your toys. *"Clean up" song	
p. 5/6					
p. 7/8	TIME BED	Time for bed.	BATHROOM	Go to the bathroom.	
p. 9/10	TIME BED	Time for bed.	BATH	Take a bath. Wash your <body part>.	Insert a body part that was introduced during Week 2 (arm, leg, hand, etc.). The verbs used on each page are carefully chosen because they are concrete and easily generalized to other activities.
p. 11/12					
p. 13/14	TIME BED	Time for bed.	BRUSH TEETH	Brush your teeth. *"Brush Teeth" song	
p. 15/16	TIME BED	Time for bed.	PAJAMAS	Put on pajamas.	
p. 17/18					
p. 19/20	TIME BED BLANKET	Time for bed. Get your blanket.			Page 20 should be covered up so it will not be a visual distraction to the children, and to emphasize the importance of the picture of the blanket.
p. 21/22	TIME BED PILLOW	Time for bed. Get your pillow.			For page 22, same as above.
p. 23/24	TIME BED	Time for bed.	SAY GOODNIGHT	Say "goodnight." *"Goodnight" song	
p. 25/26					

Book Targets:

1. To introduce/reinforce a routine for bedtime
2. To increase/reinforce bedtime vocabulary

Early CLASS Songs (words and tunes may be found in the song glossary, Appendix E):

- "Clean Up" song

- "Wash" song

- "Brush Teeth" song (from Raffi, *Singable Songs for the Very Young*)

- "Goodnight" song

Small Group: Pretend Bedtime

Scaffolded by the teachers and visual supports, the children participate in a bedtime routine that mirrors the routine introduced in the bedtime book. The following sequence is completed: brush teeth, put pajamas on, get blanket, get pillow, and sing "Goodnight."

Small Group Targets:

1. To practice a routine for bedtime
2. To facilitate symbolic play skills by participating in symbolic play routine with doll or self as agent
3. To facilitate joint play skills (waiting, watching friends, etc.)

Special Activity:

- Pretend Bedtime Dramatic Play: The bed is set up in the special activity area. Other materials needed: blanket, pillow, pajamas, pretend toothbrush, doll, stuffed animal. The basin and supplies may be set out as a continuation from last week, since both routines often go together in the child's natural environment. The child can play pretend bedtime or put a doll or stuffed animal to sleep. Using dolls/stuffed animals provides an opportunity for the child to engage in symbolic play with the object as the agent to the action rather than the child as the agent.

- Bedtime Book: The children color and glue pictures of each step in the bedtime routine onto a page. Staff should write text consistent with the book of the week and appropriate to the child's developmental level. This bedtime book can be used at home to promote discussion of the related present and also as an aid to help the child follow this routine during bedtime.

Related Songs: "Goodnight" song, "Brush Teeth" song

Additional Related Books:

- *Light* by Donald Crews

- *Maisy's Bedtime* by Lucy Cousins

- *The Napping House* by Audrey Wood

Additions to Children's Folder:

- Bedtime book supports
- Bedtime vocabulary supports

Extension Activity:

If there is a child in the class for whom bedtime is a struggle, as a service to the family, teachers and support staff might guide them in developing a joint action routine for the child's unique bedtime routine. This joint action routine should be based upon the routine presented in the Book of the Week and practiced during Small Group activities. We encourage support staff to create visual supports as appropriate to the family's routine, educate the family in their use, and send the supports home with the family to be used consistently at bedtime.

Unit 3: Bedtime
Child Book Board

	bed	time		

time	bed		clean up	toys

time	bed		bathroom	
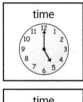				

time	bed		bath	

time	bed		brush	teeth

time	bed		pajamas	

time	bed		blanket	

time	bed		pillow	

time	bed		say	good night

Unit 3: Bedtime
Small Group: Pretend Bedtime

Targets:

1. To practice a routine for bedtime

2. To facilitate symbolic play skills by participating in symbolic play routine with self as agent

3. To facilitate joint play skills (waiting, watching friends, etc.)

Explanation of the Activity:

Scaffolded by the clinicians and visual supports, the children participate in a bedtime routine that mirrors the routine introduced in the Bedtime book. The following sequence is completed: brush teeth, put on pajamas on, get blanket, get pillow, and sing "goodnight."

Materials:

- Toothbrush, pajamas, pillow, blanket, pretend bed set-up in the middle of the Small Group circle

- Small Group activity schedules

- "Turn" support (see "Notes on Taking Turns," page 73)

How to Play:

On the first day of playing the game, the teachers model how to play.

- Teacher 1: "Time for work. It's time for pretend bedtime."
    - "Whose turn?" (talk only to the other teachers)
    - Place "turn" support in front of the Teacher 2, saying, "It's <Teacher 2>'s turn."
- Teacher 1: "Get in bed."
- Teacher 2: Gets in the bed (a blanket that is lying on the floor).
- Teacher 1: "Head on pillow."
- Teacher 2: Lays his/her head on the pillow
- Teacher 1: "Blanket on."
- Teacher 2: Puts blanket on top of himself/herself.
- Teacher 1: "Sing goodnight to teacher." (Sing "Goodnight" song.)
- Teacher 1: "Wake up! <Name>'s turn is finished."

The cycle may repeat, with each child taking a turn in the instructions as follows for the second day or stop, depending on the children's ability to pay attention.

On the second day, the children play the game.

- Teacher 1: "Time for work. It's pretend bedtime."
  - "Whose turn?" (talk only to the children)
  - "It's <name>'s turn," placing "turn" support in front of the child.
- Teacher 1: "Get in bed."
  - If the child responds: "<Name> is in bed."
  - If the child does not respond, cue the child to climb into the bed. May need to say, "Get in. Time for bed." The teacher may also need to pat the bed and guide the child to sit in the bed.
- Teacher 1: "Head on pillow."
  - If the child responds: Continue on to next step.
  - If the child does not respond: "<Name> lay head down. Head on pillow." The teacher may also need to pat the pillow and guide the child to lie down.
- Teacher 1: "Blanket on."
  - If the child responds: Continue on to next step.
  - If the child does responds: "<Name> time for blanket. Put blanket on." The teacher may also need to cover the child with the blanket because that is how it may happen at home.
- Teacher 1: "It's bedtime. Sing goodnight to <Name>." (Sing "Goodnight" song.)
  - Children and teachers: Sing to the child who is "sleeping."
- Teacher 1: "Wake up! <Name>'s turn is finished."
  - Child 1: Gets up and returns to his/her chair.
  - If the child does not respond: "Get up. <Name's> turn is finished. Get out of bed." Sing "Sit Down" song (see song glossary, Appendix E).

Advanced (Level 2)

When the children have mastered the above routine, the activity may be extended with the following steps BEFORE the first step of the previous routine.

- Teacher 1: "Brush your teeth." Give Child 1 a pretend toothbrush.
  - If the child responds: Continue to next step.
  - If the child does not respond: Model and help the child perform the action.
  - While the child is brushing, teachers sing, "Brush your teeth."
- Teacher 1: "Put pajamas on." Give Child 1 pajamas.
  - If the child responds: Continue on to next step.
  - If the child does not respond: Help the child put on the pajamas.
- Teacher 1: "Put pants on. Pull pants up. Put shirt on."

Unit 3: Bedtime
Small Group Activity Schedule – Early Level 2

pretend 	bed 	time 

one	in 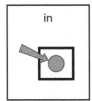	bed	
two 	head 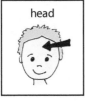	on	pillow 
three	blanket 	on 	
four	sing 	good night 	
five 	wake 	up	
six 	finish		

Unit 3: Bedtime
Small Group Activity Schedule – Level 2 (Advanced)

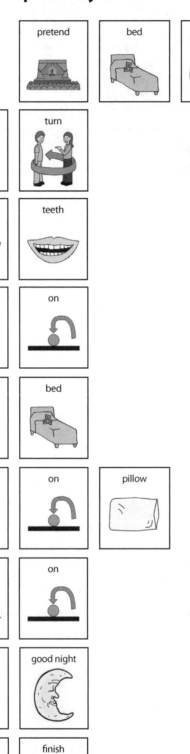

Early CLASS News

Early CLASS Office Phone Number: < > | **Date**

Welcome to the Early CLASS!

Important Dates
Dates when there will not be therapy or dates when certain clinicians will not be in Early CLASS.

Taking the Early CLASS Home

This week, we will be focusing on pretend play through the familiar routine of bedtime. During the day, you can play "pretend bedtime" and let your child pretend to go to sleep and practice putting his animals (or you!) to bed. When it's time for bed, you can sing the "Goodnight" song (to the same tune as the "Hello"/"Goodbye" song) with your child during your own bedtime routine. It's a great idea to have the steps of your bedtime routine written out and displayed for the child to follow. Remember to have fun!

Reminder:
This section can provide a reminder for the parents about an upcoming event or something that they need to bring for their child that week.

Early CLASS Policy
Note about Early CLASS policy or you can include a rationale about a certain aspect of the Early CLASS so that the parents can learn the purpose behind every decision that is made in the classroom.

Theme: Bedtime

Book: *Bedtime*
By: Elsa Warnick

Our book this week is about bedtime routines. It closely follows what may happen at your house at bedtime. The book includes the following activities: cleaning up toys, using the bathroom, taking a bath, brushing teeth, putting on pajamas, getting a blanket and pillow, and finally, going to bed.

Vocabulary
Objects, places, activities: Toy, teeth, pajamas, blanket, pillow
Social: Goodnight
Actions: Brush, say, clean up
Modifiers: Time, on

Songs: "Goodnight" song, "Brush Teeth" song

Lead: Teacher 1

Small Groups: For Small Group this week, we will "pretend" bedtime. The children will take turns following the steps of the bedtime routine and will all sing the "Goodnight" song. Participating in this activity will help your child to develop pretend play skills.

Unit 4: Happy Birthday

Overview

Many Early CLASS parents report birthday parties as being particularly stressful activities for their child. This is highly emotional for the parents, partially because birthday parties are supposed to be fun! We designed this theme week to address a functional need for the families. The "Happy Birthday" theme is designed to teach children a routine for a typical birthday party. The Book of the Week introduces birthday vocabulary and routines, as well as the concept of "waiting for friends." Symbolic play routines during Small Group feature each child as the "birthday child," so that each will have an opportunity to practice being the "birthday child" and being a guest.

Book: *Happy Birthday, Jesse Bear*
Author: Nancy White Carlstrom
ISBN-10 #: 0689833113
Publisher: Aladdin

Table 5.4
Book Narrative Unit 4

Page Spread	Pictures Left	Narrative Left	Pictures Right	Narrative Right
Cover		Happy Birthday, Jesse Bear!		
p. 1-12				
p. 13/14	TIME BIRTHDAY PARTY WAIT FRIEND	Time for the birthday party. Wait for friends. *"Waiting" song.	SAY HELLO FRIEND	
p. 15/16	TIME PRESENT	Time for presents.	SAY THANK YOU	Say "thank you."
p. 17-26				
p. 27/28	TIME BIRTHDAY PARTY SING HAPPY BIRTHDAY	Time for the birthday party. Sing "Happy Birthday." *"Happy Birthday" song	EAT BIRTHDAY CAKE	Eat birthday cake.
p. 29/30				
p. 31/32	BIRTHDAY PARTY FINISH	The birthday party is finished.	TIME HOME SAY GOODBYE FRIEND	Time to go home. Say "goodbye" to friends. *"Goodbye" song
p. 33/34				

Book Targets:

1. To introduce/reinforce birthday party routines

2. To introduce/reinforce birthday vocabulary

3. To introduce the vocabulary and a routine song for "waiting"

Early CLASS Songs (words and tunes may be found in the song glossary, Appendix E):

- "Hello" song

- "Goodbye" song

- "Waiting" song

Small Group: Pretend Birthday Party

The children participate in a pretend birthday party. One child is the "birthday boy/girl" and sits in the "birthday chair" while the other children watch. When acting as guests, the group watches the "birthday child" perform the birthday routine and sings "Happy Birthday" to him/her.

Small Group Targets:

1. To provide supported opportunities for the child to practice birthday party routines and language to use during a birthday party

2. To facilitate attention to the peer sitting in the "birthday chair"

3. To facilitate understanding of two roles in the interaction (role reversal) and to assume reciprocal and complementary roles

4. To support joint symbolic play activities with peers while taking turns, waiting, watching a friend, etc.

Special Activity:

- Birthday Cards: Provide the children with folded paper, birthday pictures/supports, crayons, and glue. The children color the birthday pictures, and glue them on to make birthday cards for friends in the classroom. Discussion surrounds what they want to put on the card and the child who will receive the card. A visual support should be provided.

- Birthday Invitations: Provide the children with folded paper, birthday pictures/supports, crayons, and glue. The children make invitations for a pretend birthday party. They may use the invitations during a "birthday party" symbolic play activity. They may also take them home to mail them to their friends or pass them out during class to encourage social interaction.

Related Songs: "Happy Birthday"

Additional Related Books:

- *Happy Birthday, Maisy* by Lucy Cousins

Additions to Children's Folder:

- *Happy Birthday, Jesse Bear* book supports
- "Happy Birthday" vocabulary supports

Extension Activity: Help parents develop a joint action routine for the child's birthday party using the routine learned in the book.

Unit 4: Happy Birthday
Child Book Board

time	birthday 	party 

wait 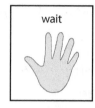	friend 	

say 	hello 	friend 

time 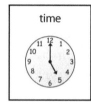	present 

say 	thank you 

time	birthday 	party 

sing 	happy 	birthday 

eat 	birthday 	cake 

time 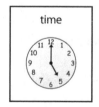	home 

birthday 	party 	finish 

say 	goodbye 	friend 

Unit 4: Happy Birthday
Small Group: Pretend Birthday Party

Targets:

1. To provide supported opportunities for the child to practice birthday party routines and language to use during a birthday party

2. To facilitate attention to peers when they are in the "birthday chair"

3. To facilitate understanding of two roles in the interaction (role reversal) and to assume reciprocal and complementary roles

4. To support joint symbolic play activities with peers while taking turns, waiting, watching a friend, etc.

Explanation of the Activity:

The children will participate in a pretend birthday party. One child is the "birthday boy/girl" and sits in the "birthday chair" while the other children watch. When acting as guests at the party (not the "birthday boy/girl"), the group watches the "birthday child" perform the birthday routine, and sings "Happy Birthday" to him/her.

Materials:

*   Pretend birthday cake with candles
*   Child-sized "birthday chair" and "birthday chair" support; the visual support is taped to the back of the "birthday chair"
*   Decorative bag containing a toy in it for the "present"
*   "Turn" support (see "Notes on Taking Turns," page 73)

How to Play:

On the first day of playing the game, the teachers model how to play.

*   Teacher 1: "Time for work. Time for pretend birthday party."
    *   "Whose turn?" (Talk only to the other teachers.)
    *   Place "turn" support in front of the Teacher 2, saying "It's <Teacher 2>'s turn."
*   Teacher 1: "<Name>, sit in the birthday chair."
*   Teacher 2: Sits in the "birthday chair."
*   Teacher 1: "Birthday hat on."
*   Teacher 2: Puts on the birthday hat.
*   Teacher 1: "Sing 'Happy Birthday' to <Name>."
*   All teachers: Sing "Happy Birthday" to the teacher.
*   Teacher 1: "Blow out candles."
*   Teacher 2: Pretends to blow out the candles.
*   Teacher 1: "<Name>'s turn is finished."

The cycle may repeat one more time with a child in the "birthday chair" (follow directions below) or stop, depending on the children's ability to pay attention.

On the second day of playing the game, the children play the game.

- Teacher 1: "Time for work. Time for pretend birthday party."
    - "Whose turn?" (Talk only to the children.)
    - Place "turn" support in front of the child, saying, "It's <name>'s turn."
- Teacher 1: "Sit in the birthday chair."
    - If the child does not respond: "<Name>, it's your turn. Sit down. Sit in the chair."
    - If the child responds: "Time for <Name's> birthday party."
- Teacher 1: "Birthday hat on."
    - If the child does not respond: "<Name>, put hat on." (Sings "Hat" song. [See song glossary, Appendix E.])
    - If the child responds: Continue to next step.
- Teacher 1: "Sing 'Happy Birthday' to <Name>."
- Teachers and children: Sing "Happy Birthday" to the child.
- Teacher 1: "Blow out candles."
    - If the child does not respond: "Time to blow." Model and use the prompting hierarchy to assist the child.
    - If the child responds: Cheer for child.
- Teacher 1: "<Name>'s turn is finished."
- Child 1: Gets up and returns to his/her chair.
    - If the child does not respond: "Stand up. <Name's> turn is finished. Find your chair." (Sings "Sit Down" song. [See song glossary.])

The cycle repeats until each child in the group gets a turn.

Advanced Activities:

For groups with emerging Level 3 and Level 3 children, the activity may be extended to include additional steps as the group's attention permits. On the following page, we outline how the activity might be extended. Modified activity supports are not provided, but the steps detailed should be a continuation of the previous routine. Therefore, the activity support on the following page may easily be modified to include additional steps.

Advanced – Modification 1: (modified support not provided)

When the children have mastered the above routine, add the following steps to the end of the routine:

- Teacher 1: "Open present." Give a bag containing a toy to the child.
  - If the child responds: "What did you get? What present?"
  - If the child does not respond: "Look in bag. Get present. Pull it out."

Vocabulary additions to provided support:

"open"   "present"

"what"   "present"

"look"   "in"   "bag"

Advanced – Modification 2: (modified support not provided)

If the children have mastered all of the above, add the following steps to the end of the above routine.

- Teacher 1: "Share with friends."
  - If the child responds: "Look at toy. What present did <Name> get?"
  - If the child does not respond: Prompt the child to pass the toy to his/her friends. Pass the toy around the circle ("Give present to friend").

Vocabulary additions to provided support:

"share"   "with"   "friends"

"look"   "toy"   "what"   "present"

"give"   "present"   "to"   "friend"

Unit 4: Happy Birthday
Small Group Activity Schedule – Level 2

pretend 	birthday 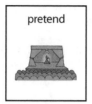	party 

one 	sit 	birthday 	chair
two 	birthday	hat	on 
three 	sing 	happy 	birthday 
four	blow 	candle 	
five 	finish 		

Early CLASS News

Welcome to the Early CLASS!

Important Dates
August 31-September 1: No Early CLASS
September 7: No Early CLASS

Taking the Early CLASS Home

Many Early CLASS parents have told us that taking their child to a birthday party or having a birthday party can be overwhelming. We hope this week's theme will help make the experience more enjoyable for everyone. The children will read a story about a birthday party and practice singing "Happy Birthday," blowing out candles, and other fun birthday activities.

If you are planning on attending a birthday party in the near future, it may be helpful to visit the site of the party before you go. If the party is at the birthday child's home, perhaps you could set up a play date before the big day. If it's at a park or restaurant, take a family trip ahead of time. Being familiar with the environment might help your child process all that's happening on party day. It is also helpful to tell your child ahead of time that it may be loud and to have a plan for what to do in case he needs a break from the action.

Reminder:
This section can provide a reminder for the parents about an upcoming event or something that they need to bring for their child that week.

Early CLASS Policy

Note about Early CLASS policy or you can include a rationale about a certain aspect of the Early CLASS so that the parents can learn the purpose behind every decision that is made in the classroom.

Theme: Happy Birthday

Book: *Happy Birthday, Jesse Bear*
By: Nancy White Carlstrom

In our book this week, Jesse Bear is having a birthday party. We will talk about the routines of a birthday party such as greeting friends, opening presents, singing "Happy Birthday," and blowing out the candles.

Vocabulary
Objects, places, activities: Present, cake, home, birthday, party, friend
Social: Hello, thank you, goodbye
Actions: Finish, wait, eat, say, sing
Modifiers: Time, happy

Songs: "Happy Birthday," "I Love You" song

Lead: Teacher 1

Small Groups: For Small Group this week, the children will play "pretend birthday party." They will take turns wearing a birthday hat, singing "Happy Birthday," and blowing out the candles on a pretend birthday cake.

Unit 5: Restaurant

Overview

Another high-stress activity noted by parents of children with ASD is a family outing to a restaurant. This theme was designed to familiarize the children with the routine of going out to eat. This week's theme and vocabulary will prepare the children for dining at a restaurant in the future. The routine presented in the book follows Barney and Baby Bop as they sit at a table, order and wait for their food, eat pizza, and go home. During Small Group, the children role play the routine, practicing appropriate behaviors as led and supported by teachers. The routine also incorporates skills that the children have been learning during Choice Time, and uses the "Sit Down," "Waiting," and "Look" songs to support comprehension and participation in the task.

Book: *Barney and Baby Bop Go to the Restaurant*
Author: Maureen M. Valvassori
ISBN-10 #: 1570642397
Publisher: Scholastic

Table 5.5
Book Narrative Unit 5

Page Spread	Pictures Left	Narrative Left	Pictures Right	Narrative Right	Notes
Cover		Barney and Baby Bop Go To the Restaurant			
p. 1/2	TIME RESTAURANT	Time for restaurant.	GO RESTAURANT	Go to the restaurant.	
p. 3/4	TIME RESTAURANT	Time for restaurant.	WAIT SIT SIT TABLE	Wait to sit. *"Waiting" song Sit down at the table. *"Sit Down" song	
p. 5/6	TIME RESTAURANT LOOK MENU	Time for restaurant. Look at the menu. *"Look" song	WHAT FOOD MAKE CHOICE	What food? Make a choice.	
p. 7/8	TIME RESTAURANT	Time for restaurant.	TELL WAITER WHAT FOOD	Tell waiter what food.	
p. 9-12					
p. 13/14	TIME RESTAURANT WAIT FOOD	Time for restaurant. Wait for food. *"Waiting" song			Cover up page.
p. 15/16	FOOD HERE	Food is here.	SAY THANK YOU	Say "Thank you."	
p. 17/18					
p. 19/20	TIME RESTAURANT	Time for restaurant.	EAT FOOD	Eat you food.	
p. 21	RESTAURANT FINISHED TIME HOME	Restaurant is finished. Time for home.			

Book Targets:

1. To introduce/reinforce a routine for going to a restaurant

2. To introduce/reinforce restaurant vocabulary

3. To introduce the routine of waiting for food at a restaurant (supported by "Waiting" song)

Early CLASS Songs (words and tunes may be found in the song glossary, Appendix E)**:**

- "Waiting" song

- "Look" song

- "Sit Down" song

Small Group: Pretend Restaurant

The children participate in a joint symbolic play routine (at the level of "self as agent") for pretend restaurant. The children will walk into the "restaurant," "wait" to be seated, sit around a table, and take turns ordering food from a teacher who is labeled the "waiter," with a picture/symbol support. After the children order their food, they wait for the food and, once served, pretend to eat it.

Small Group Targets:

1. To engage in a joint activity routine with peers for restaurant
2. To practice symbolic play skills for self as agent with visual support and clinical modeling
3. To practice the joint activity skills they learned during previous weeks (taking turns, waiting, watching a friend, etc.)

Special Activity:

- Menu: Provide construction paper, food supports, crayons, and glue so that the children can make their own menus. The menus may be used during symbolic play in the classroom or at home.
- Pretend Food: Provide paper plates, construction paper, orange yarn, glue, crayons and scissors so that the children can make their own pretend food.

  Children with fine-motor challenges or those who struggle with attention during such craft activities may require additional support from teachers. The number of steps in the activity should be determined by the developmental levels and fine-motor abilities of the children in the classroom. Construction paper foods may be prepared in advance by support staff and teachers to limit fine-motor demands for the child and shorten activity time.

  Children might "make tacos" by folding paper plates in half and gluing construction paper "meat" and yarn "cheese" inside. Children might also create plates of food by gluing construction paper foods to a paper plate. Pretend foods can then be used as part of symbolic play activities in the classroom or at home.

Related Songs: "Pizza" song, "Peanut Butter and Jelly" song

Additional Related Books:

- *Froggy Eats Out* by Jonathan London
- *Going to a Restaurant* by Melinda Beth Radabaugh
- *Hi Pizza Man!* by Virginia Walter

Additions to Children's Folder:

- *Barney and Baby Bop Go to the Restaurant* book supports
- Restaurant vocabulary supports

Extension Activity:

Help parents develop a joint action routine for going to a restaurant using the routine learned in the book.

Unit 5: Restaurant
Child Book Board p. 1/2

time	restaurant

time	restaurant		go	restaurant

time	restaurant		wait	sit
	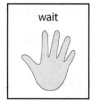			

			sit	table

time	restaurant		look	menu
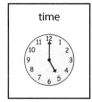				

			what	food	make	choice

time	restaurant		tell	waiter	what	food
					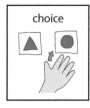	

Unit 5: Restaurant
Child Book Board p. 2/2

time 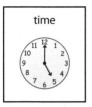	restaurant 	wait 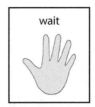	food 
food 	here 	say 	thank you
time 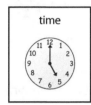	restaurant 	eat 	food
restaurant 	finish 		
time 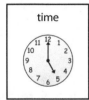	home 		

Unit 5: Restaurant
Small Group: Pretend Restaurant

Targets:

1. To engage in a joint activity routine with peers for restaurant

2. To practice symbolic play skills for self as agent with visual support and clinical modeling

3. To practice the joint activity skills they learned during previous weeks (taking turns, waiting, watching a friend, etc.)

Explanation of the Activity:

The children participate in a joint symbolic play routine (at the level of "self as agent") for pretend restaurant. The children walk into the "restaurant," wait to be seated, sit around a table, and take turns ordering food from a clinician, who is labeled the "waiter." After the children order their food, they wait for the food and, once served, pretend to eat it.

Materials:

- Table with chairs around it labeled "restaurant" with a large restaurant picture/symbol support, a menu listing typical food items (e.g., hamburger, hot dog, chicken)

- Plates with the food

- "Waiter" support for the waiter to wear. The "waiter" support should prominently feature the picture symbol for "waiter." As best fits the developmental level of the group, the "waiter" support might be a laminated picture symbol of "waiter" attached to a hat or an 8x10 laminated picture symbol for "waiter" hung around the waiter's neck.

- "Turn" support (see "Notes on Taking Turns," page 73)

How to Play:

On the first day of playing the game, the teachers model how to play, referencing picture symbol activity support throughout.

- Teacher 1: "Time for work. Time for pretend restaurant."

- Teacher 1: "Go to restaurant"

  - Teachers: May need to use the prompting hierarchy to cue the children to stand up from the Small Group table and move to the pretend restaurant area.

  - "Stand up. Go to pretend restaurant."

- Teacher 1: "Wait to sit down." (Sing "Waiting" song.)

- "Waiter": Greets children and says, "Hello! Time to sit."

- Teacher 1: "Sit at the table."
  - Teachers and children: Sit at the restaurant table. (Sing "Sit Down" song as children are being seated.)
- "Waiter": Passes out menus.
- Teacher 1: *To a teacher and all the children*: "Look at menu."
- All teachers: Individually look at the menu with their child and help them choose which food they want.

First the "waiter" asks a teacher and then moves on to the children. Repeat until all children have had their turn.

- Teacher 1: "Make a choice. What food?"
- Teacher 2: "I want chicken."
- Teacher 1: "Make a choice. What food?"
  - If the child does not respond: Use prompting hierarchy to cue the child to make a choice. "What food? Make a choice, chicken or hamburger."
  - If the child responds: "<Name> chose <food>." Move on to the next child. "It's <name>'s turn. Make a choice. What food?"
- Teacher 1: "Wait for food." (Sings "Waiting" song. The waiter gets the food ready and passes it out to the kids.)
- Teacher 1: "Pretend to eat the food."
- Teachers and children: Everyone pretends to eat the food.
- Teacher 1: "Pretend restaurant is finished."

The second day of playing the game is the same as the first, except the teachers do not order and are not served.

Unit 5: Restaurant
Small Group Activity Schedule – Level 2-3

Early CLASS News

Welcome to the Early CLASS!

Important Dates
Dates when there will not be therapy or dates when certain clinicians will not be in Early Class.

Taking the Early CLASS Home

This week, we will be using our Book of the Week, Small Group, and Special Activity to familiarize your child with the routine of going out to eat. We hope that this week's theme and vocabulary will give you valuable tools to prepare your child for dining at a restaurant in the future.

In addition to having practical application to real life, this unit offers opportunities for pretend play. You can have fun pretending to be at a restaurant with your child by sitting at a table, looking at a menu, ordering food, and our favorite skill – waiting.

Reminder:
This section can provide a reminder for the parents about an upcoming event or something that they need to bring for their child that week.

Early CLASS Policy

Note about Early CLASS policy or you can include a rationale about a certain aspect of the Early CLASS so that the parents can learn the purpose behind every decision that is made in the classroom.

Theme: Restaurant

Book: *Barney and Baby Bop Go to the Restaurant*

Author: Maureen M. Valvassori

In this week's book, Barney and Baby Bop go to their favorite restaurant for pizza. The book uses colorful photographs to familiarize children with the routine associated with going out to eat. The children will see Barney and his friend as they sit at a table, order and wait for their food, eat their pizza, and go home.

Vocabulary
Objects, places, activities: Table, menu, food, choice, restaurant, home, waiter
Social: Hello, thank you
Actions: Finish, wait, look, sit, make, eat, go, say, tell
Modifiers: Time, down, here, what

Songs: "Pizza" song, "Cookie" song, "Peanut Butter and Jelly" song

Lead: Teacher 1

Small Groups: This week the children will have fun playing pretend restaurant. They will look at a menu, make a choice, and tell the waiter what food they would like. Then they will learn to wait for the waiter to bring the food and pretend to eat it.

Unit 6: Grocery Store

Overview

Early CLASS parents frequently report difficulty going grocery shopping with their child. This theme was designed to support the child's appropriate communication and behavior while at the grocery store. The Book of the Week was adapted to introduce a grocery store routine and supporting vocabulary. The children follow a family as they push the grocery cart, look at their grocery list, search for different items throughout the store, put the purchases in bags, and pay for the items at the cashier. The Small Group activity follows the routine introduced in the book and supports a functional symbolic play activity for grocery store at the level of "self as agent." The routine also incorporates skills that the children have been learning during Look Time, and the "Look" song is sung frequently to support the children's comprehension and participation in the task.

Book: *At the Supermarket*
Author: Anne Rockwell
ISBN-10 #: 9780805076622
Publisher: Henry Holt and Company

Book Targets:

1. To introduce a routine for the grocery store

2. To introduce/reinforce vocabulary for a grocery store outing

3. To illustrate the concept of looking for and finding an item in a grocery store

Early CLASS Songs (words and tunes may be found in the song glossary, Appendix E):

- "Look" song

Small Group: Pretend Grocery Store

The children practice the routine of grocery shopping. They look at the grocery list and find items spread throughout the Small Group area. They push the cart to the item and place it in the cart. Then they push the cart to the cashier and give him/her the item.

Small Group Targets:

1. To participate in a symbolic play routine for grocery store at the level of "self as agent"

2. To reinforce routine and vocabulary for a grocery store

3. To practice the joint activity skills they learned during previous weeks (taking turns, waiting, watching a friend, etc.)

Table 5.6
Book Narrative Unit 6

Page Spread	Pictures Left	Narrative Left	Pictures Right	Narrative Right	Notes
Cover	Words read: At the Supermarket				
p. 1/2	TIME GROCERY STORE LIST	Time for the grocery store. List	LOOK LIST GROCERY LIST CHICKEN GRAPES PEANUT BUTTER MILK ICE CREAM	Look at list. Grocery list: chicken, grapes, peanut butter, milk, ice cream.	Storybook modified with addition of a teacher-created list on p. 2. Example "list" provided.
p. 3/4	TIME GROCERY STORE	Time for the grocery store.	TIME CART	Time for the cart.	
p. 5/6	LOOK LIST LOOK CHICKEN	Look at (the grocery) list. Look for chicken. *"Look" song	THERE CHICKEN IN CART	There it is! Put chicken in the cart.	Use of "Look for the <>," followed by "There it is!" was written in that order to be consistent with the already familiar, "Look" song. Place the "There" support on the page where Baby Bop is holding it in her hand.
p. 7/8	LOOK LIST LOOK GRAPES THERE	Look at (the grocery) list. Look for grapes. *"Look" song There it is!	LOOK LIST LOOK PEANUT BUTTER THERE	Look for the peanut butter. *"Look" song There it is!	
p. 9/10	LOOK LIST LOOK MILK	Look at (the grocery) list. Look for the milk. *"Look" song	THERE	There it is!	
p. 11/12	FOOD IN CART	Food in cart.			
p. 13/14					
p. 15/16					
p. 17/18					
p. 19/20	LOOK LIST LOOK ICE CREAM	Look at (the grocery) list. Look for the ice cream. *"Look" song	THERE	There it is!	
p. 21/22	TIME PAY CASHIER	Time to pay. Cashier	FOOD IN BAG GROCERY STORE FINISH(ED)	Put food in the bag. Grocery store is finished.	
p. 23/24	TIME HOME	Time for home.			
p. 25-end					

Special Activity:

- Sand Table: Teachers place grocery store-related objects in the sand table. Children scoop and pour sand at the sand table using empty milk cartons and ice cream cartons. Teachers can also hide pretend food from the Kitchen Center in the sand, to be discovered by the children during their play. The children enjoy a fun sensory activity while discovering weekly theme vocabulary.

- Hide and Find: The children look for different food items that are spread throughout the Special Activity area. The clinician sings the "Look" song to help cue the child to find the object.

Related Songs: "Pizza" song, "Peanut Butter and Jelly" song, "Look" song

Additional Related Books:

- *Max Goes to the Grocery Store* by Adria Klein
- *Our Corner Grocery Store* by Joanne Schwartz

Additions to Children's Folder:

- *At the Supermarket* book supports
- Grocery store vocabulary supports

Extension Activity: Help parents develop a joint action routine for going to the grocery store using the routine learned in the book.

Unit 6: Grocery Store
Book Board p. 1/3

time	grocery	store		list

look	list

grocery — list — chicken — grapes — peanut butter — milk — ice cream

time	grocery	store		time	cart

Unit 6: Grocery Store
Book Board p. 2/3

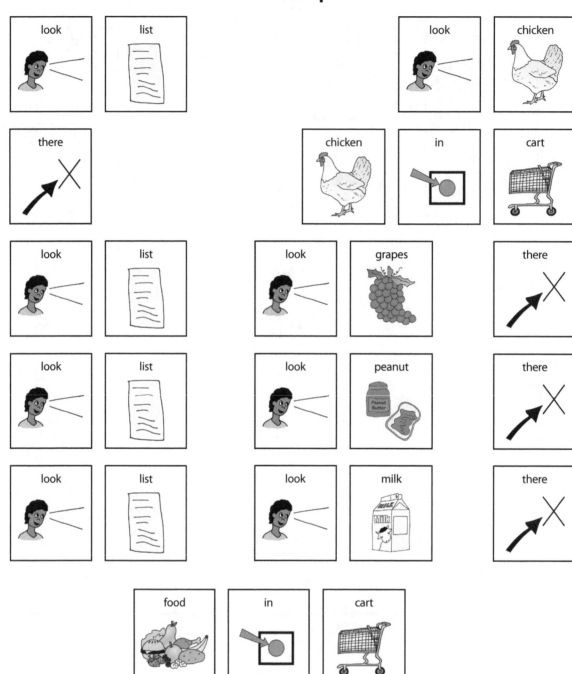

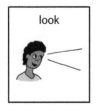  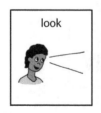  

Unit 6: Grocery Store
Book Board p. 3/3

time	pay		cashier

food	in	bag

grocery	store	finish

time	home

Unit 6: Grocery Store
Small Group: Pretend Grocery Store

Targets:

1. To participate in a symbolic play routine for grocery store at the level of "self as agent"

2. To reinforce routine and vocabulary for a grocery store

3. To practice the joint activity skills they learned during previous weeks (taking turns, waiting, watching a friend, etc.)

Explanation of the Activity:

The children practice the routine of grocery shopping. They look at the grocery list and find items spread out throughout the Small Group area. They push the cart to the item and place it in the cart. Then they push the cart to the cashier and give the item to him/her. The Small Group visual support for the week is also designed for use by parents when taking their child to the grocery store.

Materials:

*   "Turn" support (see "Notes on Taking Turns," page 73)

*   Grocery list (with apple, milk, and ice cream; these items are used because they are consistent with the Book of the Week)

*   Pretend food (or containers) that reflect the food choices on the grocery list

*   Cart

*   Cash register station

*   Support for the "cashier" to wear (such as a large laminated "cashier" picture symbol to wear on a hat, or word hung around the neck)

*   Activity schedules for all of the children

How to Play:

On the first day of playing the game, the teachers take the first turn, modeling how to play (as in the previous instructional units). Next,

*   Teacher 1: "Time for work. Time for pretend grocery store."

    *   "Whose turn?" (talks only to the children)

    *   Place "turn" support in front of the child and say "It's <name>'s turn."

*   Teacher 1: "First, look at the grocery list."

    *   If the child does not respond: Use the prompting hierarchy to cue the child to look at the list.

    *   If the child responds: Move on to the next step.

- Teacher 1: "Make a choice. What food?"
  - If the child does not respond: Use the prompting hierarchy to cue the child to look at the list. "What food? Make a choice, apple or ice cream."
  - If the child responds: Move on to the next step.
- Teacher 1: "<Name> chose <u>ice cream</u>."
- Teacher 1: "Look for the food. Find the <u>ice cream</u>."
  - If the child does not respond: Use the prompting hierarchy to cue the child to look at the list. Sing "Look" song. Remind child to push the cart to the item.
  - If the child responds: Move on to the next step.
- Teacher 1: "Put food in cart."
  - If the child does not respond: Use the prompting hierarchy to cue the child to put the food in the cart.
  - If the child responds: Move on to the next step.
- Teacher 1: "Looking for food is finished. Time to go to the cashier." The child pushes the cart to the cashier.
  - If the child does not respond: Use the prompting hierarchy to cue the child to push the cart to the cashier station.
  - If the child responds: Move on to the next step.
- Teacher 1: "Give the food to the cashier."
  - If the child does not respond: Use the prompting hierarchy to cue the child to give the food to the cashier. Sing the "Give it to _____" from the "Hat" song to the child.
  - If the child responds: Move on to the next step.
- Teacher 1: "<Name>'s turn is finished. Find your chair."
  - If the child does not respond: Use the prompting hierarchy to cue the child to finish his turn and sit in his chair. Sing the "Sit Down" song.
  - If the child responds: Move on to the next step.

The cycle repeats until each child in the group gets a turn.

Unit 6: Grocery Store
Small Group Activity Schedule – Level 2-3

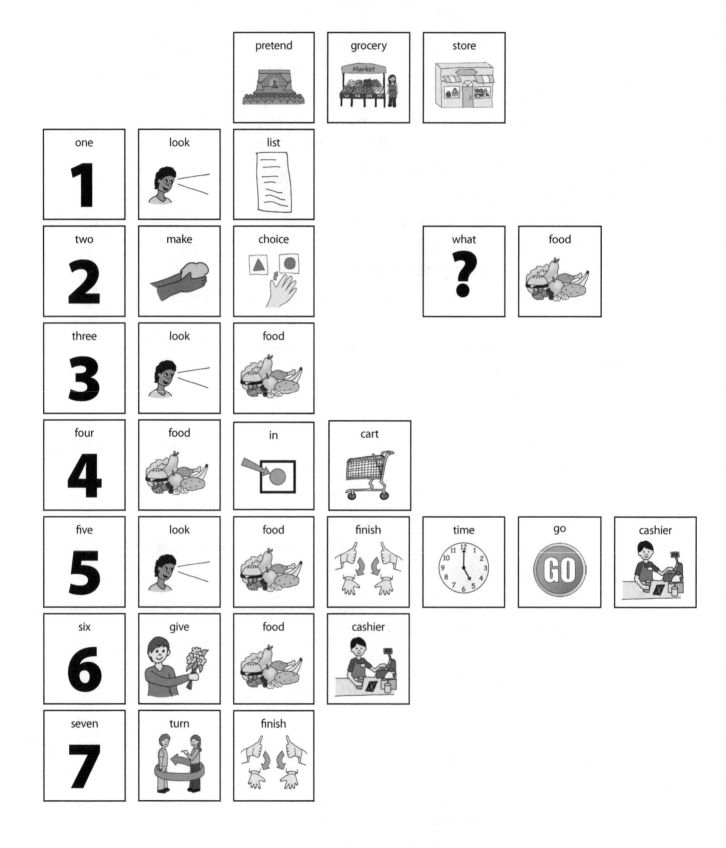

Early CLASS News

Welcome to the Early CLASS!

Important Dates
Dates when there will not be therapy or dates when certain clinicians will not be in Early CLASS.

Taking the Early CLASS Home

This week in Early CLASS, we will read a story about grocery shopping. Through a colorful book, Small Group, and Special Activity, the children will become familiar with vocabulary related to the grocery store and practice looking at grocery lists, pushing the shopping cart, and paying the cashier.

We hope this theme will help you in your own trips to the grocery store in the future. You can sing the "Look" song to enlist your child's help in finding items on your grocery list. You can also use the vocabulary we are working on this week to talk to the child about what is going on in the store as you shop, wait in line, and pay. "Pretend grocery store" is also a fun game to play at home with items you already own.

Reminder:
This section can provide a reminder for the parents about an upcoming event or something that they need to bring for their child that week.

Early CLASS Policy

Note about Early CLASS policy or you can include a rationale about a certain aspect of the Early CLASS so that the parents can learn the purpose behind every decision that is made in the classroom.

Theme: Grocery Store

Book: *At the Supermarket*

By: Anne Rockwell

In our book, a mother and son take a trip to the grocery store. They get a shopping cart and look for items on their grocery list. When they find everything on the list, they pay the cashier, put their groceries in bags, and go home.

At **Special Activity,** the kids will enjoy a fun sensory activity while using our weekly theme vocabulary. They will play in the sand table, finding and using pretend foods and food containers.

Vocabulary

Agents: Cashier
Objects, places, activities: Cart, list, chicken, grapes, milk, peanut butter, ice cream, food, bag, grocery, store, home
Actions: Finish, look, pay
Modifiers: Time, there, in

Songs: "Peanut Butter and Jelly" song, "Cookie" song

Lead: Teacher 1

Small Groups: This week in Small Group, the children will play pretend grocery store. They will look for items on a grocery list and put them in a cart. Then they will give the items to a "cashier."

Unit 7: Picnic

Overview

This theme is designed to teach the children a functional routine for how to go on a picnic. In the curriculum, this unit should be scheduled in the spring or summer months, when going on a picnic is most feasible. The book introduces a simple routine for a picnic: packing the picnic basket, laying out the blanket, and eating outdoors. This routine also incorporates skills that the children have been learning during Snack Time, such as passing out plates and cups, waiting for food, and gaining the attention of the adult to request more (as appropriate to their developmental level). Small Group offers the children an opportunity to practice a symbolic play routine for a picnic at the level of self as agent, following the routine introduced in the storybook. For extension and generalization of the routine, if the children are ready, Snack Time may take place outside in picnic format on the last day of this instructional unit.

Book: *Picnic*
Author: Emily Arnold McCulley
ISBN-10 #: 0066238544
Publisher: HarperCollins

Table 5.7
Book Narrative Unit 7

Page Spread	Pictures Left	Narrative Left	Pictures Right	Narrative Right
Cover	PICNIC	Picnic		
p. 1/2				
p. 3/4	GO PICNIC FOOD IN BASKET	Go on a picnic. Food in basket.		
p. 5-10				
p. 11/12	GO PICNIC	Go on a picnic.	OUTSIDE	Outside.
p. 13/14	GO PICNIC	Go on a picnic.	BLANKET ON GRASS	Put the blanket on the grass.
p. 15-18				
p. 19/20	GO PICNIC	Go on a picnic.	PASS PLATES PASS CUPS PASS FOOD	Pass out plates. Pass out cups. Pass out food.
p. 21/22	GO PICNIC	Go on a picnic.	WAIT EAT	Wait to eat. *"Waiting" song
p. 23-34				
p. 35/36	GO PICNIC	Go on a picnic.	EAT OUTSIDE	Eat outside.

Book Targets:

1. To introduce the routine and vocabulary for going on a picnic

2. To introduce and reinforce mealtime concepts

Early CLASS Songs (words and tunes may be found in the song glossary, Appendix E)**:**

- "Waiting" song

Small Group: Pretend Picnic

The children practice the functional routine of going on a picnic. They lay out a blanket on the floor and sit on it. A basket is nearby. The children open it, take out various items (plates, cups, food), and pass them out. Then they pretend to eat the food. This activity is designed to be adaptable to the child's natural environment. Copies of Small Group supports are provided to the parents for use on a family picnic, if desired.

Small Group Targets:

1. To introduce and support a joint routine for appropriate behaviors and language to use during a picnic
2. To practice a symbolic play routine at the level of self as agent
3. To practice the joint activity skills learned during previous weeks

Special Activity:

- Picnic Basket: Provide crayons, glue, pictures of food, and paper cutouts of picnic baskets. Children choose pictures of food to take on a picnic, color them, and glue them "in" a basket to show friends. * Please note: It is important to find a picnic basket coloring page that allows space for the child to appear to be putting it "in." Otherwise, the child is actually gluing it "on," which may be confusing when teaching prepositions ("in" vs. "on").
- Pretend Food: Provide paper plate, plate of food, construction paper, glue, crayons, and scissors so that the children can make their own pretend food.
- Children with fine-motor challenges or those who struggle with attention during such craft activities may require additional support from teachers. The number of steps in the activity is determined by the developmental levels and fine-motor abilities of the children in the classroom. Construction paper foods may be prepared in advance by support staff and teachers to limit fine-motor demands for the child and shorten activity time.

Related Songs: "Peanut Butter and Jelly" song

Additional Related Books:

- *Packing for a Picnic* by Mary Lou Roberts
- *We're Going on a Picnic!* by Pat Hutchins
- *Teddy Bears' Picnic* by Jimmy Kennedy

Additions to Children's Folder: *Picnic* book supports and picnic vocabulary support

Unit 7: Picnic
Child Book Board p. 1/2

Unit 7: Picnic
Child Book Board p. 2/2

go 	picnic 	wait 	eat
go 	picnic 	eat 	outside

Unit 7: Picnic
Small Group: Pretend Picnic

Targets:

1. To introduce and support a joint routine for appropriate behaviors and language to use during a picnic

2. To practice a symbolic play routine at the level of self as agent

3. To practice the joint activity skills learned during previous weeks

Explanation of the Activity:

Following the picnic routine introduced in the Book of the Week, the children practice a symbolic play routine for going on a picnic. They lay out a blanket on the floor and sit on it. A basket is nearby; the children open it, take out and pass around various items (plates, cups, food). Then, they pretend to eat the food. This activity is designed to be adaptable to the child's natural environment. Copies of Small Group activity supports should be provided to the parents for use on a family picnic, if desired. Each child plays a different role in the routine, rather than each child completing all steps on each turn, as in previous instructional units.

Materials:

*   Blanket, basket, pretend food (selected "picnic-appropriate" food), plates, cups, and picnic activity supports

*   "Turn" support (see "Notes on Taking Turns," page 73)

How to Play:

On the first day of playing the game, the teachers model the routine (as in the previous instructional units). The script is adapted to the number of children who are participating in the activity. Some children may have more than one turn, as they are able.

*   Teacher 1: "Time for work. Time for pretend picnic."

    *   Place "turn" support in front of Child 1 and say, "It's <name>'s turn."

*   Teacher 1: "<Child 1> Put blanket down."

    *   If the child does not respond: Use the prompting hierarchy to cue the child to lay the blanket in the Small Group area. "Blanket down. On floor. Put the blanket on the floor."

    *   If the child responds: Move on to the next step.

*   Teacher 1: "<Child 1's> turn is finished. Everyone, sit on the blanket."

    *   If any of the children do not respond: Use the prompting hierarchy to cue the child to sit down on the blanket. (Sings "Come, Sit Down" song.)

    *   If the child responds: Move on to the next step.

- Teacher 1: "It's <Child 2's> turn. Open the basket."
    - If the child does not respond: Use the prompting hierarchy to cue the child to open the picnic basket.
    - If the child responds: Move on to the next step.
- Teacher 1: "<Child 2's> turn is finished. It's <Child 3's> turn."
- Teacher 1: <Child 3>, "Pass out plates."
    - If the child does not respond: Use the prompting hierarchy to cue the child to pass out the plates. (Sings "Pass the Plates" song.)
    - If the child responds: Move on to the next step.
    - Repeat this step for passing out the cups and food, moving to Child 4 and Child 5. The steps in the activity are designed to mirror Snack Time, so the children will have an established routine to tie the new picnic routine to.
- Teacher 1: "<Child 5's> turn is finished. Time to pretend eat."
    - If the children do not respond: Use the prompting hierarchy to cue the child to pretend to eat the food.
    - After all of the children respond: Move on to the next step.
- Teacher 1: "Pretend picnic is finished. Time to clean up."
    - If the child does not respond: Use the prompting hierarchy to cue the children to clean up the Small Group area. (Sings "Clean Up" song.)

As children are developmentally ready, the routine may be extended by:

- Packing the picnic basket before the pretend picnic.
- Having a picnic during Snack Time either inside or outdoors.

Unit 7: Picnic
Small Group Activity Schedule – Level 2

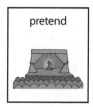
pretend

picnic

one
1

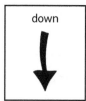
blanket

down

two
2

sit

on

blanket

three
3

open

basket

four
4

pass

plate

cup

food

five
5

pretend

eat

six
6

finish

Early CLASS News

Welcome to the Early CLASS!

Important Dates
Dates when there will not be therapy or dates when certain clinicians will not be in Early CLASS.

Taking the Early CLASS Home

We hope the beautiful weather is here to stay because this week we're learning all about going on a picnic. The children will have fun packing a picnic basket and going on a pretend picnic.

This is a great theme to take home. Please use this week's visual supports. This is a particularly fun family activity as you go on a pretend picnic inside or pack a real picnic and eat outdoors. Your child can help pack for the picnic, lay out the blanket, and pass out plates, cups, and food. Have fun!

Reminder:
This section can provide a reminder for the parents about an upcoming event or something that they need to bring for their child that week.

Early CLASS Policy
Note about Early CLASS policy or you can include a rationale about a certain aspect of the Early CLASS so that the parents can learn the purpose behind every decision that is made in the classroom.

Theme: Picnic

Book: *Picnic*
By: Emily Arnold McCully

This week's theme is "picnic." In our Book of the Week, a mouse family demonstrates the routine for a picnic. For **Special Activity**, the kids can choose pictures of food to take on a picnic, color them, and glue them in a basket to show friends.

Vocabulary
Objects, places, activities: Food, basket, blanket, grass, plates, cups, picnic, outside

Actions: Wait, go, pass, eat

Modifiers: in, on

Songs: "Cookie" song, "Peanut Butter and Jelly" song

Lead: Teacher 1

Small Groups: The children will practice a joint symbolic play routine for having a picnic. This routine may be extended to first packing the picnic basket before we have our picnic. At the end of the week, if the children are ready, we may pack our snack as a picnic to eat inside or outdoors.

Unit 8: Family

Overview

The intention of this theme is to introduce and reinforce family vocabulary concepts, as well as routines that take place in the home. Through the book, Small Group, and Special Activity, the unit will provide practice with family vocabulary and provide models for familial social routines, which will support carry-over to joint routines with family members at home.

Book: *"I Can Do It, Too!"*
Author: Karen Baicker
ISBN-10 #: 1929766831
Publisher: Chronicle Books

Table 5.8
Book Narrative Unit 8

Page Spread	Pictures Left	Narrative Left	Pictures Right	Narrative Right	Rationale
Cover	MY FAMILY	I can do it with my family.			
p. 1/2					
p. 3/4	MY DAD	With my dad	MAKE BREAKFAST	I make breakfast.	"With my …" is used as a repetitive phrase to catch the children's attention.
p. 5/6	MY SISTER	With my sister	DRESS UP	I dress up.	
p. 7/8	MY GRANDMA	With my grandma	BAKE COOKIES	I bake cookies.	
p. 9/10	MY GRANDPA	With my grandpa	READ BOOK	I read books.	
p. 11/12	MY UNCLE	With my uncle	SING SONG	I sing songs.	
p. 13/14	MY MOM	With my mom	HUG	We hug.	
p. 15/16					Skip page.
p. 17/18	MY BROTHER	With my brother	RIDE BIKE	I ride bikes.	
p. 19-22					Skip page.

Book Targets:

1. To teach/reinforce names of family members: dad, sister, grandma, grandpa, uncle, mom, brother

2. To provide a model of joint activities and routines which may be completed with a family member

Small Group: Family Lotto

The children will be matching a picture of one of their family members to the corresponding LessonPix® picture/symbol on a game board.

Small Group Targets:

1. To facilitate learning of family titles as they relate to the child's own family

2. To learn the routine of a lotto board game (drawing a card, matching it on the board, etc.)

3. To support continued learning of the foundational skills of playing a game (taking turns, waiting, watching friends)

Special Activity:

- Family Album: The children will bring pictures of their family from home and glue them to pages of a "book" to make a family album. They will also glue corresponding the Lesson Pix picture/symbol to the page to reinforce learning of family vocabulary. They may further decorate the page, if they choose.

Related Songs: "I Love You" song

Additional Related Books:

- *Who's in a Family?* by Robert Skutch

Additions to Children's Folder:

- *I Can Do It, Too!* book supports
- Family vocabulary supports

Unit 8: Family
Child Book Board p. 1/1

my

family

my	dad
my	sister
my	grandma
my	grandpa
my	uncle
my	mom
my	brother

make	breakfast
dress up	
bake	cookie
read	book
sing	song
hug	
ride	bike

Unit 8: Family
Small Group: Family Lotto

Targets:

1. To facilitate learning family titles as they relate to the child's own family

2. To learn the routine of a lotto board game (drawing a card, matching it on the board, etc.)

3. To support continued learning of the foundational skills of playing a game (taking turns, waiting, watching friends)

Explanation of the Activity:

The child matches a picture of one of her family members to the corresponding picture/symbol on the game board. It is hoped that this activity will support the child in her ability to map her mental representation of her family members to the family "title" picture/symbol, supporting carryover from the book to real life.

Materials:

- "Turn" support (see "Notes on Taking Turns," page 73)

- Lotto board (see example on p. 156) made of picture/symbol for family members surrounding the center "family" support

- Lotto cards with pictures of each member of the child's family

- Small Group activity schedules

How to Play:

On the first day of playing the game, the teachers model how to play (as in the previous instructional units). The script below addresses what the clinicians should say when only the children are participating.

- Teacher 1: "Time for work. Time to play the family game."

  - "Whose turn?"

  - "It's <name>'s turn." Place "turn" support in front of the child.

- Teacher 1: "Take card." (The cards are lying on a table near the child). The child should draw the top card.

  - If the child does not respond: Use the prompting hierarchy to cue the child to pick up the top card.

  - If the child responds: Move on to the next step.

- Teacher 1: "Look at picture."
  - If the child does not respond: Use the prompting hierarchy to cue the child to look at the picture on the card.
  - If the child responds: Move on to the next step.
- Teacher 1: "Tell who."
  - If the child does not respond: Use the prompting hierarchy to cue the child to tell her friends who the picture represents. "Who is on the picture? What person? Tell your friends."
  - If the child responds: Move on to the next step.
- Teacher 1: "Find the same."
  - If the child does not respond: Use the prompting hierarchy to cue the child to find the word that corresponds to the picture on the card. For example, match a picture of the child's mom with the visual support for "mom."
  - If the child responds: Move on to the next step.
- Teacher 1: "Put card on."
  - If the child does not respond: Use the prompting hierarchy to cue the child to put the card on the lotto board.
  - If the child responds: Move on to the next step.
- Teacher 1: "<Name>'s turn is finished."

The cycle repeats until each child in the group gets a turn.

Unit 8: Family
Small Group Activity Schedule – Level 2

play 	family	game 

one 	take 	card 
two 	look	picture 
three 	tell 	who 
four 	find 	same 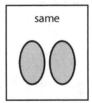
five 	card 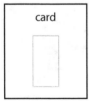	on 
six	turn 	finish 

not 

mom 	dad 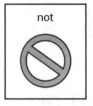
grandma 	grandpa 
aunt 	uncle 
sister 	brother

Unit 8: Family
Small Group Game Board

mom 	dad 	grandma 
brother 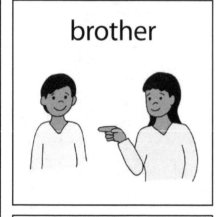	family 	grandpa 
sister 	aunt 	uncle 

Early CLASS News

Early CLASS Office Phone Number: < >   **Date**

Welcome to the Early CLASS!

Important Dates
Dates when there will not be therapy or dates when certain clinicians will not be in Early CLASS.

Taking the Early CLASS Home

This week we are focusing on the vocabulary of family. We will be using these terms to work on generalization to your family as well as the concept of matching ("same").

At home, you can look at photos or watch videos of family members while using this week's vocabulary to talk to your child about what he/she sees. You can also include family words during or in your pretend play with dolls and toys.

We've been looking forward to this week and love having your family pictures for our games. Thanks for all of your help.

Reminder:
This section can provide a reminder for the parents about an upcoming event or something that they need to bring for their child that week.

Early CLASS Policy

Note about Early CLASS policy or you can include a rationale about a certain aspect of the Early CLASS so that the parents can learn the purpose behind every decision that is made in the classroom.

Theme: Family

Book: *I Can Do It, Too!*
By: Karen Baicker

This week, we are talking about family. In our Book of the Week, the children will learn about what different family members can do and how they can do those activities too (baking cookies, reading books, etc.).

For **Special Activity**, the children will make a family album and draw family "portraits." Please use their work at home to support carryover of the family concepts we are learning this week.

Vocabulary
Objects, places, activities: Breakfast, cookie, book, song, bike, dress up

Social: Family, dad, sister, grandma, grandpa, uncle, mom, brother

Actions: Make, back, read, sing, hug, ride

Attributes: same

Songs: "I Love You" song

Lead: Teacher 1

Small Groups: The children will play a family lotto game with their friends to become familiar with names and titles of family members and work on the concept of matching.

Unit 9: Airport

Overview

We designed this unit in response to parent feedback. Many Early CLASS families were planning vacations in the summer time and were concerned about how their child would respond to the airport and traveling on an airplane. The goal of this unit is for the child to be able to establish expectations for a trip to the airport and going on an airplane, supporting his understanding and emotional regulation during real-life activities with their family. In this unit, the book introduces a routine for going on an airplane and provides a framework for a functional joint symbolic play activity. Songs and visual supports associated with the routine are utilized during classroom activities and should be made available to the family for their own excursions.

When planning the curriculum for a semester, it is recommended that this theme be placed just before a "break" (i.e., at the end of the spring semester, just before summer, just before holiday travel), so that the routine is fresh on the minds of the children and their families when needed.

Book: *Airport*
Author: Byron Barton
ISBN-10 #: 0064431452
Publisher: HarperCollins

Table 5.9
Book Narrative Unit 9

Page Spread	Pictures Left	Narrative Left	Pictures Right	Narrative Right	Notes and rationale
Cover					
p. 1/2					
p. 3/4					
p. 5/6	GO TRIP	Go on a trip.	GO AIRPORT	Go to the airport.	The phrase "Go on a trip" allows the child to become familiar with this key phrase. Repetition supports understanding and attention
p. 7/8	GO TRIP	Go on a trip.	HOLD SUITCASE STAND LINE	Hold the suitcase. Stand in line.	Introduces steps involved in boarding a plane. Knowledge of the necessary steps will help the child repeat these steps in different surroundings.
p. 9/10	GO TRIP	Go on a trip.	WAIT AIRPLANE	Wait for the airplane. *"Waiting" song	The teacher can sing the "Waiting" song to reinforce the directions the children are to follow.
p. 11/12					
p. 13/14					

Page Spread	Pictures Left	Narrative Left	Pictures Right	Narrative Right	Notes and rationale
p. 15/16	GO TRIP	Go on a trip.	WALK LINE	Walk in line. *"Following the Leader" song	The teacher may sing the "Follow the Leader" song to provide a familiar support to help the child know what to do.
p. 17/18	GO TRIP	Go on a trip.	TIME SIT AIRPLANE	Time to sit in airplane.	
p. 19/20					
p. 21/22					
p. 23/24	GO TRIP	Go on a trip.	SEATBELT ON	Put on seatbelt.	
p. 25/26					
p. 27/28					
p. 29/30	GO TRIP	Go on a trip.	AIRPLANE FAST	The airplane drives fast.	This prepares the child for what to expect when a real airplane takes off.
p. 31/32	GO TRIP	Go on a trip.	AIRPLANE SKY FLY SKY	Airplane in sky. Fly in sky.	

Book Targets:

1. To introduce the routine and vocabulary of going on a plane

2. To provide a framework for a symbolic play routine for going on a plane: going to the airport, waiting in line, sitting on the airplane, putting on the seatbelt, and flying in the air

Early CLASS Songs:

- "Waiting" song

Small Group: Pretend Airplane

The children practice a symbolic play routine of going on a plane. The children first hold their suitcase and then board/sit on the airplane. They put on their seatbelt and pretend to fly on the airplane.

Small Group Targets:

1. To practice a functional routine for going on a plane that may be generalized to real-life experiences

2. To model appropriate behaviors and language to use while on an airplane

Special Activity:

- Pretend Airport: This activity provides an additional opportunity to practice the routine set out in the book and modeled during the Small Group activity. Children can sit in the pretend airplane seats and put on their seatbelts. The teacher can model symbolic play by mimicking motions as if the plane was actually flying. The teacher can also discuss the steps involved in traveling by plane and places the children may go on a trip.

- Bean Table: The sensory activity of playing with beans is combined with opportunities to practice transportation vocabulary related to the weekly theme. A water table can be converted to a "bean table" by filling it with dried beans. Toy airplanes, cars, and trucks are placed/hidden in the beans. As children find toys hidden in the beans, they are encouraged to label them, imitate symbolic play with them, show them to friends, and share them with friends.

Related Songs: "Wheels on the Bus"

Additional Related Books:

- *Flying* by Donald Crews
- *Planes at the Airport* by Peter Mandel and Ed Miller

Additions to Children's Folder: *Airport* book supports and airport vocabulary support

Unit 9: Airport
Child Book Board p. 1/2

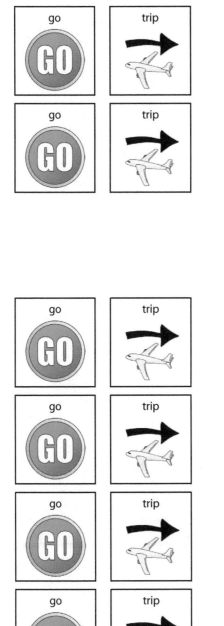

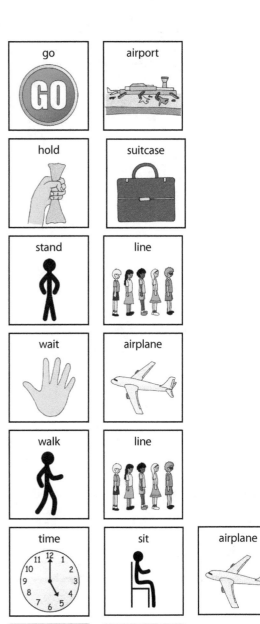

Unit 9: Airport
Child Book Board p. 2/2

Unit 9: Airport
Small Group: Pretend Airplane

Targets:

1. To practice a functional activity routine for going on a plane that may be generalized to children's real-life experience

2. To model appropriate behaviors and language to use while on an airplane

Explanation of the Activity:

The children practice a symbolic play routine which, in this case, is also a functional activity routine of going on a plane. The children first hold their suitcase and then board/sit on the airplane. They put on their seatbelt and pretend to fly on the airplane.

Materials:

- "Turn" support (see "Notes on Taking Turns," page 73)
- Chairs
- Airplane made out of cardboard
- Suitcase
- Pretend seatbelt (make out of ribbon)
- Small Group activity schedules

How to Play:

On the first day of playing the game, the teachers model how to play (as in the previous instructional units). Moving forward to child turns,

- Teacher 1: "Time for work. Time for pretending to fly in airplane."
    - "Whose turn?" (talks only to the children)
    - Place "turn" support in front of the child and say, "It's <name>'s turn."
- Teacher 1: "First, hold suitcase."
    - If the child does not respond: Use the prompting hierarchy to cue the child to hold suitcase.
    - If the child responds: Move on to the next step.
- Teacher 1: "Now, walk to airplane."
    - If the child does not respond: Use the prompting hierarchy to cue the child to walk to airplane.
    - If the child responds: Move on to the next step.

- Teacher 1: "Sit in airplane."
  - If the child does not respond: Use the prompting hierarchy to cue the child to sit in airplane. (Sings "Sit Down" song.) Remind to sit in the airplane.
  - If the child responds: Move on to the next step.
- Teacher 1: "Seatbelt on."
  - If the child does not respond: Use the prompting hierarchy to cue the child to put on seatbelt.
  - If the child responds: Move on to the next step.
- Teacher 1: "Pretend to fly in airplane." This step is designed to prepare the child for the movements of a real airplane. The clinicians and other children can say, "3, 2, 1 … blast-off" and hold out their arms as if they were flying.
  - If the child does not respond: Use the prompting hierarchy to cue and model how to pretend to fly on an airplane.
  - If the child responds: Move on to the next step.
- Teacher 1: "<Name>'s turn is finished. Find your chair."
  - If the child does not respond: Use the prompting hierarchy to cue the child to finish their turn and sit in their chair. (Sings "Sit Down" song.)
  - If the child responds: Move on to the next step.

The cycle repeats until each child in the group gets a turn. At higher developmental levels and/or as the children's learning progresses throughout the week, staff can add the step of waiting in line and walking in a line to board the plane together, rather than taking individual turns.

Example steps:

1. hold suitcase
2. stand in line
3. walking in line – follow leader (*sing "Follow the Leader" song)
4. sit airplane
5. seat belt on
6. pretend fly airplane
7. finished

Students might turns being the "leader."

Unit 9: Airport
Small Group Activity Schedule – Level 2

Early CLASS News

Welcome to the Early CLASS!

Important Dates
August 31-September 1: No Early CLASS
September 7: No Early CLASS

Taking the Early CLASS Home

As summer approaches, Early CLASS has "vacation" on the brain. This week we will be talking about taking a trip on an airplane. Throughout the week, the children will also have opportunities to talk about other types of transportation like cars, trains, and buses.

If you'll be taking a trip this summer, you can start preparing your child now. Practice the symbolic play routine we do in Small Group this week. Make a list of activities or toys your child can play with in the car or on the plane and put them in a special suitcase/travel backpack. Also, start talking about what you'll be doing and who will be there. You could make a picture book of all the things to do on vacation (download photos from the Internet of your hotel and destination or show pictures of relatives). Even if you're staying home this year, have fun pretending to take a trip.

Reminder:
This section can provide a reminder for the parents about an upcoming event or something that they need to bring for their child that week.

Early CLASS Policy

Note about Early CLASS policy or you can include a rationale about a certain aspect of the Early CLASS, so that the parents can learn the purpose behind every decision that is made in the classroom.

Theme: Airport

Book: *Airport*
By: Byron Barton

This week's theme is "airport." In our Book of the Week, we will learn the steps for taking a plane ride. The people in the book will go to the airport, wait in line, get on the airplane, and fly up in the sky.

At **Special Activity**, the kids can play with cars, trucks, and planes at the bean table. They will also have an opportunity to practice the Small Group symbolic play activity for going on an airplane.

Vocabulary
Objects, places, activities: Suitcase, line, airplane, seatbelt, sky, trip, airport
Actions: Wait, hold, go, stand, walk, sit, fly
Modifiers: Time, fast, on

Songs: "Go" song, "Wheels on the Bus" song

Lead: Teacher 1

Small Groups: The children will take turns flying on our pretend airplane. They will first hold their suitcase. Then they will sit on the plane, put on their seatbelt, and blast off.

Unit 10: Feeling Mad/Calm-Down Time

Most children with ASD have difficulties regulating their emotions. Difficulty expressing and self-regulating anger was a frequent problem observed in the Early CLASS. The intention of this unit is to model vocabulary and self-regulation strategies for "calming down" when angry. As the vocabulary of emotional regulation is abstract and, therefore, difficult to learn, activities and routines are highly simplified and highly repetitive to support comprehension. Routines and strategies implemented during this theme week may be utilized consistently throughout the classroom for the remainder of that semester, as well as implemented with the families at home.

Book: *Calm Down Time*
Author: Elizabeth Verdick
ISBN-10 #: 1575423162
Publisher: Free Spirit Publishers

Table 5.10
Book Narrative Unit 10

Page Spread	Pictures Left	Narrative Left	Pictures Right	Narrative Right
Cover		Time to calm down.		*"Calm Down" song
p. 1/2	BOY MAD	Boy is mad.	GIRL MAD	Girl is mad.
p. 3/4	BOY SAY MAD	Boy says mad.		
p. 5/6	TIME TO CALM DOWN	Time to calm down.	BREATH	Take a breath.
p. 7/8	TIME TO CALM DOWN	Time to calm down.	COUNT	Count
p. 9/10	OK	It is ok.		
p. 11/12	GIRL MAD	Girl is mad.		
p. 13/14	TIME TO CALM DOWN	Time to calm down.	HUG	Hug
p. 15/16	TIME TO CALM DOWN	Time to calm down.	BREAK OK	Take a break. It is OK.
p. 17/18	BOY SAY MAD	Boy says mad.		
p. 19/20	BREATH	Take a breath.	OK	It is OK.
p. 21/22	I HAPPY	I am happy.	TIME PLAY	Time to play.

Book Targets:

1. To introduce vocabulary to express anger

2. To model self-regulation strategies for "calming down"

Early CLASS Songs:

- "Calm Down" song

Small Group: Calm-Down Game

The children take turns choosing and practicing self-regulating behaviors to use when they are mad. The teacher then leads the group in singing the "Calm Down" song and inserts into the song the behavior the child chose. This activity will provide opportunities to practice target self-regulatory strategies with the hope of routinizing an appropriate self-regulatory response when the child feels angry.

Small Group Targets:

1. To model vocabulary related to feeling angry

2. To model appropriate self-regulatory strategies to use to calm down

3. To practice the joint activity skills learned during previous weeks (taking turns, waiting, watching a friend, etc.)

Special Activity:

• Bean Bag Toss: A bean bag toss game is modified such that for each hole there is a self-regulatory strategy presented in the book. When the child tosses the bean bag through a hole, he and the clinician will pretend/practice the corresponding strategy.

Related Songs: "I Love You" song, "If You're Mad and You Know It" song

Additional Related Books:

• *The Feelings Book* by Todd Parr

• *The Way I Feel* by Janan Cain

• *When I Feel Angry* by Cornelia Maude and Nancy Cote

Additions to Children's Folder: *Calm Down Time* book supports and feelings vocabulary support

Unit 10: Feeling Mad/Calm-Down Time
Child Book Board p. 1/2

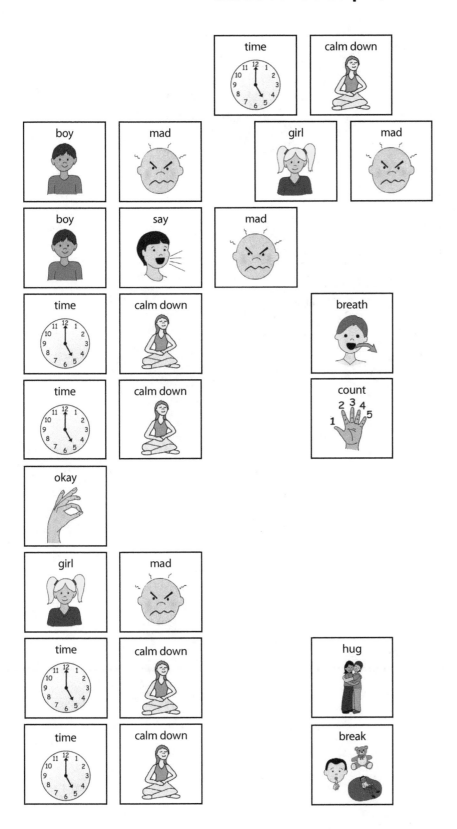

Unit 10: Feeling Mad/Calm-Down Time
Child Book Board p. 2/2

Unit 10: Feeling Mad/Calm-Down Time
Small Group: Calm-Down Game

Targets:

1. To model vocabulary related to feeling angry
2. To model appropriate self-regulatory strategies to use to calm down
3. To practice the joint activity skills learned during previous weeks (taking turns, waiting, watching a friend, etc.)

Explanation of the Activity:

This activity provides opportunities for the child to practice target self-regulatory strategies, with the hope of routinizing an appropriate self-regulatory response when the child feels angry. The children take turns choosing and practicing self-regulating behaviors to use when they are mad. The teacher then leads the group in singing the "Calm Down" song, inserting the behavior the child chose into the song. The teacher concludes the activity by saying, "It's OK."

Materials:

- "Turn" support (see "Notes on Taking Turns," page 73)
- Pictures of self-regulating activities (included in the extra Small Group support
- "Break" chair
- Small Group activity schedules

How to Play:

On the first day of playing the game, the teachers model how to play (as in the previous instructional units). For child turns,

- Teacher 1: "Time for work. Time for calm-down game."
- Teacher 1: "Whose turn?"
  - Place "turn" support in front of the child and say, "It's <name>'s turn."
- Teacher 1: "Choose how to calm down." The child chooses from the pictures provided in the Small Group materials. At the beginning of the week, and later as needed, provide the child with two choices (instead of all of the choices) to avoid overwhelming the child.
  - If the child does not respond: Use the prompting hierarchy to cue the child to choose.
  - If the child responds: Move on to the next step.

- Teacher 1: Sings "Calm Down," inserting into the song the behavior the child chose. Teachers model the behavior chosen and also encourage the children to participate in acting out the behavior chosen.
    - If the child does not respond: Use the prompting hierarchy to cue the child to sing song.
    - If the child responds: Move on to the next step.
- Teacher 1: "It's OK. <Name>'s turn is finished. Find your chair."
    - If the child does not respond: Use the prompting hierarchy to cue the child that Small Group is finished and that it is time to sit in her chair. (Sings "Sit Down" song.)
    - If the child responds: Move on to the next child.

The cycle repeats until each child in the group gets a turn.

Unit 10: Feeling Mad/Calm-Down Time
Small Group Activity Schedule – Level 2

		calm down	game

one	who	turn		breath
1	who	turn		breath

two	choose	calm down		count
2	choose	calm down		count

three	sing	calm down	song	hug
3	sing	calm down	song	hug

four	okay			break
4	okay			break

five	turn	finish
5	turn 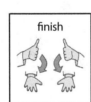	finish

Unit 10: Feeling Mad/Calm-Down Time

Extra Small Group Supports: These pictures are to be used in conjunction with the Small Group supports. They can be used as the pictures the child chooses from when selecting what to do when she is mad.

Early CLASS News

Welcome to the Early CLASS!

Important Dates
Dates when there will not be therapy or dates when certain clinicians will not be in Early CLASS.

Taking the Early CLASS Home

Many young children – and most children with ASD – have difficulty calming themselves down when angry or upset. This week we will focus on giving your child a word to express the feeling "mad," as well as offer additional strategies to help the child calm down. The children will practice taking deep breaths, stomping their feet, and taking a break when they are mad. Please let us know what strategy your child responds to best and encourage him/her to use it at home. We encourage you to support your child using these strategies at home. Feel free to use our supports!

Reminder:
This section can provide a reminder for the parents about an upcoming event or something that they need to bring for their child that week.

Early CLASS Illness Policy
Note about Early CLASS policy or you can include a rationale about a certain aspect of the Early CLASS so that the parents can learn the purpose behind every decision that is made in the classroom.

Theme: Feeling Mad

Book: *Calm Down Time*

By: Elizabeth Verdick

Based on our Book of the Week, we will discuss and practice appropriate strategies the child can do when they are mad.

Vocabulary
Objects, places, activities: Break, girl, boy
Actions: Count, play, breath, happy, mad
Modifiers: Time

Songs: "I Can Calm Down," "If You're Mad and You Know It"

Lead: Teacher 1

Small Groups: The children will practice appropriate strategies for responding when they are angry. These strategies are also presented in the book for this week.

Unit 11: Halloween

Overview

Halloween routines are frequently difficult to grasp for young children, particularly children with ASD. Many parents report frustration that an activity that was supposed to be fun, cute, and memorable was only memorable for its struggles and tears. By introducing Halloween vocabulary and breaking the trick-or-treating event down into steps in a functional activity routine, we support the child's comprehension and participation. The book introduces a routine for trick-or-treating. During Small Group, clinicians support a functional joint activity routine for trick-or-treating through songs, visual supports, and repetition. The aim of this unit is for children to be able to go trick-or-treating with their family and friends using transactional supports as necessary.

Book: *Maisy's Trick-or-Treat*
Author: Lucy Cousins
ISBN-10 #: 0763627313
Publisher: Candlewick

Table 5.11
Book Narrative Unit 11

Page Spread	Pictures Left	Narrative Left	Pictures Right	Narrative Right	Notes and rationale
Cover		Halloween			
p. 1/2					
p. 3/4	HALLOWEEN	It's Halloween.	PAINT JACK-O'-LANTERN	Paint a Jack-o'-lantern	"It's Halloween" is introduced as a key repeated phrase.
p. 5/6	HALLOWEEN TIME DRESS UP	It's Halloween. Time to dress up.	WHAT COSTUME? MAISY CHOICE COWBOY	What costume? Maisy's choice is a cowboy.	
p. 7/8	HALLOWEEN TIME TRICK OR TREAT	It's Halloween. Time to trick-or-treat.	STAND LINE WALK FRIEND	Stand in line. Walk with friend.	
p. 9/10					
p. 11/12					
p. 13/14	HALLOWEEN WALK HOUSE	It's Halloween. Walk to house.	KNOCK DOOR WAIT	Knock on door. Wait. *"Waiting" song.	
p. 15/16	SAY TRICK-OR-TREAT	Say trick-or-treat.	FRIEND TREAT IN BAG	Friend puts treat in bag.	
p. 17	SAY THANK YOU	Say thank you.	HAPPY HALLOWEEN	"Happy Halloween."	

Book Targets:

1. To introduce/reinforce Halloween vocabulary

2. To introduce a routine for trick-or-treating

Early CLASS Songs:

- "Waiting" song

Small Group: Pretend Trick-or-Treating

The children practice their routine of trick-or-treating as introduced in the Book of the Week. The children will knock on a door, say "trick-or-treat," wait for a friend to put a treat in bag, and say "thank you."

Small Group Targets:

1. To support the child's participation in a functional social routine for trick-or-treating
2. To model appropriate behaviors and language to use while trick-or-treating

Special Activity:

- Decorate Trick-or-Treat Bag: Children are provided with a brown paper sack, crayons, and additional materials to decorate the bag. To expand on this activity, the teacher can discuss trick-or-treating and what the bag will be used for.

- Play Dress-Up: Each child brings a Halloween costume or pieces of a costume from home. The child and clinicians practice putting on the costume and provide transactional supports for each child's costume, as necessary.

- Paint a Jack-O'-Lantern: The children receive small pumpkins and watercolors and paint the pumpkin. To expand on this activity, the teacher may facilitate painting a jack-o-lantern through visual supports with choices for parts of the face and colors.

Related Song: "Five Little Pumpkins"

Additional Related Books:

- *Spot's Halloween* by Eric Hill
- *Sam's First Halloween* by Mary Labatt
- *Maisy's Halloween* by Lucy Cousins

Additions to Children's Folder: *Maisy's Trick-or-Treat* book supports and Halloween vocabulary support

Unit 11: Halloween
Child Book Board p. 1/2

Halloween

Halloween 	
Halloween	
what	costume 
Halloween	
stand	line
Halloween	
knock	door 

paint	Jack O'lantern	
time	dress up 	
Maisy	choice	cowboy
time	trick or treat	
walk 	friend	
walk 	house	
wait		

Unit 11: Halloween
Child Book Board p. 2/2

say	trick or treat
say	thank you

friend	treat	in	bag
happy	Halloween		

Unit 11: Halloween
Small Group: Pretend Trick-or-Treating

Targets:

1. To support the child's participation in a functional social routine for "trick-or-treating"

2. To model appropriate behaviors and language to use while "trick-or-treating"

Explanation of the Activity:

The children practice the routine of trick-or-treating as introduced in the Book of the Week. The children knock on a door, say "trick-or-treat," wait for a friend to put a treat in bag, and say, "Thank you." At the beginning of the week, the children will walk to only one door. When they are familiar with the routine, the Small Group activity may be extended by having the children knock on multiple doors or going to different classrooms.

Materials:

Trick-or-treat bag, treats, pieces of child's costume (optional), and Halloween Small Group activity schedules

How to Play:

On the first day of playing the game, the teachers model how to play (as in the previous instructional units).

- Teacher 1: "Time for trick-or-treat."
- Teacher 1: "Stand in line."
  - If the child does not respond: Use the prompting hierarchy to cue the child to stand in line.
  - If the child responds: Move on to the next step.
- Teacher 1: "Walk with friends."
  - If the child does not respond: Use the prompting hierarchy to cue the child to begin walking with friends.
  - If the child responds: Move on to the next step.
- Teacher 1: "Walk to door."
- Teacher 1: "Knock on door."
  - If the child does not respond: Use the prompting hierarchy to cue the child to knock on the door.
  - If the child responds: Move on to the next step.
- Teacher 1: "Wait." "Wait for friend to open door." (Sings "Waiting" song to children.)
  - If the child does not respond: Use the prompting hierarchy to cue the child to wait.
  - If the child responds: Move on to the next step.

- Teacher 2: Opens the door.
- Teacher 1: Cues the child: "Say 'trick-or-treat.'"
    - If the child does not respond: Use the prompting hierarchy to cue the child to say trick-or-treat.
    - If the child responds: Move on to the next step.
- Teacher 1: "Friend puts treat in bag." Teacher 2 puts a treat in the child's bag.
    - If the child does not respond: Use the prompting hierarchy to cue the child to wait for friend to put the treat in their bag. (Sings "Waiting" song to child.)
    - If the child responds: Move on to the next step.
- Teacher 1: "Say 'Thank you.'"
    - If the child does not respond: Use the prompting hierarchy to cue the child to say "thank you."
    - If the child responds: Move on to the next step.
- Teacher 1: When all of the children have had their turn trick-or-treating, the clinician says, "Trick-or-treat is finished. Find your chair."
    - If the child does not respond: Use the prompting hierarchy to cue the child that Small Group is finished and sit in their chair. (Sings "Sit Down" song.)
    - If the child responds: Move on to the next step.

Unit 11: Halloween
Small Group Activity Schedule – Level 2

Early CLASS News

Welcome to the Early CLASS!

Important Dates
Dates when there will not be therapy or dates when certain clinicians will not be in Early CLASS.

Taking the Early CLASS Home

We are very excited to be talking about trick-or-treating this week in Early CLASS. It will be great practice for the kids to prepare for Friday, when we will go trick-or-treating around school. The treats will consist of snack items and small toys during Small Group. On Friday, some teachers may pass out candy, so let us know if there is anything we need to avoid.

If you plan to go trick-or-treating with your child this weekend, we hope you will be greatly helped by the routines and supports we use in Small Group this week. Please let us know if you need additional help.

Reminder:
Remember to bring your Halloween costumes and treat bags! We will be using them during Special Activity.

Early CLASS Illness Policy

Note about Early CLASS policy or you can include a rationale about a certain aspect of the Early CLASS so that the parents can learn the purpose behind every decision that is made in the classroom.

Theme: Halloween

Book: *Maisy's Trick-or-Treat*

By: Lucy Cousins

Our book this week is about going to Early CLASS. If your child is new to Early CLASS, this book will help teach the routines and vocabulary we use in Early CLASS. If your child is returning, this book will help reacquaint him/her with the social routines and vocabulary of Early CLASS.

Vocabulary
Objects, places, activities: Friends, pumpkin, jack-o'-lantern, costume, cowboy, leader, house, door, treat
Actions: Paint, dress up, stand, follow, say, walk, wait, knock
Modifiers: Time

Songs: "Five Little Pumpkins"

Lead: Teacher 1

Small Groups: The children will practice trick-or-treating. They will follow the steps needed to trick-or-treat, including standing in line, knocking on the door, and saying "trick-or-treat" and "thank you."

Unit 12: Train

Overview

Trains are intrinsically interesting to many young children with ASD; trains are familiar and motivating. For this unit, we use the train, a naturally motivating object, as a way to address core deficits in social skills, specifically sharing and taking turns. Within the course of the activities, we also reinforce descriptive concepts, including colors, fast/slow, and the prepositions *on* and *through*. The book was intentionally written to include only basic colors and descriptive concepts that the children likely already know. The language load of the book is kept light in order to allow the children to focus on the hard work of social interaction.

Book: *Freight Train*
Author: Donald Crews
ISBN-10 #: 0688117015
Publisher: Greenwillow Books

Table 5.12
Book Narrative Unit 12

Page Spread	Pictures Left	Narrative Left	Pictures Right	Narrative Right	Notes
Cover					
p. 1-6					
p. 7/8	RED TRAIN ORANGE TRAIN	Red train. Orange train. *On the track*	YELLOW TRAIN	Yellow train.	At higher developmental levels, on each page, "on the track" may be added as a routine phrase for extension and to facilitate carryover to the Small Group activity.
p. 9/10	GREEN TRAIN BLUE TRAIN	Green train. Blue train.	PURPLE TRAIN	Purple train.	
p. 11/12	BLACK TRAIN	Black train.			
p. 13/14	SLOW TRAIN	Slow train.			
p. 15/16	FAST TRAIN	Fast train.			
p. 17/18	TRAIN THROUGH TUNNEL	Train through tunnel.			
p. 19/20					
p. 21/22	TRAIN ON BRIDGE	Train on bridge.			
p. 23/24					
p. 25/26	GOODBYE TRAIN	Goodbye train.			

Book Targets:

1. To engage the children in a joint focus activity and provide opportunities to discuss a joint focus

2. To reinforce modifiers (colors, fast/slow) and prepositions (*on*, *through*)

Small Group: Sharing the Train

The primary goal of this activity is to facilitate participation in a joint activity with peers that involves taking turns and sharing. Each child gets a piece of the train, puts pieces of the train together, and places the train on the track. When the train is ready, the children take turns pushing it around the track. Later in the week to extend the activity, the children may be presented with a choice to push the train "fast" or "slow."

Small Group Targets:

1. To facilitate the language of social interactions with peers, specifically turn-taking and sharing

2. To facilitate success within a joint social activity with peers for sharing and taking turns

3. To facilitate understanding of "fast" and "slow"

Special Activity:

- Play With Train: The children play with the train track and trains. Clinicians facilitate sharing and taking turns (as in the Small Group activity) but in a less structured setting. The main goal of this activity is social interaction and sharing. Visual supports should be available.

- Bean Table: Toy airplanes, cars, and trucks are hidden in a bean-filled water table. The children receive sensory input from the beans, while having additional opportunities to practice transportation vocabulary. Clinicians model appropriate symbolic play with the toys and facilitate social routines for sharing and taking turns with adults and peers.

Related Songs: "Wheels on the Bus," "Train on the Track"

Additional Related Books:

- *I Love Trains!* by Philemon Sturges
- *The Little Train* by Lois Lenski
- Trains by Byron Barton

Additions to Children's Folder: *Freight Train* book supports and train vocabulary support

Unit 12: Train
Child Book Board

train

red	train	orange	train	yellow	train
green	train	blue	train	purple	train

black train

slow train

fast train

train through tunnel

train on bridge

goodbye train

Unit 12: Train
Small Group: Sharing the Train

Targets:

1. To facilitate the language of social interactions with peers, specifically turn-taking and sharing

2. To facilitate success within a joint social activity with peers for sharing and taking turns

3. To facilitate understanding of "fast" and "slow"

Explanation of the Activity:

The primary goal of this activity is to facilitate participation in a joint activity with peers that involves taking turns and sharing. Each child receives a piece of the train, puts pieces of the train together, and places the train on the track. When the train is ready, the children take turns pushing it around the track. Later in the week, to extend the activity, the children may be presented with a choice to push the train "fast" or "slow."

NOTE: For children who have particular difficulty sharing and taking turns, a simple social narrative explaining the steps and outcome of sharing may be helpful. The clinician should be ready to create and provide additional visual supports as necessary to facilitate success, as sharing may be a particularly difficult concept.

Materials:

- "Turn" support (see "Notes on Taking Turns," page 73)

- Train

- Tracks

- Visual supports. (Clinician should also supplement the Small Group support with a support with "wait," "turn," and "share")

How to Play:

On the first day of playing the game, the teachers will model how to play (as in the previous instructional units). Some children may have more than one turn.

- Teacher 1: "Time to play with the train."

  - Place "turn" support in front of the Child 1 and say, "Who's turn?" "It's <name>'s turn."

- Teacher 1: "Get train." The teacher hands a colored train to the child. These first two steps are repeated until all of the children have a piece of the train.

- Teacher 1: "Time to put the train together." "It's <name>'s turn. Put the train on track." Each child should take a turn putting his or her train on the track.

- Teacher 1: "The train is ready. Ready to play with the train."

  - Points to cues on the Small Group activity schedule.

Points to cues on the Small Group activity schedule.

- Teacher 1: "Time to share train." "It's <name>'s turn. Push the train." The teacher cues children when their turn begins and when it ends. "<Name>'s turn is finished. Time to share. Share with <friend 2>. It's <Friend 2>'s turn. Push the train."
    - If the child does not respond: Use the prompting hierarchy to cue the child to push the train and share with his friends.
    - If the child responds: Move on to the next step.
- Teacher 1: "Playing with the train is finished. Time to clean up." (Sing "Clean Up" song.)

Later in the week, the activity may be expanded by letting the children choose the color of their train, build the track, or decide whether they want to push the train fast or slow. For even higher level of language demand, the teacher might ask "Who has <color>? What friend?" as a way to choose what child's turn is next. Only expand the activity if the children are consistently succeeding with the activity at this level.

Unit 12: Train
Small Group Activity Schedule: Level 2

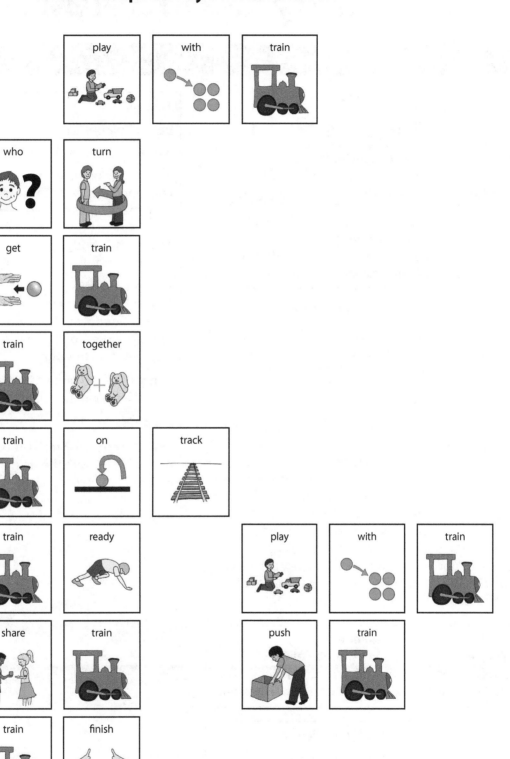

Early CLASS News

Early CLASS Office Phone Number: < >   **Date**

Welcome to the Early CLASS!

Important Dates
Dates when there will not be therapy or dates when certain clinicians will not be in Early CLASS.

Taking the Early CLASS Home

This week's theme is all about trains. We will read a fun book about a colorful freight train on a trip around town. The children will have lots of opportunities to share our train sets with friends at centers, Small Group, and Special Activity.

Many of our children love cars, trucks, and all things that "go." We hope that this week's train theme will be a motivating way to facilitate positive social interaction between the children, their clinicians, and fellow classmates. You can use the book and vocabulary from this week's theme to facilitate play with your child at home, too. You can play with your own pretend trains, building the tracks and taking turns making the trains go fast or slow around the track. You may also carry over the same vocabulary to the child's cars, trucks, and other toys that "go."

Reminder:
This section can provide a reminder for the parents about an upcoming event or something that they need to bring for their child that week.

Early CLASS Illness Policy

Note about Early CLASS policy or you can include a rationale about a certain aspect of the Early CLASS so that the parents can learn the purpose behind every decision that is made in the classroom.

Theme: Train

Book: *Freight Train*

By: Donald Crews

In our Book of the Week, a freight train makes its way along the track. The cars of the long train have many different colors, and it goes slow and fast. As the train moves, it goes through a tunnel and across a bridge. We bid farewell to the train as it goes out of sight. Goodbye, train!

Vocabulary
Objects, places, activities: Train, tunnel, bridge
Social: Goodbye
Modifiers: Red, orange, yellow, green, blue, purple, fast, slow, through, on

Songs: The "Go" song, "Train on the Track" song, and "Wheels on the Bus"

Lead: Teacher 1

Small Groups: In Small Group this week, the children will play with the train. The main focus of this activity is to practice "sharing." The children will build a long train, build the track, and take turns driving the train fast or slow around the track.

Chapter Highlights

- Each unit is a theme that, with input from the parents, was selected to be developmentally appropriate, functional, and motivating for the children.

- Each unit centers around a picture book that introduces a theme and new vocabulary. The theme and vocabulary are reinforced throughout the day during large groups (Hello Circle and Music), Small Group, and Special Activities.

- The classroom is infused with theme-related materials to be available during individual time; materials may include additional theme-related books in the book area, manipulatives in the play dough area or block center, and theme-related songs.

- The books and book boards for each unit are examples of how to utilize commercially available picture books and rewrite them to meet the needs of Level 2 and Level 3 children.

- When rewriting books for Level 2 and Level 3 children, (a) use simple language targeting developmentally appropriate core vocabulary; (b) incorporate familiar routines to facilitate increased comprehension, recognition, generalization, and attention. The book may also be a vehicle for introducing new routines, which are then generalized to the classroom through supported Small Group and individual activities; (c) use repetitive phrases to catch children's attention. Repetition also facilitates comprehension. Once the child becomes familiar with a repeated phrase, the repeated phrase becomes a carrier for a new vocabulary word, which is then emphasized and highlighted to the child; (d) new language forms/target words are embedded within repeated phrases to promote increased comprehension and attention; and (e) reinforce classroom routines and concepts.

Chapter Review Questions

1. How should weekly themes be selected?

2. What changes should be made to the classroom for each weekly theme?

3. Which activities during the classroom day change each week to reflect the theme?

References

Adamson, L., & Russell, C. (1999). Emotion regulation and the emergence of joint attention. In P. Rochat (Ed.), *Early social cognition: Understanding others in the first months of life* (pp. 281-295). Mahwah, NJ: Lawrence Erlbaum Associates.

Aldridge, M. A., Stone, K. R., Sweeney, M. H., & Bower, T.G.R. (2000). Preverbal children with autism understand the intentions of others. *Developmental Science, 3*, 294.

Aprocot. (2011). (Producer). *Peanut butter and jelly song* [Video File]. Available from http://www.youtube.com/watch?v=L39J7jCoVKY&list=FLdJJSF7qlSb3eTsPuRzkZFw&index=4

Bakeman, R., & Adamson, L. (1984). Coordinating attention to people and objects in mother-infant and peer-infant interaction. *Child Development, 55*, 1278-1289.

Baldwin, D. (1993). Early referential understanding: Infants' ability to recognize referential acts for what they are. *Developmental Psychology, 29*, 832-843.

Barney & Friends (Producers). (n.d.). *Barney: The clean-up song* [Video File]. Available from https://www.youtube.com/watch?v=WJ9uhDzN-rA#t=10

Baron-Cohen, S. (1989). Perceptual role taking and proto-declarative pointing in autism. *British Journal of Developmental Psychology, 7*, 113-127.

Bates, E. (1976). *Language and context: The acquisition of pragmatics*. New York, NY: Academic Press.

Bates, E., Benigni, L., Bretherton, I., Camaioni L., & Volterra, V. (1979). *The emergence of symbols: Cognition and communication in infancy*. New York, NY: Academic Press.

Bates, E., Camaioni, L., & Volterra, V. (1975). The acquisition of performatives prior to speech. *Merrill-Palmer Quarterly, 21*, 205-224.

Bates, E., & Goodman, J. (1997). On the inseparability of grammar and the lexicon: Evidence from acquisition, aphasia and real-time processing. *Language and Cognitive Processes, 12*(5/6), 507-586.

Bates, E., & Goodman, J. (1999). On the emergence of grammar from the lexicon. In B. Macwhinney (Ed.), *The emergence of language* (pp. 29-79). Mahwah, NJ: Lawrence Erlbaum Associates.

Bateson, M. C. (1975). Mother-infant exchanges: The epigenesist of conversation interaction. *Annals of the New York Academy of Science, 263*, 101-113.

Bloom, L., Rocissano, L., & Hood, L. (1976). Adult-child discourse: Developmental interaction between information processing and linguistic knowledge. *Cognitive Psychology, 8*, 521-522.

Bondy, A. S., & Frost, L. A. (1996). *PECS - The Picture Exchange Communication System*. Cherry Hill, NJ: Pyramid Educational Consultants.

Bratman, M. (1992). Shared cooperative activity. *The Philosophical Review, 101*(2), 327-341.

Brazelton, T. B., Koslowski, B., & Main, M. (1974). The origins of reciprocity: The early mother-infant interaction. In M. Lewis & L. A. Rosenblum (Eds.), *The effect of the infant on its caregiver* (pp. 49-76). New York, NY: John Wiley & Sons.

Bricker, D., & Cripe, J. (1992). *An activity-based approach to early intervention*. Baltimore, MD: Brookes.

Bricker, D., Pretti-Frontczak, K., & McComas, N. (1998). *An activity-based approach to early intervention* (2nd ed.). Baltimore, MD: Brookes.

Bruner, J. S. (1978). From communication to language: A psychological perspective. In I. Markova (Ed.), *The social context of language* (pp. 14-78). New York, NY: Wiley.

Bruner, J. S. (1983). *Child's talk: Learning to use language.* New York, NY: W. W. Norton.

Bruner, J. S. (1995). Meaning and self in cultural perspective. In D. Barkhurst & C. Sypnowich (Eds.), *The social self* (pp. 18-29). London, UK: Sage Publications.

Cafiero, J. (1998). Communication power for individuals with autism. *Focus on Autism and Other Developmental Disabilities, 13*(2), 113-121.

Camaioni, L. (1993). The development of intentional communication: A re-analysis. In J. Nadel & L. Camaioni (Eds.), *New perspectives in early communication development* (pp. 82-96). New York, NY: Routledge.

Carpenter, M., Nagel, K., & Tomasello, M. (1998). Social cognition, joint attention, and communicative competence from 9 to 15 months of age. *Monographs of the Society for Research in Child Development, 63* (4, Serial No. 225).

Celano, D. (Producer). (2013). *Raffi - Brush your teeth* [Video File]. Available from http://www.youtube.com/watch?v=X-JIPaxGiMp0 time 0:05-0:11

Centers for Disease Control and Prevention. (2014, March 24). *Facts about ASDs.* Retrieved from http://www.cdc.gov/ncbddd/autism/data.html

Chapman, R. S. (1978). Comprehension strategies in children. In J. F. Kavanagh & W. Strange (Eds.), *Speech and language in the laboratory, school and clinic* (pp. 308-327). Cambridge, MA: MIT Press.

Cicchetti, D., Ganiban, J., & Barnett, D. (1991). Contributions from the study of high-risk populations to understanding the development of emotional regulation. In J. Garber & K. A. Dodge (Eds.), *The development of emotional regulation and dysregulation* (pp. 15-48). Cambridge, UK: Cambridge University Press.

D'Ateno, P., Mangiapanello, K., & Taylor, B. A. (2003). Using video modeling to teach complex play sequences to a preschooler with autism. *Journal of Positive Behavior Interventions, 5*(1), 5-11.

Dagr8vixster. (Producer). (2012). *Greg and Steve's good morning song* [Video File]. Available from https://www.youtube.com/watch?v=xFFbWH3nial

Dawson, G., Rogers, S., Munson, J., Smith, M., Winter, J., Greenson, J., Donaldson, A., Varley, J. (2010). Randomized, controlled trial of an intervention for toddlers with autism: The Early Start Denver Model. *Pediatrics, 125*(1), e17-23. doi: 10.1542/peds.2009-0958

DeGangi, G. A. (2000). *Pediatric disorders of regulation in affect and behavior: A therapist's guide to assessment and treatment.* San Diego, CA: Academic Press.

Division for Early Childhood. (2007). *Promoting positive outcomes for children with disabilities: Recommendations for curriculum, assessment, and program evaluation.* Missoula, MT: Author.

Division for Early Childhood/National Association for the Education for Young Children. (2009). *Early childhood inclusion: A joint position statement of the Division for Early Childhood (DEC) and the National Association for the Education of Young Children (NAEYC).* Chapel Hill, NC: University of North Carolina, FPG Child Development Institute.

Dollaghan, C. A. (2007). *The Handbook for evidence-based practice in communication disorders.* Baltimore, MD: Paul H. Brookes Publishing Co.

Drager K.D.R., Postal V. J., Carrolus L., Castellano, M., Gagliano, C., & Glynn, J. (2006). The effect of aided language modeling on symbol comprehension and production in 2 preschoolers with autism. *American Journal of Speech-Language Pathology, 15*(2), 112-125.

Dunn, J. (1982). Problems and promises in the study of affect and intention. In Z. Tronick (Ed.), *Social interchange in infancy* (pp. 197-206). Baltimore, MD: University Park Press.

Eisenberg, A. R. (1981). *Developments in displaced reference: Language learning through routine.* Paper presented at 2nd International Congress for the Study of Child Language, Vancouver, BC, Canada.

Gray, C. (2004). Guide to bullying parts I-III: The original series of articles. *The Jenison Autism Journal, 16*(1), 1-60.

Greenspan, S., & Wieder, S. (1997). Developmental patterns and outcomes in infants and children with disorders in relating and communicating: A chart review of 200 cases of children with autistic spectrum diagnoses. *Journal of Developmental and Learning Disorders, 1,* 87-141.

Gomez, J. C. (1990). The emergence of intentional communication as a problem-solving strategy in the gorilla. In S. T. Parker & K. R. Gibson (Eds.), *Language and intelligence in monkeys and apes* (pp. 333-450). Cambridge, UK: Cambridge University Press.

Hirsh-Pasek, K., Golinkoff, R. M., & Hollich, G. (2000). An emergentist coalition model for word learning: Mapping words to objects is a product of the interaction of multiple cues. In R. M. Golinkoff, K. Hirsh-Pasek, L. Bloom, L. Smith, A. Woodward, N. Akhtar, M. Tomasello, & G. Hollich (Eds.), *Becoming a word learner: A debate on lexical acquisition* (pp. 136-164). New York, NY: Oxford University Press.

Hollich, G., Hirsh-Pasek, K., Golinkoff, R. M., Brand, R. J., Brown, E., Chung, H. L., Hennon, E., Rocroi, C., & Bloom, L. (2000). Breaking the language barrier: An emergentist coalition model for the origins of word learning. *Monographs of the Society for Research in Child Development, 65*(3), 1-135.

Hubley, P., & Trevarthen, C. (1979). Sharing a task in infancy. In I. C. Uzgiris (Ed.), *Social interaction during infancy: New directions in child development* (Vol. 4, pp. 57-80). San Francisco, CA: Jossey-Bass.

Hume, K. (2008). *Overview of visual supports.* Chapel Hill, NC: The University of North Carolina, National Professional Development on Autism Spectrum Disorders, Franklin Porter Graham Child Development Institute.

Individuals with Disabilities Education Act, 20 U.S.C. § 1400 (2004).

Ingersoll, B. R., Meyer, K., Bonter, N., & Jelineka, S. (2010). Teaching social communication: A comparison of naturalistic behavioral and developmental, social pragmatic approaches for children with autism spectrum disorders. *Journal of Positive Behavior Interventions, 12,* 33-43.

Jbrary. (Producer). (2013). *Hello and goodbye song using sign language* [Video File]. Available from http://www.youtube.com/watch?v=tKCGF2hvq3I

Keller, H., Schölmerich, A., & Eibl-Eibesfeldt, I. (1988). Communication patterns in adult-infant interactions in western and non-western cultures. *Journal of Cross-Cultural Psychology, 19,* 427-445.

Kids TV123. (Producer). (2009). Days of the week song [Video File]. Available from https://www.youtube.com/watch?v=7AvNq2CQnOI

Koegel, R. L., & Koegel, L. K. (2006). *Pivotal response treatments for autism: Communication, social & academic development.* Baltimore, MD: Brookes.

Lahey, M., & Bloom, L. (1977). Planning a first lexicon: Which words to teach first. *The Journal of Speech And Hearing Disorders, 42*(3), 340-350.

LessonPix. (n.d.). http://lessonpix.com/

Lhin Lalitha. (Producer). (2010). *Barney's I love you* [Video File]. Available from

http://www.youtube.com/watch?v=XwLLH9EZiqc

Liebal, K., Colombi, C., Rogers, S. J., Warneken, F., & Tomasello, M. (2008). Helping and cooperation in children with autism. *Journal of Autism and Developmental Disorders, 38*(2), 224-238.

Littlefoxkids. (Producer). (2013). *Who stole the cookies from the cookie jar?* Available from http://www.youtube.com/watch?v=ert9zlCx21E&list=FLdJJSF7qlSb3eTsPuRzkZFw&index=2

Lovaas, O. I. (1987). Behavioral treatment and normal educational and intellectual functioning in young autistic children. *Journal of Consulting and Clinical Psychology, 55,* 3-9.

Mandell, D. S., Novak, M. M., & Zubritsky, C. D. (2005). Factors associated with age of diagnosis among children with autism spectrum disorders. *Pediatrics, 116*(6), 1480-1486.

Mayer-Johnson. (2000). [Computer software]. *Writing with symbols.* Solana Beach, CA: Author.

McArthur, D., & Adamson, L. B. (1996). Joint attention in preverbal children: Autism and developmental language disorder. *Journal of Autism and Developmental Disorders, 26,* 481-496.

McCune, L. (1995). A normative study of representational play at the transition to language. *Developmental Psychology, 31*(2), 198-206.

Mesibov, G., & Shea, V. (2014). Structured teaching and environmental supports. In K. Dunn Buron & P. Wolfberg (Eds.), *Learners on the autism spectrum: Preparing highly qualified educators* (pp. 114-137). Shawnee Mission, KS: AAPC Publishing.

Miller, J., & Paul, R. (1995). *The clinical assessment of language comprehension.* Baltimore, MD: Brookes.

Mirenda, P., & Locke, P. A. (1989). A comparison of symbol transparency in nonspeaking persons with intellectual disabilities. *Journal of Speech and Hearing Disorders, 54*(2), 131-140.

Mizuko, M. (1987). Transparency and ease of learning of symbols represented by Blissymbols, PCS, and Picsyms. *Augmentative and Alternative Communication, 3,* 129-136.

Moll, H., & Tomasello, M. (2007). How 14- and 18-month-olds know what others have experienced. *Developmental Psychology, 43*(2), 309-317.

mommylessons101. (Producer). (2012). *Choo Choo the big train is coming down the track* [Video File]. Available from http://www.youtube.com/ watch?v=Oi974R1NiCg&list =WLYURSBXEG60obOUlhpttQ1A9buod1b7Gk

Mother Goose Club. (Producer). (2013). *If you're happy and you know it* [Video File]. Available from http://www.youtube.com/watch?v=HGsHd9RuYRg&list=WLYURSBXEG60obOUlhpttQ1A9buod1b7Gk

Mundy, P., Sigman, M., & Kasari, C. (1990). A longitudinal study of joint attention and language development in autistic children. *Journal of Autism and Developmental Disorders, 20,* 115-128.

Mundy, P., Sigman, M., & Kasari, C. (1992). Joint attention, affective sharing, and intersubjectivity. *Infant Behavior and Development, 15,* 377-381.

Mundy, P., & Thorp, D. (2008). The neural basis of early joint-attention behavior. In T. Charman & W. Stone (Eds.), *Social & communication development in autism spectrum disorders: Early identification, diagnosis & intervention* (pp. 296-336). New York, NY: The Guilford Press.

Murdoci. (Producer). (n.d.). *5 little pumpkins* [Video File]. Available from http://www.youtube.com/watch?v=xV-JFF6jfAgY

Murray, L., & Trevarthen, C. (1985). Emotional regulation of interactions between two-month-olds and their mothers. In T. M. Field & N. A. Fox (Eds.), *Social perception in infants* (pp. 177-197). Norwood, NJ: Ablex.

National Autism Center. (2009). *National standards project.* Retrieved from http://www.nationalautismcenter.org/pdf/NAC%20Standards%20Report.pdf

The National Professional Development Center on Autism Spectrum Disorders. (n.d.). *The National Professional Development Center on Autism Spectrum Disorders: A multi-university center to promote the use of evidence-based practice for children and adolescents with autism spectrum disorders.* Retrieved from http://autismpdc.fpg.unc.edu/

Nelson, K. (1974). Concept, word, and sentence: Interrelations in acquisition and development. *Psychological Review, 81*(4), 267-285.

Ninio, A., & Bruner, J. (1978). The achievement and antecedents of labeling. *Journal of Child Language, 5*, 5-15.

Ninio, A., & Snow, C. E. (1996). *Pragmatic development.* Boulder, CO: Westview.

Ninio, A., Snow, C. E., Pan, B. A., & Rollins, P. R. (1994). Classifying communicative acts in children's interactions. *Journal of Communication Disorders, 27*(2), 157-187.

Odom, S. L. (2009). The tie that binds evidence-based practice, implementation science, and outcomes for children. *Topics in Early Childhood Special Education, 29*(1), 53-61.

Odom, S. L., Boyd, B. A., Hall, L. J., & Hume, K. (2009). Evaluation of comprehensive treatment models for individuals with autism spectrum disorders. *Journal of Autism & Developmental Disorders, 40*(4), 425-436. doi:10.1007/s10803-009-0825-1

Odom, S., Collet-Klingenberg, L., Rogers, S., & Hatton, D. (2010). Evidence-based practices in interventions for children and youth with autism spectrum disorders. *Preventing School Failure, 54*(4), 275-282. doi:10.1080/10459881003785506

Oh my genius. (Producer). (2013). *Wheels on the bus go round and round* [Video File]. Available at http://www.youtube.com/watch?v=_gR_CB8Mz9I

Owens, R. E., Jr. (2008). *Language development: An introduction* (7th ed.). Boston, MA: Pearson Education, Inc.

Paul, R. (2001). *Language disorders from infancy through adolescence: Assessment & intervention* (2nd ed.). St. Louis, MO: Mosby, Inc.

Pine, J. (1994). The language of primary caregivers. In C. Gallaway & B. Richards (Eds.), *Input and interaction in language acquisition* (pp. 15-37). Cambridge, UK: Cambridge University Press.

Prizant, B. M., Wetherby, A. M., Rubin, E., Laurent, A. C., & Rydell, P. J. (2006). *The SCERTS model: A comprehensive educational approach for children with autism spectrum disorder.* Baltimore, MD: Brookes.

Prizant, B. M., Wetherby, A. M., & Rydell, P. J. (2000). Communication Intervention issues for young children with autism spectrum disorders. In A. M. Wetherby & B. M. Prizant (Eds.), *Autism spectrum disorders: A transactional developmental perspective* (pp. 193-224). Baltimore, MD: Brookes.

Reichow, B. (2012). Overview of meta-analyses on early intensive behavioral intervention for young children with autism spectrum disorders. *Journal of Autism and Developmental Disorders, 42*(4), 512-520. doi:10.1007/s10803-011-1218-1219.

Rochat, P., Querido, J., & Striano, T. (1999). Emerging sensitivity to the timing and structure of protoconversation in early infancy. *Developmental Psychology, 35*(4), 950-957.

Rochat, P., & Striano, T. (1999). Social cognitive development in the first year. In P. Rochat (Ed.), *Early social cognition* (pp. 3-34). Mahwah, NJ: Lawrence Erlbaum Associates.

Rogers, S. J. (2006). Evidence-based interventions for language development in young children with autism. In T. Charman & W. Stone (Eds.), *Social and communication development in autism spectrum disorders: Early identification, diagnosis, & intervention* (pp. 143-179). New York, NY: Guilford.

Rogers, S. J., & Dawson, G. (2010). *Early start Denver model for young children with autism promoting language, learning, and engagement.* New York, NY: Guilford Press.

Rogers, S. J., Dawson, G., & Vismara, L. A. (2012). *An early start for your child with autism: Using everyday activities to help kids connect, communicate, and learn.* New York, NY: Guilford Press.

Rollins, P. R. (1994a). *A case study of the development of language and communicative skills for six children with autism.* Unpublished doctoral dissertation, Harvard Graduate School of Education, Cambridge, MA.

Rollins, P. R. (1994b). Language of children with specific language impairment. In J. L. Sokolov & C. E. Snow (Eds.), *Handbook of research in language development using CHILDES* (pp. 372-407). Hillsdale, NJ: Lawrence Erlbaum Associates.

Rollins, P. R. (1999). Early pragmatic accomplishments and vocabulary development in preschool children with autism. *American Journal of Speech-Language Pathology, 8*(2), 181-190.

Rollins, P. R. (2003). Caregiver contingent comments and subsequent vocabulary comprehension. *Applied Psycholinguistics, 24,* 221-234.

Rollins, P. R. (2009). Developmental pragmatics. In L. Cummings (Ed.), *The Routledge pragmatics encyclopedia* (pp. 110-112). London, UK: Routledge.

Rollins, P. R. (2013). A developmental behavioral, parent-mediated, translational research intervention for toddlers with autism spectrum disorder. Retrieved from http://www.dads.state.tx.us/tarrc/publications/toddlerswith-asd-august2013.pdf

Rollins, P. R. (2014). Developmental pragmatics. In Y. Huang (Ed.), *Handbook of pragmatics.* Oxford, UK: Oxford University Press.

Rollins, P. R., & Greenwald, L. C. (2013). Affect attunement during mother-infant interaction: How specific intensities predict the stability of infants' joint attention. *Imagination, Cognition and Personality, 32*(4), 339-366.

Rollins, P. R., & Snow, C. E. (1998). Shared attention and grammatical development in typical children and children with autism. *Journal of Child Language, 25*(3), 653.

Rollins, P. R., & Trautman, C. H. (2011). *Caregiver input before joint attention: The role of multimodal input.* International Congress for the Study of Child Language (IASCL), Baltimore, MD.

Rollins, P. R., Wambacq, I., Dowell, D., Mathews, L., & Reese, P. B. (1998). An intervention technique for children with autistic spectrum disorder: Joint attentional routines. *Journal of Communication Disorders, 31*(2), 181-193.

Shattuck, P. T., Durkin, M., Maenner, M., Newschaffer, C., Mandell, D. S., Wiggins, L., et al. (2009). Timing of identification among children with an autism spectrum disorder: Findings from a population-based surveillance study. *Journal of the American Academy of Child and Adolescent Psychiatry, 48*(5), 474-483.

Skinner, B. F. (1957). *Verbal behavior.* New York, NY: Appleton-Century-Crofts.

Smith, T. (2001). Discrete trial training in the treatment of autism. *Focus on Autism and Other Developmental Disabilities, 16*(2), 86-92. doi:10.1177/108835760101600204

Snow, C. E. (1977). The development of conversation between mothers and babies. *Journal of Child Language, 4,* 1-22.

Snow, C. E. (1999). Social perspectives on the emergence of language. In B. MacWhinney (Ed.), *Emergence of language* (pp. 257-276). Hillsdale, NJ: Lawrence Erlbaum Associates.

Snow, C. E., Burns, S., & Griffin, P. (Eds.). (1998). *Preventing reading difficulties in young children.* Washington, DC: National Academy Press.

Snow, C. E., Pan, B., Imbens-Bailey, A., & Herman, J. (1996). Learning how to say what one means: A longitudinal study of children's speech act use. *Social Development, 5,* 56-84.

Snow, C. E., Perlman, R., & Nathan, D. (1987). Why routines are different: Towards a multiple-factor model of the relation between input and language acquisition. In K. E. Nelson & A. Van Kleeck (Eds.), *Children's language* (Vol. 6, pp. 65-98). Hillsdale, NJ: Lawrence Erlbaum Associates.

Snyder-McLean, L. K., Solomonson, B., McLean, J. E., & Sack, S. (1984). Structuring joint action routines: A strategy for facilitation communication and language development in the classroom. *Seminars in Speech and Language, 5*, 213-228.

Spitz, R. A. (1965). *The first year of life: A psychoanalytic study of normal and deviant development of object relations.* New York, NY: International Universities Press.

Sprout. (Producer). (2013). *Kids song: Learn how to sing the Peanut Butter & Jelly Song* [Video File]. Available from http://www.youtube.com/watch?v=ApVMDLyx5j8&list=FLdJJSF7qISb3eTsPuRzkZFw

Stern, D. N. (1977). *The first relationship: Infant and mother.* Cambridge, MA: Harvard University Press.

Stern, D. N. (1985). *The interpersonal world of the infant: View from psychoanalysis and development psychology.* New York, NY: Basic Books.

Super Simple Songs. (Producer). (2013). *Head, shoulders, knees & toes (Sing It)* [Video File]. Available from http://www.youtube.com/watch?v=ZanHgPprl-0

Sussman, F. (1999). *More than words: Helping parents promote communication and social skills in children with autism spectrum disorder.* Toronto, ONT, Canada: The Hanen Centre.

Tomasello, M. (1995). Joint attention as social cognition. In C. Moore & P. Dunham (Eds.), *Joint attention: Its origins and role in development* (pp. 103-130). Hillsdale, NJ: Lawrence Erlbaum Associates.

Tomasello, M. (2000). Perceiving intentions and learning words in the second year of life. In M. Bowerman & S. Levinson (Eds.), *Language acquisition and conceptual development* (pp. 132-158). Cambridge, MA: Cambridge University Press.

Tomasello, M. (2003). *Constructing a language: A usage-based theory of language acquisition.* Cambridge, MA: Harvard University Press.

Tomasello, M., & Barton, M. (1994). Learning words in nonostensive contexts. *Developmental Psychology, 30*, 639-650.

Tomasello, M., & Call, J. (1997). *Primate cognition.* New York, NY: Oxford University Press.

Tomasello, M., Carpenter, M., Call, J., Behne, T., & Moll, H. (2005). Understanding and sharing intentions: The origins of cultural cognition. *Behavioral and Brain Sciences, 28*, 675-691.

Tomasello, M., Carpenter, M., & Liszkowski, U. (2007). A new look at infant pointing. *Child Development, 78*, 705-722.

Trevarthen, C. (1977). Descriptive analysis of infant communicative behavior. In H. R. Schaffer (Ed.), *Studies in mother-infant interaction* (pp. 227-270). London, UK: Academic Press.

Trevarthen, C. (1979). Instincts for human understanding and for cultural cooperation: Their development in infancy. In M. V. Cranach, K. Foppa, W. Lepenies, & D. Ploog (Eds.), *Human ethnology: Claims and limits of a new discipline* (pp. 530-571). Cambridge, UK: Cambridge University Press.

Trevarthen, C. (1980). The foundations of intersubjectivity: Development of interpersonal and cooperative understanding in infants. In D. Olsen (Ed.), *The social foundations of language and thought* (pp. 316-342). New York, NY: W. W. Norton & Company.

Trevarthen, C. (1993). The function of emotions in early infant communication and development. In J. Nadel & L. Camaioni (Eds.), *New perspectives in early communicative development* (pp. 48-81). New York, NY: Routledge.

Trevarthen, C., & Aitken, K. (2001). Infant intersubjectivity: Research, theory and clinical applications. *Journal of Child Psychology and Psychiatry, 42*, 3-48.

Trevarthen, C., & Hubley, P. (1978). Secondary intersubjectivity: Confidence, confiding and acts of meaning in the first year. In A. Lock (Ed.), *Action, gestures and symbol* (pp. 183-229). London, UK: Academic Press.

Troy DaBoss. (Producer). (2011). *Greg & Steve – Days of the week* [Video File]. Available from http://www.youtube.com/watch?v=ZyUNjiac_Mw

Uccelli, P., Hemphill, L., Pan, B. A., & Snow, C. E. (2005). Conversing with toddlers about the nonpresent: Precursors to narrative development in two genres. In L. Balter & C. S. Tamis-LeMonda (Eds.), *Child psychology: A handbook of contemporary issues* (pp. 215-237). New York, NY: Taylor & Francis Group.

Wallace, K. S., & Rogers, S. J. (2010). Intervening in infancy: implications for autism spectrum disorders. *Journal of Child Psychology and Psychiatry, 51*(12), 1300-1320. doi: 10.1111/j.1469-7610.2010.02308.x

Warren, Z., McPheeters, M. L., Sathe, N., Foss-Feig, J. H., Glasser, A., & Veenstra-VanderWeele, J. (2011). A systematic review of early intensive intervention for autism spectrum disorders. *Pediatrics, 127*(5), e1303-e1311. doi: 10.1542/peds.2011-0426

Wetherby, A. M. (1986). Ontogeny of communication functions in autism. *Journal of Autism and Developmental Disorders, 16*, 225-316.

Wetherby, A. M., Cain, D. H., Yonclas, D. G., & Walker, V. G. (1988). Analysis of intentional communication of normal children from the prelinguistic to the multiword stage. *Journal of Speech and Hearing Research, 31*, 240-252.

Wetherby, A. M., Yonclas, D. G., & Bryan, A. A. (1989). Communicative profiles of preschool children with handicaps: Implications for early identification. *Journal of Speech and Hearing Disorders, 54*, 148-158.

Wolff, P. H. (1987). *The development of behavioral states and the expression of emotions in early infancy.* Chicago, IL: University of Chicago Press.

Yoder, P. J., & McDuffie, A. S. (2006). Treatment of responding to and initiating joint attention. In T. Charman & W. Stone (Eds.), *Social and communication development in autism spectrum disorders: Early identification, diagnosis, & intervention* (pp. 117-142). New York, NY: Guilford Press.

Glossary

A

Adult directed – the adult directs what the child will learn by presenting the child with materials for learning and requiring a pre-specified targeted response from the child.

Autism spectrum disorder – a heterogeneous neurodevelopmental disorder that severely compromises the development of social relatedness, reciprocity, social communication, joint attention, and learning.

B

Behavioral regulations – communicative acts intended to regulate or control the behavior of another person, such as requests and protests.

Breakdowns – a language-stimulation technique in which adults gradually decrease the complexity of their utterance into several phrase-sized elements.

Buildups – a language-stimulation technique in which the adult gradually expands the child's sentence to the full grammatical form.

C

Commenting – communicative act intended to share information with another person.

Complex joint anticipatory system – a system such as a routine where an individual can make decisions based on predictions, expectations and beliefs about the future.

Comprehensive treatment model – a set of intervention practices designed to achieve broad learning or developmental impact on the core deficits of ASD.

Context-embedded communication – communication that occurs in a context of shared understanding where the meaning is tied to the specific situation (e.g., communication within routines).

Cooperative intersubjectivity – active sharing of thoughts and emotions about an outside entity.

Coordinated joint engagement – a type of engagement in which the infant coordinates his attention between the caregiver and an object of mutual interest.

D

Decontextualized communication – communication in which the language is not tied to the present environment (i.e., no clues from gestures, pictures, or context).

Discrete programs – a method of adult-directed teaching whereby isolated skills are taught in structured steps using the principles of behaviorism.

Discussing a joint focus of attention – communicative acts focused on comments (or questions) about objects and events in the immediate environment.

Discussing a nonpresent – discussing objects or events that are not in the environment and have no perceivable reference in the environment.

Discussing a related present – discussing objects or events that are not in the environment but are related to objects, events or pictures that are present.

Division for Early Childhood (DEC) – one of 17 divisions of the Council for Exceptional Children (CEC). CEC is the largest international professional organization dedicated to improving educational outcomes for individuals with exceptionalities, students with disabilities, and/or the gifted.

Dyads – two individuals who are paired in interaction.

E

Early semantic relations – early developing semantic roles expressed in children at the one-word stage.

Evidence-based practice (EBP) – the use of current best evidence in making decisions about the care of an individual. This includes scientific evidence, child/caregivers' characteristics, and expert professional opinion.

Expansion – a language-stimulation technique in which the adult repeats the child's communicative attempt/utterance back to her with the grammatical markers and semantic details that would make it an acceptable adult utterance.

Extension – a language-stimulation technique in which the adult comments on the child's utterance while adding semantic information.

F

Focused interventions – intervention practices that are used to promote a specific outcome.

J

Joint attention – shared focus of attention of two individuals on an object by means of eye gaze, pointing, or other nonverbal or verbal ways of communication.

L

Labeling – noncommunicative speech act where the word produced is not intended to be for the benefit of anyone besides the child him/herself.

N

National Association for the Education of Young Children (NAEYC) – the largest accrediting organization for preschool programs in the United States.

Naturalistic behavioral approaches – intervention approaches that are rooted in the theory of applied behavioral analysis (ABA) but are influenced by developmental social-pragmatic theory in that teaching is initiated by child's focus and motivation within a naturalistic environment.

Naturalistic programs – based on developmental and social-pragmatic theory, programs focus on the child interacting with a communicative partner within the context of her surroundings.

Negotiating mutual attention – communicative acts directed towards a person to get her to look at the speaker (e.g., calling the person's name, tapping someone on the shoulder).

Nonlinguistic comprehension strategy – using contextual clues observed from the environment to derive meaning of unknown words.

P

Parallel talk – a language-stimulation technique in which the adult comments on the child's actions.

Passive joint engagement – a dyadic interaction whereby the adult manipulates or talks about objects the child is focused on, but the child is unaware of the adult as a social partner.

Preverbal – developmental stage at which the child has not yet acquired language forms.

Protests – communicative acts that express objection to an activity or event.

Proto-conversations – a universal feature of caregiver-infant interaction that involves a range of affect, emotions, social expectations, and rounds of vocal turn-taking.

Proto-declarative – a preverbal intention of a declarative statement, such as showing an object to another person.

Proto-imperative – a preverbal intention of an imperative statement, such as nonverbal requesting and protesting.

Pseudo-conversations – a conversational interaction where the child continually initiates new topics of conversation.

R

Recasting – a language-stimulation technique in which the adult reformulates the child's utterance so that it is grammatically correct.

Referent – the object or idea to which a picture symbol, word, or phrase refers.

Repair strategies – strategies used to repair a communication when the original message is not understood by the listener.

Request – communicative act intended to get someone to give you an object or engage in an activity.

Responding to joint attention (RJA) – the child looking in the direction that the adult is looking in or pointing to.

S

Self-talk – a language-stimulation technique in which the adult comments on his own actions.

Shared intentionality – an interaction in which participants share information about objects, events, thoughts, or feelings and know that they are sharing with each other.

Shared understanding – both interaction participants realize that they have shared goals and can interact in a relationship together.

Social affective signaling – conveying emotional information to another person through the use of facial expressions.

Social cognition – the ability to gather information about our social interactions as well as understand the rules and concepts that direct them.

Social cues – verbal or nonverbal signals that help us know how to act around others. Nonverbal cues include gestures, facial expressions, and vocal tone.

Social reciprocity – being aware of another's emotions and social cues when participating in a back-and-forth interaction.

Social sensory routines – routines that are created from sensory activities like tickle games, swinging, or bouncing on a large ball. They may also include finger plays like "pattycake," "open, shut them," and "I'm going to get you."

Social-pragmatic – social use of language and communication.

Social-pragmatic approach – an intervention approach that aims at facilitating social communication within affectively based reciprocal social interactions.

Social-pragmatic theory of language – focuses on social/emotional and communication development within the context of the child's everyday interactions, describes language and communication as a usage-based system.

Symbolic play – play that occurs when children substitute one object for another or use one object to symbolize another.

T

Telegraphic speech – agrammatic speech that omits function words, leaving only the most essential content words.

Transactional approach – social-pragmatic intervention that uses some teaching strategies rooted in behaviorism. These approaches focus on intentional communication and respond to all communicative attempts, including unconventional forms.

Triadic interactions – interactions that involve two participants focusing on an outside entity, such as an object or an event.

Answers to Chapter Review Questions

Answers to Chapter 1 Review Questions

1. The three types of evidence that make up evidence-based practice are scientific evidence, professional expertise, and child/caregiver characteristics.

2. A focused intervention is a practice that is used to promote a specific skill.

3. The principles of a discrete trial program are as follows:
   a. The program is adult-directed because the therapist or teacher identifies the skill to be taught and the targeted correct response from the child.
   b. Correct responses are followed by something that is motivating to the child to reinforce the behavior.
   c. The program relies on one-to-one drills of preselected tasks outside of the child's natural environment.
   d. It treats language and communication just like any other behavior that can be trained in discrete steps using Skinner's analysis of verbal behavior.

4. The three main principles of the developmental social-pragmatic approach are:
   a. All children, including children with ASD, develop social communication and language skills in a similar sequence.
   b. Communication is viewed within affectively based reciprocal social interactions.
   c. The focus is on the child interacting with a communicative partner within the context of his or her surroundings.

5. The naturalistic behavior approach is similar to the transactional approaches in that they both include components of ABA and social-pragmatic theory. Both approaches:
   a. Target social communication within more naturalistic and ongoing activities
   b. Set up the environment to maximize teaching/facilitative techniques
   c. Follow the child's focus of attention to choose materials/activities
   d. Use natural reinforcers

   These approaches differ in what motivates communication and language development as well as what is reinforced.

   Naturalistic behavioral approaches:
   • Target isolated measurable skills, and only the targeted skill is reinforced
   • Are adult-directed (teacher identifies the skill to be taught and the targeted correct response from the child)
   • Reinforce correct responses with an external or internal reinforcer

   Transactional approaches:
   • Focus on intentional communication and respond to all communicative attempts, including unconventional forms

- Use the developmental sequence of a particular skill as the road map for intervention
- View communication within affectively based reciprocal social interactions
- Focus on the child interacting with a communicative partner within the context of his or her surroundings
- Do not consider overt response necessary for learning

6. The three core principles of a universally designed curriculum are:
   a. Multiple means of representation
   b. Multiple means of engagement
   c. Multiple means of expression

7. The developmental social-pragmatic approach most closely aligns with the principles of a universally designed curriculum (DEC) as well as NAEYC's philosophy of developmentally appropriate practices. This approach incorporates principles of a collaborative teaching model involving therapists and teachers, consistent with NAEYC standards and DEC recommendations.

Answers to Chapter 2 Review Questions

1. The three stages of early social cognition during the first two years of life are:
   a. Sharing Emotions
   b. Sharing Perceptions and Pursuing Goals
   c. Sharing Attention and Intention

2. In Sharing Perceptions and Pursuing Goals, children are goal directed and understand that others have goals. They can share an experience but cannot yet share attention. They develop communicative intent by using proto-imperatives and can regulate behavior. In Sharing Attention and Intention, children have a mutual understanding with their communicative partner. They understand that they have shared goals and can interact together in a relationship. They begin to form true language and towards the end begin to use decontextualized language.

3. In Sharing Perceptions and Pursuing Goals, children learn words by the temporal pairing of hearing the word while looking at perceptually salient objects and events.

4. In Sharing Perceptions and Pursuing Goals, children use protesting, requesting, and labeling. They do not yet have the communicative intentions of directing attention or commenting needed for communication.

5. In Sharing Attention and Intention children are able to direct another's attention and share attention by commenting on items in the environment. Later in this phase, they are able to participate in a discussion about objects and events that are not present in the environment but are somehow related to it and to engage in objects and events with no perceivable referent in the environment.

6. Commenting denotes that the child is sharing information with another person; labeling does not.

7. The goal of intervention for the Level 1 child stresses social-emotional reciprocity and requests. Once the child is at Level 2, the goal changes to sharing together in relationships with others using joint cooperative activities with shared goals and shared intentions.

Answers to Chapter 3 Review Questions

1. Any two of the following eight key components:
    a. Individualized goals with a developmental approach to goal hierarchy – It is important to write goals that address the child's developmental levels across the various domains of social communication and language. Children are variable in their communicative competency with changes in the social situation and communicative contexts, and goals must reflect that.
    b. Activity-based intervention – This component is important because each child's individual goals must be embedded into classroom activities for the activities to be developmentally appropriate for the child.
    c. A core functional vocabulary – This simplifies the language used when addressing a Level 2 or 3 child on the spectrum. The simplification ensures that the child receives multiple exposures to each word in multiple contexts.
    d. Visual graphic symbols – Pairing spoken core vocabulary with visual graphic symbols during engaging and motivating classroom activities capitalizes on the word learning strategy available to Level 2 children.
    e. Joint activity routines – Routines facilitate comprehension and function as a scaffold to the joint cooperative activity principle of mutual knowledge.
    f. Discussion about objects or events not in the immediate environment but somehow related to it – This promotes mutual knowledge and helps with topic maintenance when talking about future and past events. It also promotes complex language forms and literacy development.
    g. A naturalistic prompt hierarchy – This keeps the conversation moving forward while giving the child opportunities to communicate within activities. It allows for scaffolding the child's response, facilitating successful communication by reducing the level of linguistic demand when needed.
    h. Strategies to keep the child regulated – Supporting a child's emotional regulation is important because it is essential for optimal attention and social and communication development.

2. The four criteria for goals are specifiying communicative means, communicative intention, conversational move, and the specific social condition. Example: <Child's name> will respond to turn-taking routines for 3 turns with a familiar child when playing with table toys by saying "my turn," when provided with a picture symbol of "turn," 2 times/days for 2 weeks.

3. To choose words to include in a child's core functional vocabulary, you would pick words related to objects and actions relevant to the child's daily routines, as well as early semantic relational words. You would choose one word for each function and focus on words that can be used across various activities.

4. Routines facilitate context-embedded, shared meaning that may scaffold joint cooperative activities. They are embedded into meaningful activities that can occur across the child's various activities and environments, which facilitates comprehension and mutual knowledge and helps the child to predict what is coming next.

5. A nonlinguistic strategy is a strategy where a child uses contextual cues from the environment to understand what another person is saying without comprehending the words used.

6. When using picture symbols to facilitate language, use only one word per picture symbol and ensure that the picture symbol used to represent an individual word is always the same across various contexts.

7. Within an activity, you would use the prompt hierarchy to scaffold a child's response by reducing the level of linguistic demand after giving the child an opportunity for spontaneous communication. You would start with giving the least amount of prompting and then add more as the child needs it.

8. Discuss a Related Present is an important communicative intention because it facilitates shared knowledge to which participants are jointly committed to discussing together. It promotes topic maintenance and facilitates complex language and literacy development.

9. Emotional regulation is when a person's arousal level is directed, controlled, modulated, and modified to enable the person to function adaptively. It is important to keep a child regulated so that he is available for learning.

10. Some classroom strategies are:
    a. Using calm interactions
    b. Preorganizing by providing a predictable structured routine and visual supports
    c. Simplifying language
    d. Using clearly labeled areas
    e. Ensuring everything in the classroom has a designated place to avoid clutter
    f. Having a designated spot for the child to sit or stand
    g. Having a relaxing area to use if the child is feeling dysregulated (a break room)

Answers to Chapter 4 Review Questions

1. In order to keep the children emotionally regulated, it is important to alternate Small Group, Large-Group, and 1:1 time with a teacher, alternate focusing activities with movement activities, and alternate less challenging, preferred activities with more challenging, less preferred activities.

2. Having a mixture of small- and large-group activities as well as 1:1 activities allows children to use their communication, language, and social skills within a variety of social contexts.

3. The "Hello" song facilitates the understanding that there are reciprocal roles in the interaction and that these roles can be reversed. Using a Hello Chair provides the children with a visual cue that there is both a sender and a receiver of the hello message.

4. When rewriting a book, you would use repetitive phrases, core vocabulary, and core vocabulary routines to increase the children's comprehension of functional activities and concepts represented in the book. You would simplify the language to increase the child's ability to attend.

5. Structuring transitions helps keep the child emotionally regulated. This helps children understand the organization of the transition and know what is coming next.

6. Some activities that increase children's use of cross-context communication between the home and school environments are:
    a. Talk About Bags
    b. Picture Diaries
    c. My Day at School form

Answers to Chapter 5 Review Questions

1. Weekly themes should be selected to be developmentally appropriate, functional, and motivating for the children and with input from the parents.

2. The classroom is infused with theme-related materials to be available during individual time, such as theme-related books, manipulatives in the play dough area or block center, and theme-related songs in music center.

3. Activities that change during the classroom day to reflect the weekly theme include Small Group, Special Activities, Book of the Week and Music.

Index

Appendices

Appendix A: Early CLASS Functional Communication Assessment

Appendix B: Hello Circle Script

Appendix C: Strategies for Varied Repetition With the Book of the Week

Appendix D: Sample "My Day at School" Form

Appendix E: Song Glossary

Appendix A: Early CLASS Functional Communication Assessment

Adapted from Schuler, Prizant, and Wetherby (1997).

This criterion-based, performance-oriented assessment may be used to gather information about a child's developmental level across and within the various aspects of social communication and language. The author suggests many materials and tasks that can be used to elicit social communication and language skills directly. Information may also be gleaned by direct observation of the child in the classroom or with his/her caregivers.

Once the assessment is complete, goals should be written that flow naturally from the assessment and focus on the child's social communication and language capabilities. Further, the classroom should be structured so that each child's goals can be embedded within the context of the ongoing routines and activities.

Suggested Materials and Tasks:

Symbolic Play Set:

Baby food set: cup, spoon, fork, bowls/plates

blanket, bottle, toothbrush, brush, comb,

Elmo®

- Picture book (e.g., *Elmo G-nite, G-nite Baby*)
- Bubble gun
- "No-spill" bubbles
- Balloons
- Stacking cups
- Bus and Little People
- Picture symbols: "more," "want," "finished," clean up," "mad." Additionally, have available symbols of words you will use when assessing comprehension
- Pop on Pals®

Snack Set:

Animal crackers, Goldfish®,

Tupperware®, plate, cup,

water and picture symbols

Suggested Tasks

Make observations of social communication and language at any time during the observation period. Below are some suggestions to help elicit social communication and language.

1. Warm-up and interaction with parent – Give the child a few toys – Pop on Pals, bus with people, nesting cups – and observe what he/she does. If the caregiver is present, observe how the child interacts with the caregiver. Don't put demands on the child but interact naturally if child tries to engage with you.

2. Means for relating to objects and combinatorial play – Give the child nesting cups, blocks, two small cars, and other toys and observe what the child does.

3. Symbolic play

   a. Spontaneous – Give the child a symbolic play set (see above) and observe what he/she does.

   b. Imitation – After you observe the child's spontaneous symbolic play, model the next highest level of play and see if the child imitates you.

4. Comprehension – Use the comprehension probes listed in the comprehension section. Identify if the child is using nonverbal comprehension strategies rather than language to comply with the tasks.

5. Routine with object – Use a balloon or bubbles to establish a routine with the child. See if the child will participate in the routine and anticipate their move in the routine.

6. Point to a picture on the wall – When the child's is looking at you, point to a picture on the wall and say, "Oh look." Observe if the child responds to joint attention by looking in the direction of your point.

7. Social Routine with Person – Engage in a routine without an object such as "peek-a-boo" or a tickle game as a social routine. See if the child will participate in the routine and anticipate his/her move in the routine.

8. Bubble gun – Using a bubble gun, observe if the child initiates, comments, responds to comments and/or requests more. In addition, observe if the child uses a three-point gaze shift (i.e., the child looks at the object, looks at a person and then looks back at the object) denoting coordinated joint attention; CJA).

9. Book sharing – Share a book with the child to observe if the child initiates comments, responds to comments, directs your attention to pictures, or engages in CJA.

10. Snack – Give the child a snack item and wait for him/her to request more.

11. Interest in/ability to use picture symbols – Try doing parts of the assessment with picture symbols. Identify if the child will use the symbols to request more. Identify if the child understands the pictures better than the spoken word during comprehension probes.

Early CLASS Functional Communication Assessment
Adapted from Schuler, Prizant, and Wetherby (1997).

Child's Name:_____ **Date of Birth:** _____

Date of Interview: _____

Person(s) Participating: _____

Chronological Age: _____

Person Completing Assessment: _____

Case History Notes

_____

_____

_____

_____

_____

_____

_____

Warm-Up Period/Initial Observations (What is the child drawn to?)

Communication Observations

Articulation/Phonology

(Note all sounds and syllable formations the child makes during the session. If the child is making few sounds try to get him/her to imitate you.)

- Speech sound repertoire (circle):

Early 8:	/m/	/b/	/j/	/n/	/w/	/d/	/p/	/h/
Middle 8:	/t/	/ŋ/	/k/	/g/	/f/	/v/	/tʃ/	/dʒ/
Late 8:	/ʃ/	/θ/	/s/	/z/	/d/	/l/	/ʒ/	/r/

- Syllabic formation (circle all that apply and give examples):

Consonant-Vowel (CV):

Vowel-Consonant (VC):

Consonant-Vowel-Consonant (CVC) :

CVCV reduplications (mama, dada):

Language Comprehension (based on Miller & Paul, 1995)

Children often do not understand the words addressed to them but pick up clues from the context of the environment. These contextual clues help the child figure out what people are talking about without the child having to understand words and sentences. These contextual cues are called "***non-linguistic comprehension strategies***"(Chapman, 1978; Paul, 2001). Chapman (1978) outlined several nonlinguistic comprehension strategies that young children use in the first two years of life. When assessing the child's language comprehension, determine if the child is using nonverbal comprehension strategies instead of comprehending the words and sentences addressed to the child. The following is a list of nonlinguistic comprehension strategies you may observe and suggestions for how to circumvent them while assessing language comprehension:

1. Child looks at an object the adult looks at or moves (to circumvent this strategy look directly at the child, do not look or touch the objects you are asking the child to locate).

2. Child acts on objects the adult notices or that are next to the child (to circumvent this strategy look directly at the child, do not ask the child to locate objects that are next to them or that the child is holding or reaching for).

3. The child imitates an ongoing activity (to circumvent this strategy do not ask the child to engage in an activity that others in the room are doing).

4. The child does what is typical in the situation (to circumvent this strategy ask the child to perform an unusual action on an object. For example, ask the child to "kiss the ball" rather than "throw the ball". Remember when assessing words such as in, on and under it is typical to put object *in* to a container and *on* a horizontal surface).

Comprehension Probe Checklist

When filling out the comprehension probe checklist below, give at least one example for each item the child is capable of doing correctly without relying on nonlinguistic comprehension strategies. Note if you would or would not expect this level of word/sentence understanding given the child's chronological age. Make a statement indicating the child's developmental level for word/sentence comprehension. Next, document if the child uses any nonlinguistic comprehension strategies (rather than relying on understanding the words and sentence) to perform a task.

____ Locates sound (6-7 mos.)

____ Responds to name (8 mos.) _____
(When the child is not looking towards you, call his/her name. Ask the caregiver if the child responds to name.)

____ Names for objects with contextual cues (8-12 mos.) _____
(The child may understand a few words in context, such as "bottle" when in kitchen and hungry, or when someone points or gestures at the object. Sitting on the floor or at a table, place several common objects in front of the child. Without looking at the objects, ask the child to give you each object. Because you are interested in determining whether or not the child understands the object word and not the action of giving, it is permissible to put your hand out or gesture that you want the child to give you an object. Watch to see if the child is using nonlinguistic comprehension strategies to locate objects in his/her environment.)

____ Action words within contexts of routines (8-12 mos.) _____
(e.g., Understands "Splash" within bath routine or waves "bye-bye" when leaving). Ask the caregiver if the child knows any routines such as "wave bye bye" or "peek- a- boo." If the child is

reported to play one or more of these games, engage in the game with the child without using motor behaviors to cue the child.)

____ Names of objects without contextual cues (12-18 mos.) _____
(Place several common objects in the room that are behind the child or obstructed from view. Ask the child "Where's the x?" See if the child gets, hands over or shows you the object.)

____ Familiar person in view (12-18 mos.) _____
(Ask the child to locate familiar people in the room whom he can see from where he is located; for example, "Where's mommy?")

____ Action words, without nonlinguistic comprehension strategy (12-18 mos.) _____
(Ask the child to perform simple actions—kiss, hug, blow, smell, throw—with **objects she is holding.** Do not ask the child to perform the "typical action" with the object, such as throwing the ball, but something atypical, such as kissing the ball.)

____ Possessor-possession (18-24 mos.) _____
(Ask the child to touch body parts on him/herself and others. You can also use a doll or stuffed toy, (saying "Show me dolly's nose" vs. "show me mommy's nose.")

____ Action-object (18-24 mos.) _____
(Ask the child to perform an action on a specified object—kiss, hug, blow, smell, throw. The child should **not be engaged with the object** when the direction is given. As before, do not ask the child to perform the "typical action" with the object, such as throwing the ball but something atypical, such as kissing the ball.)

Schemes for Relating to Objects

(Give at least one example for each item checked.)

____ Undifferentiated actions on objects (2-6 mos.) _____
(The child bangs, mouths, or shakes objects without regard to their affordance properties. For example, a rattle affords shaking whereas a sponge affords squeezing.)

____ Approximating objects (5-9 mos.) _____
(The child brings two or more objects, including self [e.g., clap hands], into contact with each other in ways not organized around the function of the objects. Other than approximating, no other action is involved.)

____ Exploration and differential actions on objects (5-9 mos.) _____
(The child explores objects and performs actions on objects according to their affordance properties. For example, a rattle affords shaking whereas a sponge affords squeezing.)

___ Manipulation of physical properties of objects (10-16 mos.) _____
(The child manipulated a moveable, yet attached part of an object. The action is isolated in that it is not related to other actions the child may be doing.)

___ Combinatorial play (10-15 mos.) _____
(Combining stacking blocks, nesting cups, or stacking rings regardless of order.)

___ Grouping objects (10-16 mos.) _____
(The child creates a group of at least three objects. The grouping is based on either the functional or perceptual similarity of the objects. Some evidence must be present that he child is deliberately creating a group. Do not code behaviors as grouping if objects are subsequently placed into a receptacle or container.)

Symbolic Play (based on McCune, 1995)

Give at least one example for each item checked. For the first skill the child is not capable of doing, note if you would expect/not expect this given child's chronological age. End the section with a statement indicating the child's developmental age level in this domain. *Note:* If children demonstrate the skill following a model or verbal instruction, the skill is beginning to emerge with the guidance of an adult or more capable peer.)

___ None _____

___ Differed imitation; e.g., hairbrush to head but not playful (9-12 mos.)

    ___ Spontaneous

    ___ Following a model or verbal cue

___ Auto-symbolic action schemes/actions towards self; e.g., hairbrush to head appears playful (12-18 mos.)

    ___ Spontaneous

    ___ Following a model or verbal cue

___ Single schemes that include others/action schemes; e.g., brushes own hair/brushes mom's hair) (15-22 mos.)

    ___ Spontaneous

    ___ Following a model or verbal cue

___ Activities of others; e.g., pretends to mop floor (15-22 mos.)

    ____ Spontaneous

    ____ Following a model or verbal cue

___ Single scheme combination; e.g., drinks from toy bottle, then feeds doll from bottle (20-26 mos.)

    ____ Spontaneous

    ____ Following a model or verbal cue

___ Multi-scheme combinations; e.g., successive schemes such as kisses doll, puts it to bed, puts blanket on (24-30 mos.)

    ____ Spontaneous

    ____ Following a model or verbal cue

___ Planned single-act schemes (30-38 mos.)

    ____ Spontaneous

    ____ Following a model or verbal cue

___ Planned multi-scheme symbolic acts (30-38 mos.)

    ____ Spontaneous

    ____ Following a model or verbal cue

___ Symbolic identification; e.g., picks up screwdriver and begins to brush teeth (30-38 mos.)

    ____ Spontaneous

    ____ Following a model or verbal cue

___ Combination of planned elements (30-38 mos.)

    ____ Spontaneous

    ____ Following a model or verbal cue

Social-Emotional Signaling

(Give at least one example for each item checked.)

Eye Gaze

____ Use of two-point gaze shifts; i.e., child looks at an object and then to a person (6-9 mos.)
    a. For regulating interactions (*and to whom?*)
    b. For social referencing

____ Follows gaze/point; i.e., response to joint attention (10-12 mos.)

____ Uses three-point gaze shifts; i.e., the child looks at the object, looks at a person and then looks back at the object (12-24 mos.)

Affective Signals

(In this section, it is important that the children demonstrate affect. Sharing affect and emotional signals begins at 2 months of age and continues.)

____ Expression of positive affect

____ Expression of negative affect

____ Shares positive affect (requires looking at you when expressing affect)

Expressive Language

Communicative Means

(Report examples of communicative means below and make sure to indicate how the child is using his/her communicative means in the communicative intentions section on the next page. *Note:* The child does not have to perform all the different types of communicative means. Besides, you would not expect the child to use the aberrant means if he is typically developing.)

____ Conventional gesture

____ Vocalizations

____ Words (different words or approximations)

____ Phrases (different multi-word combos)

____ Sentences

____ Push/pull/tool use

____ Reach

____ Point

_____ Distal point (in distance)

_____ Proximal point (touch)

_____ Eye gaze _____

_____ Preservative speech _____

_____ Immediate echolalia _____

_____ Delayed echolalia _____

_____ Unconventional gesture _____

Communicative Intentions

(Give at least one example for each item checked. For the first skill the child is not capable of doing, note if you would expect/not expect this given child's chronological age. End the section with a statement indicating the child's developmental age level in this domain. Note: Behavior regulations, social routines, directing a joint focus of attention, and sharing a joint focus nonverbally or verbally develop at 9-12 months of age; discuss a related present and nonpresent begins at 20 and 32 months, respectively.)

_____ No intention

_____ Behavior regulation

_____ Requests object/action

_____ Protests

_____ Requests termination

_____ Requests help

_____ Requests comfort (from parent)

_____ Engage in social routine (greetings or other social interaction) _____

_____ Negotiates mutual attention (seeks attention of adult) _____

_____ Shares a joint focus of attention (nonverbally, comments on the here and now, gives information)

_____ Directs others' attention

_____ Discusses a related present _____

_____ Discusses a nonpresent_____

_____ Asks others to gain information _____

Reciprocity (Engages in Reciprocal Verbal/Vocal Interactions)

a. Conversational Turn-Taking
(Does the child Initiate conversation or just respond to conversation?)

____ Vocal (preconversational) turn-taking _____

____ Verbal turn-taking _____

____ Responds to questions _____

____ Responds to comments _____

____ Initiates comments: _____

b. Topic Maintenance

____ Number of turns

____ Turn length (number of words/turn)

c. Repair Strategies
(What happens when a child is not understood or does not understand? Does he/she persist? How does he/she repair breakdown?)

____ Repeats communication

____ Modifies communication

____ Recognizes breakdown and requests information

d. Nonverbal/Vocal Turn-Taking

____ Initiates interactions/play with others

____ In routines

____ Out of routines

____ Responds to/interacts/play with others

____ In routines

____ Out of routines

Emotional Regulation and Sensory Processing

Oral Peripheral Examination

Summary and Impressions

(Remember to comment on the following: Comparison of chronological age with developmental level in each domain, including the level of social cognition (i.e., sharing perceptions and pursing goals or sharing attention and intention) indexed by what you found in your assessment.)

Appendix B: Hello Circle Script

Hello Circle Sample Script

(words and tunes to all songs are in the song glossary, Appendix E):

"Hello, friends! It's time for Circle!"
(Point to the symbol on large classroom schedule.)

"It's time to say 'hello.'"
(Point to "hello" schedule card on pocket chart.)

Show a picture of the first child. "Time to say hello to _____."

Put the "my turn" support in front of first child. See if the child will sit in the "hello chair" spontaneously before you go through the prompt hierarchy: "_____, sit in hello chair!" Sing "Sit Down" to help the child. The "hello chair" is labeled with a hello symbol and faces the rest of the group.

When the child is sitting in the "hello chair," everyone sings the "Hello" song. "Hello _____. Hello _____. Hello _____, it's time to say hello." Allow the child in the "hello chair" time to spontaneously say, "Hello, friends." If he does not, show the child the "hello friends" visual support and move through the prompt hierarchy. Child goes back to his seat. (This sequence is repeated for all children in the class. If someone is absent, ask, "Who is not here today?" and go through the response hierarchy, showing pictures of children who are absent. Finish this segment by saying "hello is finished" *and* turn over "Hello" schedule card on pocket chart.)

- Point to Days of the Week schedule card.
    - It's time for "Days of the Week"
    - Sing "Days of the Week"
    - Look at calendar
    - Model moving "not" and "today" symbols to appropriate days. "Today is not_____. Today is _____."
    - Have "day helper" move large "not" and "today" symbols. "Today is not_____. Today is _____."
    - Turn schedule card over. "Day of the week is finished."

- Point to "look" schedule card. "Now it's time to look."
  - "Today we will look for _____" (Point to model picture or object what they are to look for.)
  - Move the model picture over to the wall singing "♪♫♫Look, look, look for the _____, look, look look for the _____.♪♫♫"
  - When you find the picture (taped to the wall), everyone points and say, "there it is."
  Turn schedule card over. "Look is finished."

- Point to "Book" schedule card. "Now it's time for Book."
  - Introduce book.
  - Read Book of the Week (may base reading on plan for varied repetition found in Appendix C).
  - Turn schedule card. "Our book is finished."

- Place "Special Activity" card and supports on pocket chart; describe.

- Point to large schedule: "Hello Circle is finished (turn over schedule card). It's time for Centers. Check your schedule."

Appendix C: Strategies for Varied Repetition With the Book of the Week

Reading the book of the Week

The Book of the Week is an example of varied repetition. Repetition provides reinforcement of the target core and theme vocabulary and supports the children in predicting what comes next. The use of variation maintains interest and supports joint attention. The beginning and ending of the activity is defined by the use of a clear introduction and closure. (Remember to point to the illustrations when reading, *not* to the picture symbols. The picture symbols are there to ensure that the language used is consistent.)

- **Day 1:** Show the book cover and give a general idea of what the book is about and/or how it relates to the theme (e.g., for *The Napping House*: "Our book is about a family. A family takes a nap. [point to cover] It's *The Napping House*."). Read the book slowly, as written, to provide the template for the week. Conclude by repeating the link to the theme or the general idea. (For *The Napping House*: "The family took a nap. Everyone was sleeping.")

- **Day 2:** For the second reading, remind the children of the general idea of the book: "Here's our book. It's *The Napping House*. Everyone was sleeping." Book reading might be the same or only slightly different than Day 1. Conclude with a summary statement with a pause. ("In *The Napping House*, [pause] everyone was sleeping.")

- **Day 3:** Begin to focus a little more on the details of the book: "Here's our book, *The Napping House*. Who was sleeping?" During the reading, you might pause to point out details in the illustrations. Think about any questions, open-ended statements, anything you plan to point out about the pictures or add at the end of the reading.

- **Day 4:** You can now expect the children to be familiar enough with the book to "help" with the reading. Set the stage for their help. ("Today you can help me. Help me read *The Napping House*.") Pause on each page to give an opportunity for the children to say the repeated refrain. Conclude by saying, "Today you helped me read."

- **Day 5**: Again, the children can "help" with the reading. Introduce the book again: "Our book is about a family. The family takes a nap. A nap means that everyone is _____." Pause on each page for the children to name the character, objects or events. You could also emphasize concepts or vocabulary (e.g., "the boy is *on* Granny, dog is *on* boy, etc."). Or you could ask simple questions about the story.

Appendix D: Sample "My Day at School" Form

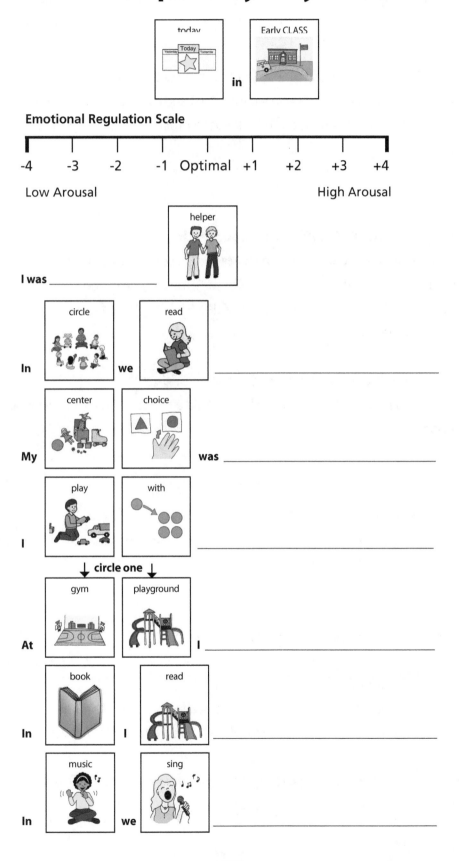

Appendix E: Song Glossary

Many of the songs and chants in the song glossary are part of core functional vocabulary routines (see Chapter 3, Implementing Functional Routines). They can be used as part of the naturalistic prompt hierarchy to reduce the level of linguistic demand a child needs to process during ongoing activities (see Chapter 3, Naturalistic Prompt Hierarchy).

B

"Brush Teeth" Song (to the tune of "Raffi - Brush Your Teeth")
"♪ ♫ ♫You brush your teeth ch,ch,ch,ch,ch,ch,ch,ch. You brush your teeth ch,ch,ch,ch,ch,ch,ch,ch. ♪ ♫ ♫"
We only use the refrain portion of Raffi's "Brush Your Teeth." Tune may be found at 0:05-0:11.
Celano, D. .(Producer). (2013). *Raffi -- Brush Your Teeth* [Video File]. Available from http://www.youtube.com/watch?v=XJIPaxGiMp0. Time 0:05-0:11

"Build a Tower Up So High" Song (to the tune of "London Bridge")
"♪ ♫ ♫Build a tower up so high, up so high, up so high. Build a tower up so high. All fall down. ♪ ♫ ♫"
Repeated as necessary.

C

"Calm Down" Song (to the tune of "Frère Jacques")
"♪ ♫ ♫ I can calm down, I can calm down. Yes, I can! Yes, I can! I can calm down. I can calm down. Yes, I can. Yes, I can! ♪ ♫ ♫"
Repeated as necessary.

"Check Your Schedule" Song (to the tune of "Frère Jacques")
"♪ ♫ ♫ Check your schedule, check your schedule. Check it now, check it now. Time to check your schedule, time to check your schedule. Check it now, check it now. ♪ ♫ ♫"
The song is repeated until the majority of the children have checked their schedule. If a child requires more time, an assistant may continue singing to the child while the rest of the class moves on to the next activity.

CHOO CHOO (to the tune of "Choo Choo the Big Train Is Coming Down the Track")
"♪ ♫ ♫ Choo Choo the big train is coming down the track . . . CHOO CHOO

Choo Choo the big train is coming down the track ... CHOO CHOO

Stop, Look and Listen (do hand motions)

Stop, Look and Listen (do hand motions)

Choo Choo ♪ ♫ ♫."

This is a good song to sing when playing with a train. After the song is established the "Stop, Look and Listen" portion of the song can be sung to get the children's attention.

mommylessons101 (Producer). (2012). *Choo Choo the Big Train Is Coming Down the Track* [Video File]. Available from http://www.youtube.com/watch?v=Oi974R1NiCg&list=WLYURSBXEG60obOUlhpttQ1A-9buod1b7Gk

"Clean Up" Song (to the tune of "Barney: Clean-Up" song)

"♪ ♫ ♫ Clean up, Clean up, Everybody, Everywhere, Clean up, Clean up, Everybody Do Your Share. ♪ ♫ ♫"

The song is repeated until everyone has finished cleaning up.

Barney & Friends (n.d.). (Producers). *Barney: The Clean-Up Song* [Video File]. Available from https://www.youtube.com/watch?v=WJ9uhDzN-rA#t=10

D

"Days of the Week" Song (to the tune of "Days of the Week" song or "Greg & Steve – Days of the Week")

"♪ ♫ ♫ Sunday, Monday, Tuesday/ Wednesday/ Thursday/ Friday, and Saturday/ Sunday comes again. ♪ ♫ ♫"

Kids TV123 (Producer). (2009). *Days of the Week Song* [Video File]. Available from https://www.youtube.com/watch?v=7AvNq2CQnOI

Troy DaBoss (Producer). (2011). *Greg & Steve – Days of the Week* [Video File]. Available from http://www.youtube.com/watch?v=ZyUNjiac_Mw

The class sings the entire song one time before calendar time.

F

Five Little Pumpkins (from Raffi's "Five Little Pumpkins" song)

"♪ ♫ ♫ Five little pumpkins sitting on a gate/ First one said, "Oh my, it's getting late"/ Second one said, "There are witches in the air."/ Third one said, "But we don't care."/ Fourth one said, "Let's run and run and run."/ Fifth one said, "I'm ready for some fun."/ Ooh went the wind, and out went the light/Five little pumpkins rolled out of sight. ♪ ♫ ♫"

Murdoci (Producer). (n.d.). *5 little Pumkins* [Video File]. Available from http://www.youtube.com/watch?v=x-VJFF6jfAgY

G

"Goodbye" Song (to the tune of "Hello and Goodbye Song Using Sign Language")

The class sings the goodbye song one time to the target child using the target child's name.

"♪ ♫ ♫ Goodbye, _____. Goodbye, _____. Goodbye, _____. It's time to say, "Goodbye."

The target child responds back to the class by saying "Goodbye friends. ♪ ♫ ♫"

Goodbye is repeated until each child has a turn to be the target child.

Jbrary (Producer). (2013). *Hello and Goodbye Song Using Sign Language* [Video File]. Available from http://www.youtube.com/watch?v=tKCGF2hvq3I time 1:03-1:15

Note that the actors in the Jbray youtube video are using sign language. While we advocate waving goodbye during the song, we do not advocate the use of sign language. Goodbye song tune may be found at time 1:03-1:15.

Greg and Steve's Good Morning Song (to the tune of "Greg and Steve's Good Morning" song)

"♪ ♫ ♫ Good morning, good morning, good morning to you/ Today is beginning. There's so much to do. ♪ ♫ ♫"

Dagr8vixster (Producer). (2012). *Greg and Steve's Good Morning Song* [Video File]. Available from https://www.youtube.com/watch?v=xFFbWH3nial

"Goodnight" Song (to the tune of "Hello and Goodbye Song Using Sign Language")

The class sings one time, to the target child using the target child's name. The song is repeated for each child.

"♪ ♫ ♫ Goodnight, _____. Goodnight, _____. Goodnight, _____. It's time to say, 'Goodnight'. ♪ ♫ ♫ "

Jbrary (Producer). (2013). *Hello and Goodbye Song Using Sign Language* [Video File]. Available from http://www.youtube.com/watch?v=tKCGF2hvq3I time 1:03-1:15

Note that the actors in the Jbray youtube video are using sign language. We do not advocate the use of sign language.

H

"Hat" Song (chant and elongating the word "give" in the last line)

"♪ ♫ ♫ (Target child's name) has a hat.

What do you think of that?

He takes off his hat and gives it to (second child's name). ♪ ♫ ♫"

Head, Shoulders, Knees and Toes (to the tune of "Head, Shoulders, Knees and Toes")
"♪ ♫ ♫Head, shoulders, knees and toes, knees and toes/ Head, shoulders, knees and toes, knees and toes/ eyes and ears and mouth and nose/ head, shoulders, knees and toes, knees and toes. ♪ ♫ ♫ "
Super Simple Songs (Producer). (2013). *Head Shoulders Knees & Toes (Sing It)* [Video File]. Available from http://www.youtube.com/watch?v=ZanHgPprl-0

"Hello" Song (to the tune of "Hello and Goodbye Song Using Sign Language")
The class sings one time, to the target child using the target child's name. The song is repeated for each child.
"♪ ♫ ♫ Hello, _____. Hello, _____. Hello, _____. It's time to say, 'hello'. ♪ ♫ ♫"
The target child responds back to the class by saying "Hello friends".
Hello song is repeated until each child has a turn to be the target child.
Jbrary (Producer) (2013). *Hello and Goodbye Song Using Sign Language* [Video File]. Available from http://www.youtube.com/watch?v=tKCGF2hvq3I at time 1:03-1:15
Note that the actors in the Jbray youtube video are using sign language. While we advocate waving hello during the song, we do not advocate the use of sign language.

I

If You're Happy and You Know It, Clap Your Hands (to the tune of "If You're Happy and You Know it, Clap Your Hands")
"♪ ♫ ♫ If you're happy and you know it clap your hands/ If you're happy and you know it clap your hands/ If you're happy and you know it and you really want to show it/ if you're happy and you know it clap your hands. ♪ ♫ ♫"
Substitute other actions for clap your hands, like "stomp your feet" or "pat your knee."
Mother Goose Club (Producer). (2013). *If You're Happy and You Know It* [Video File]. Available from http://www.youtube.com/watch?v=HGsHd9RuYRg&list=WLYURSBXEG60obOUlhpttQ1A9buod1b7Gk time 34-2:13

If You're Mad and You Know It (to the tune of "If You're Happy and You Know It")
"♪ ♫ ♫ If you're mad and you know it, stomp your feet.
If you're our mad and you know it, stomp your feet.
If you're mad and you know it then your face will surely show it,
If you're mad and you know it, stomp your feet. ♪ ♫ ♫"
Substitute other actions that you are teaching the child in order to redirect anger (e.g., take a breath, count to 10, take a break).
Mother Goose Club (Producer). (2013). *If You're Happy and You Know It* [Video File]. Available from http://www.youtube.com/watch?v=HGsHd9RuYRg&list=WLYURSBXEG60obOUlhpttQ1A9buod1b7Gk time 34-2:13

"I Love You Song" (to the tune of "Barney's I Love You" song)

"♪ ♫ ♫I love you. You love me. We're a happy family. With a great big hug and a kiss from me to you, won't you say you love me too. I love you. You love me. We're best friends like friends should be. With a great big hug and a kiss from me to you, won't you say you love me too. ♪ ♫ ♫"

Lhin Lalitha (Producer). (2010). *Barney's I Love You* [Video File]. Available from http://www.youtube.com/watch?v=XwLLH9EZiqc. Time :0:09-0:57

L

"Look" Song (to the tune of the first line of "Skip to My Lou")

"♪ ♫ ♫ Look, look, look for _____, look look look for _____. ♪ ♫ ♫"

The song is repeated until the target object/picture is found. Children are encouraged to point to the target and say, "There it is." Or "here it is."

P

"Pass the Plates" Song (to the tune of "Skip to My Lou")

Pass, pass, pass the plates/Pass, pass, pass the plates/ Pass, pass, pass the plates/pass the plates at snack. Sing while child is passing out plates. Names of other items (cups, napkins) can be substituted for plates.

Pizza Song (to the tune of the "Peanut Butter and Jelly Song")

"♪ ♫ ♫ Pizza, Pizza, Pizza and cheese / First you take the sauce and you spread it, you spread it, you spread it, spread, spread it/Pizza, Pizza, Pizza and cheese/Then you take the cheese and sprinkle, you sprinkle, you sprinkle, sprinkle, sprinkle/Pizza, Pizza, Pizza and cheese/Then you take the pizza and you eat it, you eat it, you eat it, eat it, eat it/Pizza, Pizza, Pizza and cheese. ♪ ♫ ♫"

Sing while children are making pretend or real pizza (do the correct motions for spread, sprinkle, and eat). If eating pizza only sing the last line of the song and the chorus.

Aprocot (Producer). (2011). *Peanut Butter and Jelly Song* [Video File]. Available from http://www.youtube.com/watch?v=L39J7jCoVKY&list=FLdJJSF7qlSb3eTsPuRzkZFw&index=4

Or

Sprout (Producer). (2013). *Kids Song: Learn How to Sing the Peanut Butter & Jelly Song* [Video File]. Available from http://www.youtube.com/watch?v=ApVMDLyx5j8&list=FLdJJSF7qlSb3eTsPuRzkZFw

S

"Sit Down" Song (to the tune of "London Bridge Is Falling Down")

"♪ ♫ ♫Everybody come sit down, come sit down, come sit down/Everybody come sit down/Find your chair. ♪ ♫ ♫"

The song is repeated until the majority of the children sit down.

T

The Train on the Track Goes Choo Choo Choo (to "The Wheels on the Bus" song)

"♪ ♫ ♫ The train on the track goes choo choo choo

choo choo choo

choo choo choo

The train on the track goes choo choo choo

All around the track. ♪ ♫ ♫"

Oh My Genius. (Producer). (2013). *Wheels on the Bus Go Round and Round* [Video File]. Available at http://www.youtube.com/watch?v=_gR_CB8Mz9I

W

The "Wash" Song (chanting)

"♪ ♫ ♫ Dirty _____, gonna wash, wash, wash

Dirty _____, gonna wash, wash, wash

Dirty _____, Dirty _____, gonna wash, wash, wash. ♪ ♫ ♫"

Repeat for each body part

The "Waiting" Song (chanted with falling intonation)

"♪ ♫ ♫ Waiting (*clap, clap*), Waiting (*clap, clap*). ♪ ♫ ♫"

Chant whenever the children (or a child) needs to wait. Repeat until waiting is finished.

The Wheels on the Bus

"♪ ♫ ♫ The wheels on the bus go round and round/round and round/round and round/the wheels on the bus go round and round all day long. ♪ ♫ ♫"

Repeat with other actions like "the horn on the bus goes beep," "the people on the bus go up and down," "the door on the bus goes open and shut."

Oh My Genius (Producer). (2013). *Wheels on the Bus Go Round and Round* [Video File]. Available at http://www.youtube.com/watch?v=_gR_CB8Mz9I

"Where" Song (To the tune of "Where Is Thumbkin")

The class sings one time, to the target child using the target child's name. The song is repeated for each child.

♪ 🎵 🎵"Where is _____, where is _____" ♪ 🎵 🎵 pausing after two repetitions of "where is _____," leaving space for the child to say, "Here I am."

Who Stole the Cookies From the Cookie Jar? (to the tune of "Who Stole the Cookies From the Cookie Jar?")

"♪ 🎵 🎵 Who stole the cookies from the cookie jar?/ (child's name) stole the cookies from the cookie jar/Who me?/ Yes you/Not me/Then who? ♪ 🎵 🎵"

Repeat until all the children have had a turn to be the cookie thief. Using a visual support, have the target child say "Who me?" and "not me" and the rest of the class say "yes you" and "then who??"

Littlefoxkids (Producer). (2013). *Who Stole the Cookies From the Cookie Jar?* Available from http://www.youtube.com/watch?v=ert9zlCx21E&list=FLdJJSF7qISb3eTsPuRzkZFw&index=2

Consult AAPC Textbooks for All Your Teaching and Inservice Needs

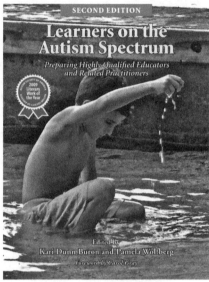

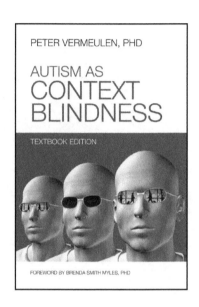

The Comprehensive Autism Planning System (CAPS) for Individuals With Autism Spectrum Disorders and Related Disabilities

Integrating Evidence-Based Practices Throughout the Student's Day

by Shawn A. Henry and Brenda Smith Myles, PhD

This system allows educators to understand how to implement an instructional program for students with ASD. Known as CAPS, the model answers common questions about finding the right supports to fit a child's learning style in order to help him reach his full potential. Used with *The Ziggurat Model*, CAPS enables educators and other professionals to address adequate yearly progress (AYP), response to intervention (RTI), and positive behavior support (PBS).

ISBN 9781937473761 | Code 9510 |

Price: $44.95

Also available as an ebook!

Learners on the Autism Spectrum

Preparing Highly Qualified Educators and Related Practitioners; Second Edition

Edited by Kari Dunn Buron and Pamela Wolberg

The second edition of this highly popular text has been updated and expanded with chapters on evidence-based practices, special interests, sensory processing, and more. This textbook responds to the escalating need to prepare educators with essential knowledge and practical skills to support diverse learners on the autism spectrum. Covering a range of critical topics and themes, this edited volume brings together leading experts representing diverse disciplines and perspectives (i.e., researchers, therapists, educators, parents, and adults on the autism spectrum) for a comprehensive look at the core issues related to individuals with autism spectrum disorders. Perfect for introductory classes, *Learners on the Autism Spectrum* covers the foundations and characteristics of individuals with ASD.

ISBN 9781937473945 | Code 9504A |

Price: $85.95

Hardcover

Autism as Context Blindness

by Peter Vermeulen, PhD

According to Peter Vermeulen, treatment of autism is still too focused on behavior and minimally focused on observation or determining the way of thinking that leads to the behavior. In this groundbreaking book, inspired by the ideas of Uta Frith, internationally known psychologist and a pioneer in theory of mind as it relates to autism, Vermeulen explains in everyday terms how the autistic brain functions, with a particular emphasis on the apparent lack of sensitivity to and awareness of the context in which things happen. Full of examples, often humorous, the book goes on to examine "context" as it relates to observation, social interactions, communication and knowledge. The book concludes with a major section on how to reduce context blindness in these various areas, vital for successful functioning.

ISBN 9781937473457 | Code 9508 |

Price: $44.95

Also available as an ebook!

Visit aapcpublishing.net for more information.

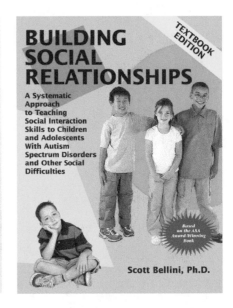

Quality Literacy Instruction for Students With Autism Spectrum Disorders

edited by Christina Carnahan, EdD, and Pam Williamson, PhD; foreword by Kathleen Quill, PhD

Textbook Excellence Award "Texty" Winner (2011)

Quality Literacy Instruction for Students With Autism Spectrum Disorders brings together experts from both the autism and reading fields to provide a detailed discussion of literacy instruction, thus supporting professionals and families alike in building lifelong literacy instruction geared to the needs of students on the autism spectrum.

Using case examples, the textbook brings theory and research to practice, thus meeting the mandate for evidence-based practice and illustrating that having effective literacy skills enhances the quality of life of all individuals, including those with ASD. If you're teaching a college course or preparing for an in-house training, turn to *Quality Literacy* to cover the essential area of literacy.

ISBN 9781934575666 | Code 9506 |

Price: $75.95

Also available as an ebook!

Designing Comprehensive Interventions for High-Functioning Individuals With Autism Spectrum Disorders

The Ziggurat Model, Release 2.0

by Ruth Aspy, PhD, and Barry Grossman, PhD; foreword by Gary Mesibov, PhD, director of Division TEACCH

It is relatively easy to find information describing specific interventions, but it is difficult to find information on how to develop a comprehensive intervention plan. This textbook presents a process and framework for designing interventions for individuals of all ages with ASD while staying consistent with recent special education trends, including response to intervention (RTI), evidence-based practices, and positive behavioral supports. This updated and expanded version includes the latest research, a special section on Ziggurat-CAPS integration (written by Brenda Smith Myles and Shawn Henry), and a new version of the Underlying Characteristics Checklist for Early Intervention (UCC-EI).

ISBN 9781934575963 | Code 9502 |

Price: $75.95

Also available as an ebook!

Building Social Relationships

A Systematic Approach to Teaching Social Interaction Skills to Children and Adolescents With Autism Spectrum Disorders and Other Social Difficulties

by Scott Bellini, PhD

Based on an ASA Award winner!

Building Social Relationships: A Systematic Approach to Teaching Social Interaction Skills to Children and Adolescents With Autism Spectrum Disorders and Other Social Difficulties addresses the critical need for social skills programming for children and adolescents with ASD and other social difficulties. The book is unique in presenting a comprehensive model that incorporates five fundamental steps: assess social functioning, distinguish between skill acquisition and performance deficits, select intervention strategies, implement intervention, and evaluate and monitor progress. Rather than promoting a single strategy, the model details how to organize and make sense of the myriad social skills programs and resources available.

ISBN 9781934575055 | Code 9500

Price: $75.95

Also available as an ebook!

P.O. Box 23173
Shawnee Mission, Kansas 66283-0173
www.aapcpublishing.net

CPSIA information can be obtained
at www.ICGtesting.com
Printed in the USA
BVHW011500300419
546942BV00011B/401/P